CHINA AND THE GLOBAL ECONOMY SINCE 1840

UNU WORLD INSTITUTE FOR DEVELOPMENT ECONOMICS RESEARCH (UNU/WIDER) was established by the United Nations University as its first research and training centre and started work in Helsinki, Finland, in 1985. The purpose of the Institute is to undertake applied research and policy analysis on structural changes affecting the developing and transitional economies, to provide a forum for the advocacy of policies leading to robust, equitable and environmentally sustainable growth, and to promote capacity strengthening and training in the field of economic and social policy-making. Its work is carried out by staff researchers and visiting scholars in Helsinki and through networks of collaborating scholars and institutions around the world.

— — — — — —

UNU World Institute for Development Economics Research (UNU/WIDER)
Katajanokanlaituri 6 B, FIN-00160 Helsinki, Finland

China and the Global Economy since 1840

Lu Aiguo
Research Fellow
Institute of World Economics and Politics
Chinese Academy of Social Sciences
Beijing
China

Foreword by Giovanni Andrea Cornia

in association with
UNU/WIDER

First published in Great Britain 2000 by
MACMILLAN PRESS LTD
Houndmills, Basingstoke, Hampshire RG21 6XS and London
Companies and representatives throughout the world

A catalogue record for this book is available from the British Library.

ISBN 0–333–77721–2

First published in the United States of America 2000 by
ST. MARTIN'S PRESS, INC.,
Scholarly and Reference Division,
175 Fifth Avenue, New York, N.Y. 10010

ISBN 0–312–22628–4

Library of Congress Cataloging-in-Publication Data
Aiguo, Lu.
China and the global economy since 1840 / Lu Aiguo.
p.   cm.
Includes bibliographical references and index.
ISBN 0–312–22628–4 (cloth)
1. China—Foreign economic relations.   2. China—Economic
policy—19th century.   3. China—Economic policy—20th century.
4. China—Economic conditions—19th century.   5. China—Economic
conditions—20th century.   6. International economic relations.
I. Title.
HF1604.L825   1999
337.51—dc21   99–15427
                                                                        CIP

© The United Nations University/World Institute for Development Economics Research 2000
Foreword © Giovanni Andrea Cornia 2000

This book is printed on paper suitable for recycling and made from fully managed and
sustained forest sources.

10   9   8   7   6   5   4   3   2   1
09   08   07   06   05   04   03   02   01   00

Printed and bound in Great Britain by
Antony Rowe Ltd, Chippenham, Wiltshire

Contents

List of Tables   vi

Foreword   vii

List of Acronyms and Glossary   ix

Introduction: A Framework for Analysis   1

Part I: Westernization (1840–1949)   13

  1 The Westernization Movement   16
  2 Foreign Trade   28
  3 The Dual Structure of the Economy   42
  4 Falling Behind: The Lessons   55

Part II: Delinking and Self-reliance (1949–78)   69

  5 The Formation of a Strategy for Catching Up   72
  6 Industrialization   86
  7 Trade and Trade Performance   96
  8 Outcome: A Mixed Package   108

Part III: Reintegration (1978 and Beyond)   117

  9 A Different Game   121
 10 Economic Restructuring   130
 11 The State   141
 12 The Overseas Chinese Capitalist Diaspora   152
 13 Catching Up?   162

Conclusion   172

Notes   183

Bibliography   193

Index   215

List of Tables

2.1	China's major exports, 1871–1936	35
2.2	China's major imports, 1871–1936	36
2.3	The share of principal countries in China's foreign trade	37
2.4	China's imports, exports and total trade, 1871–1929	39
4.1	Comparative performance of Western Europe and China in per capita GDP, 1400–1950	57
4.2	Per capita GDP in advanced capitalist countries and other selected countries, 1900–50	58
4.3	Average tariff levels, 1913–25	64
6.1	The structure of investment in capital construction, 1952–78	90
6.2	Employment structure of the labour force, 1952–78	91
7.1	The China–US trade, 1972–80	101
7.2	China's foreign trade, 1971–78	102
7.3	Shares in China's imports and exports, 1979	103
7.4	Shares in China's imports and exports, 1934	103
7.5	China's share of world exports, 1950–79	106
8.1	Annual average real GDP growth in selected countries and regions, 1900–73	110
8.2	Economic performance, 1900–87	113
10.1	China's foreign trade, 1978–95	134
13.1	Average annual growth rate, 1980–95	163
13.2	Changes in China's share of GDP, merchandise exports and private consumption, 1980–95	164
13.3	Index of per capita GNP/GDP relative to the rich countries	165
13.4	Index of per capita GDP relative to the US	165

Foreword

This book is a timely contribution to an expanding literature on China and China's integration into the world economy, as well as to the current debate on alternative strategies of transition from the plan to market economy.

This work deals with one of the most important economic events of the twentieth century, that is, the rise of China. The uniqueness of the book is that the recent trajectory of China's development is placed within the historical context of the evolving relationship between China and the world economy. The book takes a long-term perspective, which is the proper way to undertake such an exercise, providing a systematic account of China's reaction to the expansion of the world capitalist economy from the early-nineteenth century to date.

Since the beginning of the 1990s, a great deal of attention has been paid to the anticipated 'rise of China', a rise which is hailed by some and feared by others. China's impressive economic growth since the introduction of the economic reforms in 1978 has been viewed by many as the result of the liberalization of the economy. This approach highlights implicitly the merits of free market as opposed to these of central planning, the declining role of the government as opposed to state-led industrialization, and the advantages of the free flow of capital and of economic openness generally speaking as opposed to inward-looking development strategy. This book addresses these issues not so much by engaging in current debate as by deriving insights and lessons from the historical development of China over the last two centuries.

It deals critically with the scholarship on China's performance under the impact of Western imperialism in the pre-1949 period. Based on the analysis of the process of China's opening up, the book suggests that China's integration into the world economy on the terms set up by Western powers did not lead to its development but to its marginalization. The book goes on to provide a careful account of the Maoist period, outlining its many development successes as well as its problems in terms of China's limited 'catching up' with the most advanced nations. Overall, the author assesses this period as one of de-linking from the world economy. The volume further analyses the reasons for and results of the post-Mao opening up, and China's renewed attempt to 'catch up'. Each of these periods is interpreted from a relevant analytical perspective, emphasizing the difficulties China faced throughout these years. The author brings to our attention the peculiarities of each period, as well as the elements of continuity throughout the entire period, especially the Maoist and the post-Maoist development paths.

This is one of the first books, if not the first, which in a convincing way applies the 'world-system interpretation' to China's modern history and current development, covering such a long historical time period within such a compass. To be sure, not everything the author argues will be convincing to all. Indeed the study reaches some provocative conclusions, which will no doubt feed the critical debate on the participation of China. But these viewpoints are entirely valid. They need to be understood, especially at the current juncture in international relations and the structural change of the world economy.

The book is a part of the 1994–95 research programme of UNU/WIDER on the globalization process. Its publication will contribute to and stimulate the development of our interdisciplinary research.

Giovanni Andrea Cornia
Director
UNU/WIDER

List of Acronyms and Glossary

ACRONYMS

ASEAN	Association of Southeast Asian Nations
CCP	Chinese Communist Party
GMD	Guomindang or Kuomintang (KMT), the Nationalist Party
MFN	most-favoured-nation treatment
NIEs	newly industrialized economies
PPP	purchasing power parity
RMB	renminbi (national currency)
TVEs	township and village enterprises

GLOSSARY

Angang xianfa	the Charter of the Anshan Iron and Steel Company
fu qiang	wealth and power
gaige	reform
guan shang he ban	joint government and merchant enterprises
guanban	government enterprises
guandu shangban	privately owned and government supervised enterprises
hong	business firm
kaifang	openness
qian zhuang	'money house', old-style Chinese private bank
qiufu	the pursuit of wealth
taban	general manager of a *hong*
tael	Chinese ounce (the equivalent of 1.208 British ounces) of silver as a former monetary unit
Yangwu yundong	Westernization movement
yuan	current Chinese monetary unit (valued approximately $ 0.12)
zhuan kou	transit or entrepôt trade
zili gengsheng	regeneration or reconstruction through one's own efforts
ziqiang	self-strengthening

Introduction: A Framework for Analysis

China's burgeoning presence in the global economy over the last two decades has been drawing attention from the world economic and political community. Indeed, according to almost every major indicator, China's economy has expanded considerably since the initial reforms in 1978. The country's real GNP growth rate is nearly 10 per cent annually. The overall standard of living has been on the rise, as demonstrated in the improvements in diets, clothing, housing, transportation and telecommunications, as well as in the greater access to modern consumer goods among both urban and rural residents. However, what impresses the world more is the rapid advance in China's foreign trade. Since 1978, the level of foreign trade has climbed more quickly than has GNP. This has led to a jump by a factor of three in China's share in international merchandise trade. China appears to have become an important player in the world market.

Not surprisingly, in view of China's economic development through reform and an open door policy, particularly its remarkable performance in trade and foreign direct investment, the country's integration into the world economy has become a much-discussed topic. A great many publications have dealt with the subject. The findings are frequently similar. A basic argument running through these publications can be summarized as follows.

Initiated by a reform programme in 1978, China's shift away from a centrally planned economy has been undertaken concurrently with an economic adjustment in the foreign-trade sector. First steps which have played a major role in the opening up of the economy include the elimination of the state monopoly over foreign trade, the creation of special economic zones, the lifting of the ban on foreign direct investment, the devaluation of the domestic currency (the renminbi, or RMB), and gradual movement towards the convertibility of the currency. All these changes have been carried out through measures involving decentralization and aimed at economic liberalization and the establishment of a market-oriented economy.

With regard to the general strategy of reform, the pragmatic attitude of China's policymakers – contrary to what many people expected – appears to have been superior to the 'big bang' approach. The reform

1

programme has been adopted and carried out without any clearly defined blueprint or timetable. The strategy of 'feeling for the stones while crossing the river' – known as 'gradualism' or 'incrementalism' – is now considered quite successful. In China, this strategy has been accompanied by an experimental approach. The gradual and experimental approaches have not only given society the time and the room to adjust to change, thus avoiding social breakdowns, but they have also offered policymakers plenty of opportunity to make modifications in the various reforms through a process of trial and error. Consequently, although there have been ups and downs, the move towards an open market economy has been smooth and steady. Moreover, the strategies and the concrete measures involved in economic liberalization have pushed China into the ranks of the most rapidly developing countries in the world.

China's reforms are thus usually seen as a success story. The rise of China within the world economy is viewed with particular satisfaction because it contrasts favourably with the experience in developing countries and in transition economies. For this reason, many people have sought to draw lessons from China's reform process. The 'model' of China is referred to in discussions about the most effective ways to address a number of the concerns and problems facing other nations searching for economic growth or successful economic transition. In such discussions, one main conclusion seems to be that economic openness, liberal economic policies and free play for market forces are the keys to economic prosperity.

However, such 'lessons' drawn from the Chinese experience with reform and integration reveal at best only half the truth. They seem to raise more questions than they answer. Why has such therapy worked in some cases, but not in others, or during one period of time, but not always? Moreover, the issue of just how China has achieved rapid world-market integration and a high economic growth rate through partial, far-from-complete market reforms seems still to be a puzzle. Apparently, before any more 'lessons' are learned, more work is needed simply to understand the process.

With regard to China's integration into the world economy, a number of methodological topics needs to be addressed. As a first concern, there is the question of perspective. China's current move towards integration into the world economy is frequently thought to reflect the needs of China's trade relations with other countries and is thus viewed overwhelmingly or exclusively in terms of international trade and capital flows (for example, see Lardy, 1987, 1994). Since foreign trade and capital investment have most obviously been affected by the reforms, studies which take this slant tend to concentrate on state policies in order to find the cause of the changes and to explain China's integration into the world economy. Many of these studies conclude or imply that economic liberalization, openness and closer integration with the world economy are essential to economic growth. This idea underlies a strategy often recommended to transition and developing economies: to achieve economic growth, a nation must strive for 'total openness' and 'full' integration within the world economy.

Yet, devoid of a historical context, such a conclusion may prove to be misleading. There are plenty of instances in which free trade or marketization has been associated with underdevelopment and economic failure. Instead of a focus on economic policies and short-term development, a historical perspective is needed to reveal and explain current patterns of socioeconomic development. In the case of China, integration into the world economy has been a long historical process involving attempts to establish free trade and marketization that have produced different results at different times. Recent developments represent but one stage in this historical process, although, under the circumstances, they seem more conspicuous and more successful.

Another theoretical–methodological problem is the definition of 'world economy'. Discussions about China and the world economy cannot be fruitful unless it is clear what is being discussed. However, despite the voluminous literature on the subject, it appears that 'world economy' actually means different things to different people.

One use of the term suggests that the world economy is an aggregate of all national economies. In this sense, China is and always has been a component of the world economy. Still, a problem arises: How can one talk about China's integration into a world economy of which China is already a part?

Another common use of the term involves the idea that the world economy is 'outside' China, that the world economy is an aggregate of all national economies except the Chinese economy. This raises other questions: What kind of 'world' economy is it if it lacks (one of) its component parts? How is China's relationship with this incomplete totality to be seen? Based on this definition, China's relationship with the world economy has to be viewed mainly in terms of international economic relations. It is thus not surprising that many studies are focusing on foreign trade and capital flows across national boundaries.

This book takes a somewhat different tack. It uses the term 'world economy' in the sense adopted in the world-system analysis approach

(Hopkins and Wallerstein, 1982; Wallerstein, 1974, 1979a, 1980, 1989). According to this approach, the modern 'world economy' – that is, the capitalist world system – originated in Europe. Eventually, it expanded beyond Europe to other parts of the world, incorporating ever larger territories into its orbit until, at the end of the nineteenth century, it encompassed the entire globe.

This world economy is not simply the aggregate of national economies; it is an economic totality, for it is based on a single division of labour, and it is reproducing itself in a process of endless capital accumulation on a worldwide scale. The capitalist world economy, however, is not a single political unit. It functions within the 'inter-state' system, that is, the 'world economy' operates across the boundaries of the jurisdictions of the different nation-states. It is a system of production for profitmaking on markets and the appropriation of the profit on the basis of individual or collective ownership. Nation-states are far from being equal and free competitors; their status within the world economy depends on their position in the worldwide process of capital accumulation, which in turn is structured into three layers: a core, a periphery and a semiperiphery. This structure functions to assure the uninterrupted accumulation of capital on a global scale; thus, during the accumulation process, the core areas appropriate the surplus produced within the entire world economy, and this serves as the basis for the ongoing reproduction of the structure.

National economies become part of the world economy, thus defined, when they are 'incorporated', that is, when they become integrated in the single division of labour of the system. Prior to their incorporation, they are not part of the world economy; but belong to what Wallerstein called the 'external arena'.

A detailed description of the process by which the core of the world economy was formed and the ways in which non-core states are incorporated would require many pages. According to the world-system analysis approach, the gist of the story is as follows.

The core of the world economy emerged in Northwestern Europe during the sixteenth century. By taking advantage of strong state mechanisms, the European-led world economy expanded rapidly into areas on the periphery, creating very weak state mechanisms in these areas. The differing strengths of the state machinery of the core and other areas supported the operation of unequal exchanges. The modern capitalist world economy therefore involves, in addition to the appropriation of surplus value based on class relationships, an appropriation of the surplus of the whole world economy by the core.

Over time, the core-periphery-semiperiphery structure of the modern world economy has remained quite stable, and there has not been much change in the geographical profile of the structure (Arrighi, 1990, 1991, 1994a). During the 500-year existence of the modern world economy, the US, Canada and Japan are the only countries outside the 'traditional' core area that have been able to 'upgrade' to core status. It seems to be extremely difficult, though not absolutely impossible, for a country to change its position in the hierarchical structure either up, or down.

From the conceptual point of view, the strength of the world-system analysis approach is obvious. In the world economy so understood, China remained an 'external arena' until the early nineteenth century. Only later, around the 1840s, after the Western core countries had forced their way into China, did the long historical process of the nation's incorporation into the single division of labour of the capitalist world economy begin.

China's changing relationship with the world economy, as defined above, constitutes the starting point for discussion in this study. However, to lay out the overall process of integration is a tremendous task, partly because of the difficulty in situating China properly within the three-layered structure of core, periphery and semiperiphery. One can say with certainty only that China has never been a core country in the capitalist world economy. It is less clear whether China was incorporated into the world economy as a 'periphery', and, if it was, how long it remained a 'periphery'. This is the case for several reasons.

Politically, unlike many other similarly large areas on the periphery, such as India, the incorporation of China has never involved colonialization either by a single Western power, or by several Western powers. Instead, China was a 'semi-colonial, semi-feudal' society before the successful Communist Revolution in 1949; it was always governed by a national ruling elite with which foreign powers had to consult, although it was constantly faced with the risk of foreign intervention via war, subversion or big-power diplomacy. By the beginning of the twentieth century, China had to be recognized as a factor in world affairs. Following World War II, China, together with the most important Western powers, including the USSR, became one of the five permanent members of the UN Security Council, as well as a signatory member of the General Agreement on Tariffs and Trade. For a substantial period after the 1949 Revolution, China remained outside international organizations such as the UN, the International Monetary Fund and the World Bank. Yet, the weight of China in world affairs in this century has been evident.

One needs only look at China's role in the Cold War or its significant position in the post-Cold War world order.

To be sure, there are other countries which have been incorporated into the world economy without being colonized. However, China's position in the politics of the 'inter-state' system is not a gauge of its economic strength relative to the capitalist world economy. China may have more weight in international politics than Japan, though Japan is a core country, and China is not.

None the less, while it is not common for countries on the periphery to play such an important role in the inter-state relationships of the world system, the difficulty of classifying China as a periphery country has more to do with the characteristics of its economy.

For the 100 years up to 1949, China was an empire in slow but accelerating decline *vis-à-vis* the West. It was backward economically because it lacked modern industries, while its state apparatus was extremely weak. However, China's economy was not typical of the economies of the periphery. Although it was largely agricultural, the economy was not monocultural, as are many peripheral economies. The country's economy remained very diverse, with well-developed handicraft industries able to meet virtually all domestic needs.

Since the 1949 Revolution, China has become a unified country with a very strong state. State-led industrialization has resulted in the establishment of a relatively comprehensive industrial base. In light of the country's progress in science, technology, industry and agriculture, the production sector does not appear to be based merely on 'periphery-like' activities, as described in world-system analysis.[1] Some economic sectors may seem more 'peripheral'; however, others certainly do not.

Moreover, China as a nation-state presents rather unique features. For example, China is 'continental' in terms of surface area, population and the long history of its civilization. More important according to some is China's historical position at the centre of Asia. Despite dynastic decline and the disintegration of the Sino-centric order in Asia during China's incorporation in the world economy, the 'core–periphery' relationship between China and its former tribute-paying neighbours was not totally replaced; rather, it was transformed (Hamashita, 1988, 1993, 1994).

None the less, the last 150 years have seen the growing involvement of China in the world economy either through the intervention of outside forces, or, more recently, through the country's own initiatives. To be sure, this process has been first and foremost a result of the expansion of the capitalist world economy. The world economy encompassed more and broader territory in the nineteenth century. China was among the last to be incorporated. This demonstrates not that China was more peripheral, but the increasing strength of the world economy, which was able to reach further afield and assimilate even relatively powerful states like China.

The purpose of this study is not, however, to map out the entire history of China's incorporation. This would require an examination of the capitalist world economy as an active force with respect to China, which at one time was in the 'external arena'. Instead, this study takes a different angle by focusing on China's responses to the incorporation process and evaluating the outcomes of these responses. By following this approach, the study views the Chinese themselves as the active agents who have been attempting to withstand the pressure of incorporation by means of resistance, emulation, selective adaptation, and so forth, in order to improve the position of China in the world economy, so that China can become like the West and perhaps finally regain the great power status which it held for centuries, if not a millennium, before the rise of the West.

If there is a key phrase to describe the essence of China's responses to the expansion of and incorporation by the world economy, it has to be 'catching up'. The effort to catch up with the core countries reflects a fundamental concept in China's world view and underlies China's long-term struggle to achieve a prominent position in the modern world economy.

For many centuries before the appearance of the ascending Western core countries, the 'outside world' for China was largely limited to Asia, mainly East and Southeast Asia, of which China was the centre. The Asian world order was based on and evolved from a 'regional tributary trade system', in which neighbouring countries paid tribute to China. This system was 'an external expression of basic domestic relations of control which saw a hierarchical division of power – from the provinces [of China] downward and outward' (Hamashita, 1994).

In the integrated system in Asia, China had a core-like position. Its main goal within the region was to preserve the Sino-centric order by conferring titles on and confirming the succession of foreign rulers, maintaining the tributary relationship, granting the use of the Chinese calendar, providing troops on request to protect rulers, and so on. It has therefore been argued that, for a long period before China began to be incorporated into the world economy, the attempts of tributary states such as Vietnam, Korea and Japan to alter the Sino-centric order and China's efforts to maintain it constituted the principal dynamism in East and Southeast Asia (Hamashita, cited in Ikeda, 1996).

The situation was slowly but drastically altered following the expansion of the capitalist world economy into Asia. The Sino-centric order of East and Southeast Asia collapsed (for some observers, it was transformed), and China's 'periphery' was gradually and via various routes and in varying degrees incorporated into the ascending Europe-centred world system (Moulder, 1977; So and Chiu, 1995). China had to face a new world order which functioned on principles unknown to it. The rules of the game were changed. The West, that is, the core of the capitalist world economy, now presented itself as the main challenge to China's survival and destiny. This is the backdrop against which China has been labouring over the last 150 years.

Leaving aside the issue of whether or how completely China has been incorporated into the world economy, we can confidently characterize the historical process since the first half of the nineteenth century as the 'peripheralization' of China. The major force behind incorporation has been the capitalist world economy, which is driven by an innate need for the worldwide expansion of capital accumulation. At least from the point of view of the areas being peripheralized, the centre of capital accumulation, that is, the Western core countries, has been the leading agent in the incorporation of the 'external arena'.

To China, the world economy appears largely identical with the wealthy Western nations. Therefore, China's response to its incorporation within the world economy has been basically directed at the core, that is, by the so-called 'Western countries' (including Japan). This response has included China's long-term efforts to change the country's peripheral status relative to the core by 'catching up' with the West, mainly in terms of economic development. It can be argued that the attempts of the capitalist core to incorporate China as a 'periphery' country and China's efforts to rid itself of this peripheral status constitute the principal dynamism behind China's development since the nineteenth century.

The present study explores this dynamism by focusing on the roads China has taken in the past 150 years. The research is based on the assumption that China's responses to the expansion of the capitalist world economy are the cornerstone of any understanding of the dynamic processes behind the country's socioeconomic development. The study evaluates the general outcome and the socioeconomic consequences of the effort to 'catch up'.

Strictly speaking, the experience of China over the past 150 years cannot be adequately described under the single general heading of 'catching up'. In terms of the organization of the forces for change, these years can be divided into a period of incorporation and a period of catching up. The incorporation of China into the world economy took place after the so-called 'treaty ports' started to operate in the mid-nineteenth century. During the 'century of humiliation', that is, from 1840 to 1949, from the Opium War to the establishment of the People's Republic, China was gradually incorporated into and peripheralized within the world economy. The years since 1949 can be viewed as a period of catching up, during which a unified China under a strong government has vigorously sought the reversal of China's peripheralization and nurtured the hope that 'upward mobility' is possible in the hierarchy of the world economy.

The two periods are distinct in terms of the dominant ideology and the 'official' response to the expansion of the world economy. During the period of incorporation, China slowly recovered from the 'shock' which had been delivered by the British (the hegemonic power within the world economy at the time) and eventually administered a therapy which can be described as 'Westernization'. Although Westernization represented a reluctant admission of the country's weakness and reflected the willingness of the ruling elite to emulate the West, a clearly defined, official policy of catching up with the West was absent. Only since 1949 has catching up become a national goal.

The second period, that is, the period since the Communist victory in 1949, can be further divided into two stages, the pre-reform stage and the reform stage, 1978 being the decisive year of the onset of reform. While catching up has remained an official policy during the entire period, there has been a considerable change in ideology and in key strategies. During the pre-reform stage, catching up, under Mao, was understood in a socialist sense, that is, China should narrow the economic gap with the West through socialism. Social development and economic development were pursued with an antisystemic orientation in an effort not to play by the rules of the capitalist world economy. Hence, the country witnessed large-scale social movements carried out under the banner of 'continuous revolution', industrialization based on the principle of self-reliance, delinking from the world economy, and so forth.

The reform stage of catching up has been conducted 'Deng style'; it has involved a striving towards a mixture of capitalist and socialist elements. 'Modernization' has been a keyword. The reform ideology has emphasized learning from the West, while winding down the self-reliant approach and adapting to the rules and codes of behaviour accepted in international business, with the aim of boosting China's competitiveness and its upward mobility within the world system. Social movements have largely disappeared as organized reactions against the expansion of the capitalist world economy.

Overall, China has travelled a winding road in its quest for a new identity with respect to the capitalist world economy, and the results have varied. This study is organized so as to outline the major characteristics of the changes, active forces and socioeconomic outcomes of the period of incorporation and the period of catching up, the latter including a pre-reform stage and a reform stage.

The state, the social and economic legacies of the past and the Chinese overseas diaspora are examined in the section dealing with developments during the current, reform stage so as to highlight some of the aspects of China's present situation that have appeared favourable and even unique to the country. It will be argued that, although the recent rapid growth in foreign trade and investment has been directly linked to the reform policies of the state, particularly the policy of economic openness, evolving social and economic conditions, including geopolitical changes, have permitted these reform policies to be formulated and implemented, with the apparently positive result that, in contrast to the past, important strides have been made in the effort to catch up. In other words, the economic gains during the reform stage are viewed as a product of historical factors as much as of design.

Throughout modern history, China has constantly tried to strengthen its position in the world economy. From the first contest with the Western powers during the Opium War up to the eve of the victory of the Communist-led Revolution, all China's attempts ended in humiliating defeat and the further weakening of the country. Neither the 'open door' policy forced on China by the capitalist core countries in the nineteenth century, nor the subordinate collaboration with them during the first half of the twentieth century worked to the advantage of the country. On the contrary, China not only fell from its self-proclaimed status as 'Middle Kingdom' of the world; it also became the 'sick man of Asia'. China grew so weak that it was a victim in every major imperialist war in which it was involved, even when it happened to be on the winning side, such as during World War I. Its early experiences with integration into the world economy through Westernization did not result in prosperity and ascendance, but in dependence and further economic backwardness.

Drawing on these lessons, the new leadership brought to power by the Communist-led Revolution has undertaken a serious effort to reposition China within the world system. 'Delinking' and 'self-reliance' were the keywords during the first round of economic development. While the strategy which they describe was adopted partly because of the pressure of the world order during the Cold War, it also appeared to the new policymakers to represent an attractive alternative path which their predecessors over the previous 100 years had never been able or willing to follow. Since 1978, the government has initiated a new series of efforts to catch up, including vigorous steps to relink China with the world market.

Of course, this is an oversimplified version of the modern economic history of China. None the less, it can shed light on the ongoing debate over the issue of economic integration. For example, economic openness and delinking can appear to be in opposition irrespective of historical context. Economic openness is believed to be superior in promoting development. Thus, the current economic growth of China seems to be tied to the country's recent pursuit of economic openness. However, this description fails to take into account the important connection between openness and delinking. China's advances under 'self-reliance' – the so-called 'autarchic policy' – have played a rather positive role in the recent growth of the country. Because it favoured political independence, self-reliance led China to achieve a higher degree of economic autonomy, permitting domestic control over capital accumulation, resource allocation and the distribution of wealth. When China re-opened to the outside world in the late 1970s, it was able to assume a much stronger political and economic position within the world community than would have been otherwise possible. Although, like regions outside the core area of the world economy, China continues to be at a disadvantage in terms of the world division of labour, the foundations laid during the pre-reform stage have none the less enabled China to re-enter the world economy not only as a strong state, but also with a structurally more coherent and more firmly grounded economy.

Geopolitics and geoculture have always been important contributing factors in defining China's position in the world, and they seem to have been especially favourable to China's ascendance during the reform years. In particular, the relative success of China's current efforts to enter the world market must be understood within the context of the changing conditions in the world system, the substantial contribution of the Chinese overseas diaspora, and the rise of East Asia as an economically significant region.

Given its huge size and advanced civilization, China occupies an important position in the world, but especially with respect to Asia. The establishment of Western dominance in the world economy coincided with the collapse of the Chinese empire. Eventually, not only were China's tribute-paying neighbours in East Asia incorporated into the world system, but also the territory of China proper was encroached upon. China was forced to lease Hong Kong to Great Britain. In 1949 Taiwan's temporary but *de facto* separation from the mainland was backed by the US-led Western powers.

These two parts of China embarked on distinct paths to development. The same has been true of other East Asian countries. By the end of the 1970s, when China began to pursue a policy of economic openness, some of the surrounding East Asian nations had already begun to move upward within the world economy. Japan became the only non-Western country to join the core. The four so-called 'Asian tigers' – South Korea, Taiwan, Hong Kong and Singapore – experienced such rapid economic growth that they have often been referred to as 'economic miracles', and they were able to join the ranks of the 'semiperiphery'.

By operating in the world economy rather successfully, the Asian tigers have accumulated considerable physical and human capital, know-how, management skills and trading networks. These assets have proved of great value to China, while historical bonds, cultural similarities and geographical proximity have begun to encourage closer economic cooperation between China and other East Asian economies. The intense and growing economic relations among mainland China, Hong Kong and Taiwan are especially salient. Once tragically separated from China because of the weakness of the country, Hong Kong and Taiwan in the 1980s and 1990s have become instrumental to China's efforts to establish an open economy. The surrounding East Asian economies, particularly Hong Kong and Taiwan, have performed a crucial service by acting as channels and bridges between China and world markets at a time when Asia is achieving economic development and the world economy is being restructured.

With the rapid re-entry of China into the world market, a new pattern of regional integration is appearing in Asia. Whether this new regional pattern can be compared to the historical Asian model is open to speculation. In any case, one can expect that an emerging Asia will have a strong impact on the existing regional configuration of the world economy.

These and other issues and questions will be discussed in detail in this book. Hopefully, the following analyses of long-term and large-scale changes will help us not only to understand how the integration of China in the world economy has taken place, but also to discern the direction in which China is moving.

Part I: Westernization (1840–1949)

PART I: WESTERNIZATION (1840–1949)

Part I discusses China's reaction to its incorporation into the capitalist world economy during the approximately 100 years from the Opium War to 1949. These 100 years occupy a special place in China's long history. Among Chinese, they are widely referred to as the 'century of humiliation'.

At one time Asia, especially the 'Middle Kingdom' of China, enjoyed a higher level of culture, civilization and economic, scientific and technological development, as well as more advanced social organizations, than did Europe, which was geographically and economically marginal with respect to Africa–Eurasia (Abu-Lughod, 1989; Frank, 1994, 1998; Wallerstein, 1974).

European-centred capitalism emerged in the sixteenth century and by the nineteenth century had come to dominate the world. Consequently, regions outside Europe, including China, were in relative decline. None the less, China remained central to Asia and an 'external arena' in the world economy until the early-nineteenth century. The Opium War in 1840–42 heralded the era of China's incorporation into the world economy and precipitated the process of the country's marginalization and peripheralization.

Like other parts of the world outside the European core countries, China's incorporation into the world economy was not a voluntary act undertaken by China. The process of incorporation was initiated and led by Great Britain, the 'hegemonic power' of the period, and, to break China's resistance, all possible means were resorted to, including 'legal trade', outright smuggling, diplomatic manoeuvring and political pressure. Most typically, when economic penetration alone was not able to do the job, wars were waged to clear the way for the exercise of economic power.

On the other hand, incorporation was not a unilateral process. China's responses also had a profound impact on the overall socioeconomic dynamics of the process. The reaction of China to its incorporation into the world economy after the Opium War is discussed in this book under the heading 'Westernization'. The word 'Westernization' was employed formally by the first organized movement to confront the challenge of incorporation and captures well the nature of successive government responses, both formal and informal, before 1949. These responses involved attempts to emulate Western methods of industrial development and to reproduce the perceived advantages of the West.

1 The Westernization Movement

By the time the Europeans launched an intensive drive to incorporate China at the beginning of the 1840s, the capitalist world economy was already completing the incorporation of other major new zones into its division of labour, most importantly, the Indian subcontinent, the Ottoman empire, the Russian empire, and West Africa. In the case of the Indian subcontinent and West Africa, incorporation went hand-in-hand with colonialization, while the Ottoman empire and the Russian empire were drawn into the world system without formal colonization, although with different results: while the Ottoman empire was fragmented, the boundaries of Russia remained relatively unchanged (Wallerstein, 1989).

In the case of China, incorporation took the form of 'semi-colonialization'. China was not formally colonized by a single country, as happened to India, its Southern neighbour. Nor did it totally escape colonialization, as did Japan, its neighbour to the Northeast (Moulder, 1977; So and Chiu, 1995). Rather, China became a semi-colony in the sense that, although it formally remained a sovereign state, it resembled a colony in terms of power structure and the economy. This was made possible by a treaty system which was imposed and maintained not by a single country, but by all the major Western core countries.

In this process, the significance of the Opium War between Great Britain and China can hardly be overestimated. A dispute between the Chinese authorities and British traders over the flourishing opium trade, or rather, over opium smuggling into China, was the ostensible spark that touched off the war. For the Chinese authorities, the war was a crusade against an illegal trade in drugs which were extremely harmful not only to the physical and mental health of the nation, but also to the coffers of the Qing imperial government. For the British, the issue was a matter of free trade, and the use of force was considered legitimate in this 'just' cause of opening up the Chinese market, which until then had been a source of frustration for foreign traders.[1]

The consequences of the war were far-reaching and more profound than initially expected by either side. The victory by Great Britain in the war provided unprecedented opportunities for the incorporation of China into the world trading framework and the world division of labour. However, it is also true that, for numerous reasons, this process was

16

much less rapid and more difficult than the West had anticipated. For China, the total defeat of the country in the war forced it to open up to the world market. Now exposed to the dynamics of the world economy, China entered the most turbulent period of its modern history. In the midst of economic integration, there was persistent social unrest in the intervals between wars, revolts and revolutions. Increasingly, economic and social development in China became heavily influenced by external forces.

During the course of the war, the British military had occupied several coastal cities from the old port of Canton to Shanghai. The war ended with the signing of the Treaty of Nanking on 29 August 1842. Other Western powers, such as the US and France, immediately came forward to demand trading rights similar to those acquired by the British, and treaties were signed with these powers in short order. These treaties provided for the abolishment of the officially sanctioned and controlled monopolistic system of trade, the opening of a number of ports to foreign trade, extra-territoriality, most-favoured-nation status for Western powers, the cession of Hong Kong to Great Britain, and a fixed tariff.[2]

China's defeat in the Opium War turned out to be but the first step in the country's peripheralization. Great Britain and the other Western powers were quicker than the Chinese ruling class to realize the extent to which the 'Middle Kingdom' had already fallen behind, and they intensified their efforts to incorporate China. During the decades that followed, the Western powers launched repeated assaults on China's sovereignty, scrambling for political and economic concessions. Foreign military and economic invasion and, in particular, the utter incompetence of the Qing government in facing up to the outside challenge perplexed both the ruling class and the populace.

To be sure, China had been invaded by other nations or peoples before the Opium War. The Qing Dynasty was controlled by the Manchu minority long before and after the Opium War. For nearly five centuries up to the late-fourteenth century, minorities had ruled large territories within what is China today or had established central authority over the entire country; the latter had been the case of the Yuan Dynasty (1271–1368) under the Mongols. However, these previous events had not derailed China from the main course of its historical evolution. These peoples who had invaded or ruled China had been less well developed economically and socially, and they had not been able to provide alternative modes of production or social structure that were sufficiently powerful to change either the general perception of 'Chineseness', or the country's habitual manner of conducting domestic and foreign affairs. The modern capitalist world economy was quite different. Not only did it appear to be far more advanced in terms of technology, but it also demonstrated ways of thinking and behaving that were alien to the Chinese. For example, the Chinese ruling elites were surprised that 'barbarians' considered foreign trade so essential that they wanted to affect it by waging war and conduct it exclusively on their own terms.

The Opium War was indeed a 'shock', and it took the Chinese a long time to devise a 'therapy'. Initially, the imperial government had great difficulty understanding the significance of the war and did not know how to respond. Most officials and scholars viewed the war as merely an historical accident. Only after the second Opium War in 1860 – during which the Qing imperial court was chased from the capital, great damage was inflicted on Chinese property and many Chinese were killed – did the country begin to awaken from its torpor.

In response to the foreign menace, a movement known as *Yangwu yundong* ('Westernization movement') was started by government officials. The Westernization movement had two major goals: *ziqiang* ('self-strengthening') and *qiufu* ('pursuit of wealth'). It had become clear by this time that China was no longer the 'Middle Kingdom'. The country's very survival was at the mercy of Western nations, the most powerful 'barbarians' it had ever encountered. Something had to be done if China was ever to become the equal of the Western powers and recover its status as a great nation in the new world order. Changes were required, and, in the eyes of officials, the changes which needed to be introduced were those that would make China stronger and richer.

However, there was no consensus as to what had caused China to stumble behind the West. Few, if any, officials at the time recognized that the problem was the lack of industrialization, although this eventually became the firm conviction of all government leaders after the fall of the Qing Dynasty.[3] In reality, even long after the 1840s, not many things offered by the industrialized West were admired by the Chinese. On the eve of the Opium War, the only imported Western 'goods' that could be said to have had a significant impact on the Chinese market was opium. As a result of industrialization, Manchester became the main source of manufactured goods for the entire world, but it found no market in China. A few Western manufactured goods, such as watches and clocks, did find their way into a small number of homes (those of the ruling elites) in China, but they were enjoyed rather as exquisite and exotic curiosities and may not have even been considered comparable to similar products of skilled Chinese craftsmen and artists. Tangible evidence of the lack of appreciation in China of the achievements of the 'industrial revolutions' in the West is provided by the long-term imbalance in trade that favoured China. In fact, China had little awareness of the 'industrial revolutions' and did not come to understand their significance until very late.

However, in one area China's inferiority *vis-à-vis* the West was obvious to all: arms. This was the major and perhaps the only lesson the Qing government learned from its wars with the West. This perception led to the conclusion that China had 'to use the superior abilities of the barbarians to dominate the barbarians' (*shi yi zhi changji yi zhi yi*). In a word, the ruling elites believed that China needed to catch up to the West in terms of military power, especially advanced weaponry.

How much change would be needed for this purpose? Not much, at least not so much as to shake the socioeconomic foundations of the dynasty's power. The Westernization movement would borrow a few practical things from the West, but would not modify the Chinese (Confucian) essence. 'Self-strengthening' meant the strengthening of China through the strengthening of the Qing court, and the way to achieve this was to return to Confucian principles, while adopting advanced technology in selected areas, especially the arms industry. This approach was described as letting 'the wisdom of China serve as substance and the learning of the West serve in practice' (*zhongxue wei ti, xixue wei yong*).

The desire to improve the military did not merely reflect a need to defend the country from foreign aggression. During the late Qing period, China was confronted with serious threats from the outside, but the ruler of the dynasty and the entire ruling class also faced serious challenges from within. Domestic rebellions kept rattling the dynasty. The Qing government was quite willing to ally itself with foreign military forces in order to crush domestic rebellion and maintain its rule. Thus, immediately after a settlement had been reached with the Anglo–French invaders following the second Opium War, the Qing government appealed to them for help in putting down peasant rebellions, particularly the Taiping rebellion, and it succeeded. In case after case, the Qing government's handling of domestic and foreign challenges to its rule suggested that no serious cultural or ideological barriers existed to its willingness to collaborate with Western powers if such collaboration would help maintain the dynasty. The Westernization movement in fact had as much to do with strengthening the regime as with strengthening China as a nation.

Formally undertaken in the 1860s, the Westernization movement initially focused on the military. The lessons learned from the repeated defeats by superior Western arms and the fresh memory of the suppression of the Taiping rebellion with the help of Western weaponry supported the government's belief that a modern, well-equipped military force would be able to put a halt to both foreign invasion and domestic rebellion. The government-led development of an arms industry, particularly shipbuilding and the manufacture of guns, formed the basis of the country's modern industrial sector. The first production facilities – a few small workshops in arsenals – were opened in the early 1860s. Jiangnan Arsenal, the first large-scale military enterprise, was established in Shanghai in 1865. Over a dozen military enterprises were set up in the next few years. The nascent military industry was mainly created and managed by provincial governments and financed by the state.

The effort to build a military industry based on the Western model depended heavily on foreign technology, expertise and materials. Foreigners were hired as supervisors and technicians. Almost all machinery and equipment, as well as raw materials, were imported.

After the 1870s the government's programme of Westernization was extended from the military to civilian industries. The government became involved in the creation of enterprises in shipping, mining and textile production. Government participation took different forms in terms of ownership and management. While the military sector was mainly government financed and managed (*guanban*), civilian industries were usually privately owned but supervised by the state (*guandu shangban*) or jointly owned by the state and private merchants (*guan shang he ban*). In fact, all these enterprises were controlled by the government to some degree. However, this government control focused on the tradition of tax-farming, that is, the distribution of profits rather than reinvestment, and profiteering rather than industrialization.

During the early period of industrialization, the machine production of cotton goods was a leading industry in the Western countries, and cotton mills were proving very successful in Japan by the 1880s. In China, the first and largest cotton textile mill was established in Shanghai in 1878. A few others were set up in the following years. The government helped finance the mills and granted tax exemptions and temporary monopoly status to mills producing cotton cloth and yarn. There was a handful of such mills in operation by the early 1890s. Privately owned enterprises in filature, shipbuilding, machinery and other light industries had begun to appear earlier, while privately owned cotton textile factories remained relatively undeveloped until after the 1880s.

The government involvement in the establishment of a modern civilian industrial sector had little to do with a desire or a strategy to create comprehensive national industries. It was largely prompted by the need to develop a strong military. For the Qing government, the development of civilian industries represented a way to 'pursue wealth' in order to finance the arms industry. The government also became involved in coalmining, the production of iron and machinery, railroad construction and so forth with the immediate aim of obtaining raw materials for military industries, which were then heavily dependent on foreign markets. Civilian industries were under the strict supervision of government officials who, more often than not, were either corrupt or ignorant of management and production methods. Although these enterprises were supposed to be run for profit, earnings were frequently siphoned off by the Qing government for other purposes. When enterprises encountered financial difficulties, they tended to borrow heavily from foreign financial institutions, and some of them eventually became foreign owned.

The support of the Qing court for even this limited level of industrial development was at best half-hearted. A conservative element within the government resisted it. As long as there was no immediate military threat, many people at the top preferred to spend only to maintain their extravagant lifestyles.[4] Moreover, for the ruling class as a whole, despite the small scale and the partial nature of industrialization, the change seemed too extreme and took place too rapidly, and this generated a fear of unwanted disturbances to the existing social order.

The Westernization movement, with its focus on the development of a military industry, proved a failure. The military industry did produce ships, guns and cannons, but it failed the test during each of the subsequent wars with the Western powers. The Qing army was defeated during a French invasion in 1884 and again in the Sino–Japanese War in 1894, in which the Japanese were victorious over the Qing Northern Ocean Navy, armed with Chinese-made ships and guns.[5] After the Sino–Japanese War, the Westernization movement was brought to an end.

The Westernization movement had lasted for three and a half decades. It was initiated following a military defeat and ended after a military defeat. It failed most obviously in its primary goal of building a strong military force. However, for the government, the effort was not a total failure, since the military, which proved so incapable of punishing foreign aggression, helped maintain order at home. The arms were put to 'good' use by the Qing government in the suppression of popular rebellions, such as the Nian rebellion, a Muslim rebellion in the Northwest, and minority rebellions in the Southwest. The defeat in the Sino–Japanese War and the collapse of the Chinese military industry also dealt a severe blow to civilian industries which were closely associated with the military.

Why did China fail so utterly in its attempt to avoid being peripheralized, while Japan succeeded? There is no simple answer. The development of a military industry might have guided China through the critical phase of industrialization and fostered a breakthrough into self-sustaining growth. Why this did not happen has been pondered by generations of thinkers. It is generally agreed that success in industrial development would have required more central support and a more comprehensive approach. It would have required a whole set of circumstances that was lacking in China, including clearly defined national economic and political goals, more determined and stronger state leadership and more large scale and more rational resource mobilization and allocation. Government-sponsored or government-supervised enterprises were relatively small and were concentrated in a few small enclaves within the treaty ports. This limited their potential role in fostering industrialization nationwide. Although there was a certain amount of development among nongovernment-owned enterprises, these were unable to generate growth momentum because of a lack of capital and the difficulties of market entry caused by government policies which, in order to protect state monopolies in certain areas, were discriminatory against private undertakings. The Westernization movement, as the core concept in an early effort at industrialization, remained the concern of only a small segment of the ruling elites and was alien to the vast majority of the Chinese people. Thus, while Japan grew into a powerful nation at China's doorstep, able to carry out successful military actions against China so as to further its own ambitions in Asia, the industrialization of China was ultimately doomed.

In 1898, following the failure of the Westernization movement, a political reform, known as the 'hundred-day' reform, was initiated in order to generate institutional change from above. This reform grew partly from a lesson learned from the Westernization movement: without certain political and institutional changes, there could be no genuine economic progress. However, while the reform was sufficiently radical to invite a decisive reaction from the rulers who easily crushed it, it was too conservative – it did not tackle the fundamental problems of the regime – to gain wide popular support. Failure was unavoidable. A revolution, not a reform, would be needed to change the regime.

When the competition among the Western powers over colonial expansion intensified at the turn of the century, China went up for grabs. In the ten years following the Sino–Japanese War, China was forced to lease territory to the Germans, Russians, British, Japanese, and French during 1897–98, was plundered by an alliance of eight

Western powers that marched into its capital in 1900, and suffered through the 1904–05 Russo–Japanese War over control of its Northeastern provinces. According to Chinese historians, each of these events caused far more damage to China than had the two Opium Wars. They resulted in large losses of territory and huge war indemnities. Major harbours in coastal areas and along inland rivers fell under the control of Westerners, and the number of treaty ports increased from 15 in 1870 to 40 in 1900 (Luo, 1991). China became a 'semi-colony' of all the major Western powers, including Japan.

In the early-twentieth century, China sank further into crisis and at times seemed about to fall apart as it fought seemingly impossible battles against peripheralization. The 1911 Revolution, resulting in the establishment of the Republic, finally ended the dynastic cycle and, from this viewpoint, represented a breakthrough in the country's history. However, the legacy of the Qing Dynasty continued to haunt post-dynastic China. The country was militarily divided under warlords until the late 1920s, when the Nanjing (Nanking) regime of Guomindang (Kuomintang or KMT, hereinafter, GMD) unified a large part of China and established control over major urban centres.

This central government soon came under siege because of renewed Japanese imperialism. Japan annexed the Northeast in the early 1930s and then in 1937 waged a full-fledged eight-year war against China that ended in 1945. At the same time, the Nanjing regime, like the Qing imperial court before it, faced constant domestic unrest, especially the long-lasting and increasingly powerful challenge of the Communist-led Revolution. The GMD government finally lost to the Communists in the Civil War of 1945–49.

Not surprisingly, during most of its existence, the GMD regime had been preoccupied with consolidating its power, and this consumed much of its energy. The government was constantly engaged in military actions to eliminate the domestic armed opposition led by the Communists in the 1930s. Its focus on fighting Communists instead of resisting foreign expansion, especially the Japanese military occupation of the Northeastern provinces, eventually cost it popular support in the face of a surging nationalism.[6]

None the less, the Nanjing government was able for a short period before World War II to implement a few economic development programmes in the urban centres under its control. These programmes concentrated on financial policies and were carried out by Western-trained officials, who tried to apply the knowledge they had obtained from the West. The government undertook a financial reform to establish a unified fiscal and budget system. One of the most notable changes was the substitution of the silver dollar for the tael (an ancient unit of account) in 1933 and the introduction of paper currency as legal tender in 1935 (So and Chiu, 1995, p. 124; Xu and Wu, 1993, pp. 59–84). National banks were developed, and some of these were authorized to buy and sell foreign currencies. This meant that, for the first time in China's history, the foreign exchanges were controlled by government banks.

These reform measures brought the modern sector of the economy increasingly under the government's financial influence and made it possible for the government to control credit. However, the government's financial reform brought about few achievements in terms of savings and investment for long-term industrial growth. Capital was not mobilized, while available resources went mainly for the support of military actions against the domestic opposition.

Telecommunications and transportation, especially railroad transportation, were two other areas that saw major government effort. The Ministry of Railways was established to be responsible for railroad construction and improvement. A few new rail lines were completed. Airlines were created, and the postal service and telecommunications network were extended.

One significant accomplishment during this period was the restoration of national sovereignty. In the late 1920s, tariff autonomy was partially recovered. A number of foreign concessions in Chinese cities were gradually revoked. In 1943, the Western powers, led by the US and Great Britain, desiring to associate China in the war and construct the postwar world order, agreed to relinquish extra-territoriality in China. This was an important step in China's effort to shake off its semi-colonial status, although it was made possible as a result of big-power rivalry and undertaken as 'a symbolic gesture to counter Japanese propaganda about Anglo-American imperialism' (Iriye, 1986, p. 533).

The economy improved during this period. It has been estimated that, from 1920 to 1936, the rise (adjusted for inflation) in agricultural output was 17.5 per cent, industrial output, 52.3 per cent, transportation output, 97.6 per cent, and in total output in the modern industrial sector, 172.5 per cent. Textiles, agricultural processing and a few other areas in light industrial manufacturing performed more satisfactorily. However, the growth was quite uneven among industrial sectors and from year to year. The world economic crisis in the early 1930s led to decline in a number of industries (Xu and Wu, 1993, pp. 120–1, 738–44).

Overall, the degree of industrial development was well short of what might be characterized as a beginning of industrialization. The modern industrial sector was left largely to its own devices, although industrialization was generally recognized as being essential to the national economy and the public was becoming aware of the crucial importance of modern science, technology and industry. If a lack of direct government control and regulation over economic activities is a feature of a 'free economy', then the early experience in industrial development in China appears to have been quite a good example of this approach. However, the amount of industrial development this approach generated was far from significant.

In view of state policies and the development pattern during this period, a certain level of continuity can be discerned in the ideas adopted and the choices made. Although the GMD government never formally or officially advocated a Westernization campaign, it did turn to Western models in the attempt to achieve 'national salvation', as the Qing government had tried to do. The main difference was the fact that, despite the absence of an official campaign, Westernization proceeded much further under the GMD regime than it had under the Qing Dynasty. The regime depended heavily on Western-trained personnel in the management of economic initiatives and on Western models in charting the economic course of the country.

The government relegated land taxation, which had been the principal source of revenue under the dynasties, to provincial administrations, while relying for its own revenue on customs duties, the salt tax and commercial taxes, which accounted for 42 per cent, 17 per cent and 9 per cent, respectively, of total government revenue in 1935. However, government revenues were able to cover only 80 per cent of expenditures, of which 40 per cent went to the military and 25 to 37 per cent to debt servicing (Hsu, 1990, p. 573). This fiscal policy caused a chronic budgetary imbalance that eventually led to hyperinflation, which produced disincentives for industrial development.

The disastrous fiscal policy of deficit spending, coupled with other factors such as government corruption and the lack of popular support, showed that the GMD regime, like the one before it, was incapable of providing leadership in the industrialization of the country. This was so despite the fact that the Nanjing government found itself in a better international environment than had the Qing Dynasty, since the world economic depression in the 1930s and the scramble for supremacy among the Western powers that culminated in the two world wars had created room for manoeuvre.

The dependence on Western models also fostered a community of interests between the ruling GMD and the West. Government economic policies supported favourable conditions for those foreign forces which had benefited under the old regime. In particular, the Western powers gained as many privileges and benefits by ostensibly supporting the GMD regime as they had once gained by pressuring the Qing government.

The GMD government generated its power through the military; its economic policies were formulated in accordance with capitalist concerns, and it had a vested interest in collaboration with foreign forces and in cooperation between bureaucrat capital and comprador capital.[7] In short, it was as remote from most of Chinese society, that is, rural society, as were the foreign capitalists operating in the country.

The GMD government 'often understood modern finance, foreign trade and exchange, transport and telecommunications better than it understood its own hinterland. Its modern-minded officials seldom felt at home in the villages' (Fairbank *et al*., 1965, p. 692). The vested interest of the Nanjing regime in maintaining landed property and the superficial understanding the Western-trained government bureaucrats had of China's problems were most clearly demonstrated in the government indifference towards land problems in rural areas. For the government, agricultural backwardness and the poor living conditions of peasants were not stumbling blocks. Industrial development was never undertaken outside urban boundaries and contributed little to improving conditions in rural areas, where the majority of the people lived.

From the mid-nineteenth century to the mid-twentieth century, there were several stages in the response of the successive regimes in China to the military and economic expansion of the world economy. The initial stage involved a doomed attempt to meet the demands of the Western powers by giving up some national sovereignty in the misguided hope that China would then be left free of further interference. Realizing that autarchy was no longer an option, the regimes subsequently sought to emulate the West and achieve 'self-strengthening' in order to reach a better position within the world 'inter-state' system and the world economy. At first, the focus was on the development of an arms industry dependent on Western technology, equipment, materials, and personnel. This approach failed to improve either the country's position in the inter-state system, or its economic strength. The GMD government also applied Western methods in finance and certain areas of industrial production.

The overall result seems to have been that, while China gained some recognition of its political independence and token admission to the club of big nations in world affairs, it became further integrated into the world economy as a periphery country. The fate of China remained largely at the mercy of foreign powers, the changing friendships and rivalries of which had a decisive influence on the pattern of China's economic and political development. In other words, China's development was not so much the result of the nation's efforts; rather, it was despite the nation's efforts.

Among the Chinese people, questions were frequently raised about the disappointing outcome of the country's endeavours, especially with regard to the aggressive behaviour of the West, which China, swallowing its pride, had tried so hard to emulate. 'Why do Western countries thrive, while China continues to decline by pursuing Westernization?', Liang Qichao, a famous reformist under the Qing Dynasty at the turn of the century, asked after the failure of the Westernization movement.[8] Mao Zeodong (1949, p. 413) later discussed the popular sense of frustration. 'Imperialist aggression shattered the fond dreams of the Chinese about learning from the West', wrote Mao. 'It was very odd – why were the teachers always committing aggression against their pupils? The Chinese learned a good deal from the West, but they could not make it work and were never able to realize their ideals. All their repeated struggles, including such a country-wide movement as the Revolution of 1911, ended in failure. This was indeed a painful question which troubled many reform-minded people.

None the less, despite all the frustrations, at that time few wondered whether Westernization, even if pursued more vigorously and more extensively, could ever be achieved, much less permit China to become a power in the world economy. People seemed not to be asking the right questions, and they were clearly not finding the right solutions to the ongoing failures. The right answer to the question of why China was not able to develop Western-type capitalism cannot be found by looking exclusively at the internal factors within China. In response to this question, Mao (1965, p. 310) offered a most insightful comment. 'It is certainly not the purpose of the imperialist power invading China to transform feudal China into capitalist China,' he said. 'On the contrary, their purpose is to transform China into their own semi-colony or colony.'

2 Foreign Trade

The Opium War initiated a period during which, under the pressure of armed conflict, diplomatic manoeuvring and political and military blackmail, China was locked into an iron-clad treaty system, from which it was not freed until 1943, a little more than 100 years later. The treaties were signed by the Chinese government and individual countries, but the privileges acquired by any Western country through a single treaty were automatically conferred on other Western countries because of the most-favoured-nation clause.

To be incorporated into the world economy, China's trade regime and institutions had to be remodelled so that they would be accessible to the expansion of foreign trade, that is, the Chinese domestic market had first to be opened up to Western goods. During these 100-odd years, the treaty-port trade system became one of the most important features of China's trade regime. Immediately after the end of the Opium War, in addition to the traditional trading port of Canton, four other coastal cities, Amoy (Xiamen), Fuzhou, Ningpo and Shanghai, were opened to trade. During the first half of the twentieth century, the system came to include around 90 treaty ports or open ports and about 25 ports of call for steamships. These ports were open not only to foreign trade, foreign consular representation and the residence of foreigners, but also offered foreigners other privileges and gave them control over certain administrative functions under the legal institution of 'extra-territoriality'.

This system, which had begun as a legal device mainly to help Westerners avoid the Chinese judiciary, became a tool to protect foreign firms and corporations from the payment of taxes to China. As Westerners took more control, Western legal practices, with their special tailoring for commerce, such as legal incorporation and proceedings for the enforcement of contracts, became more common.

The *de facto* foreign control over port concessions was instrumental in making these ports the nodes for the entry of foreign trade into other parts of China. As they gained access to more ports and extended their influence along the coasts of the country, the Western powers formed a nurturing matrix for modern-style Chinese trade and enterprise, although they kept the Chinese bureaucracy largely away from the new businesses. The ports became points of entry for international commercial networks and were centres of foreign commerce, capital investment and other economic activities.

Judged from various angles, foreign trade in China during most of this period was predominantly the affair of Westerners. The trade in the treaty ports was conducted essentially by Western trading firms, often in partnership with Chinese. The Westerners generally functioned as business executives, while the Chinese partners, or 'compradors', acted as the domestic agents who executed the transactions or filled the orders.

At first, Western firms monopolized the export markets, while the Chinese merchants and commercial organizations were involved basically in supplying the goods for export. In the late-nineteenth century the Chinese began to establish their own organizations to obtain goods and engage in the preliminary sorting and processing of products for export. Chinese merchants and trading organizations traditionally played a more important role in the exportation of tea. Foreign traders usually bought tea in bulk from Chinese dealers at the ports. Under the Western monopoly over exports for the world market, the port cities were actually the 'foreign' market for the Chinese. Chinese participation normally concluded there. The first Chinese firms to undertake foreign trade were founded mainly by two types of people: the compradors, who eventually established commercial firms independently of the foreign firms to which they had provided services, and Chinese merchants, who either started new trading firms, or expanded their previous businesses into foreign trade. In general, Chinese foreign trading companies were modelled on their foreign rivals. They began to acquire some significance only after the 1920s.

Foreign firms also handled most of China's import trade. Chinese merchants became involved usually after the goods had already been delivered at the treaty ports. Their role was more important in small ports, where they acted as distributors of imported goods, particularly staples. Gradually, there was a sort of division of labour whereby the tasks of the Westerners and the Chinese merchants tended to diverge, rather than converge. For example, taking advantage of the development of steamshipping beginning in the 1860s, Chinese dealers in imported cotton textiles or opium began to bypass the Western offices in the smaller ports and make their purchases directly in Shanghai or Hong Kong. As a result, while some Western offices were closed, those that remained dealt in goods for export and the sale of more specialized imports, leaving the distribution of staples largely in Chinese hands.

Thus, 'the business of the foreign trading firms in the early Republic had become heavily concentrated in the major treaty ports – in the actual importation (typically as commission agents) of foreign goods for sale to Chinese dealers and in the exportation of Chinese goods (with some processing) from these same places' (Feuerwerker, 1983, pp. 195–6).

Like China's external trade, the country's modern financial institutions were also 'foreign' in nature in the sense that they had been established and developed by Westerners, were concentrated almost exclusively in the treaty ports and initially provided services to further the import and export business of Western firms. They reflected a financial structure which had little to do with traditional Chinese banking institutions, the *qian zhuang* ('money house'). At first, Western merchant houses themselves undertook to provide the services, such as banking, foreign exchange and insurance, that were essential to their businesses. By the second decade of the twentieth century, 12 foreign banks were operating in China. These banks financed the import and export trade operated by Western firms. As in foreign trade, a dual structure emerged in the financial sector as well, with Western and Chinese banking institutions operating in different areas, although the linkages between them somehow increased. Foreign banks sometimes advanced credit more or less directly to Chinese merchants, notably through short-term loans to the *qian zhuang*, which in turn lent money to the merchants. Before it was abolished in 1911, this practice had given Western banks considerable leverage over the money market in China's emerging financial centre, Shanghai.

Since the banks active in the port trade were largely in the hands of Western concerns and the trade itself was dominated by Western firms, neither the Chinese government, nor Chinese businesses exercised much influence over the foreign exchange market. In fact, Western banking institutions in the port cities practically controlled the foreign exchange market in China. Because of the frequently large fluctuations in the exchange rate between Chinese silver currency and gold (the world standard), foreign exchange dealings and international arbitrage provided substantial profits to Western banks, especially the Hong Kong Bank, a well-established British-owned concern, which announced daily exchange rates that were accepted as official by the entire Shanghai market.

Modern banks and insurance companies based on Chinese capital began to emerge early in the twentieth century, especially after 1911. It took more than 20 years for Chinese banks to break into the existing foreign trade and financing networks. By 1925, the number of Chinese banks had surpassed that of foreign banks and joint-venture banks.[1] According to one study, Chinese banks accounted for about 41 per cent of the total capital, foreign banks for 32 per cent, *qian zhuang* for 23 per cent, and joint-venture banks for the remaining 5 per cent (Du, 1991). Because of this, Chinese banks were able to finance a number of domestic firms engaged in import and export. Chinese banks became one of the main sources of credit for domestic foreign-trade firms. As a result, Western banks began to lose their privileged position with respect to Chinese banks, especially after 1928. However, they continued to be pre-eminent in the area of foreign trade, which remained monopolized by Western firms. The influence of the Western banks on the Chinese economy outside the foreign-trade sector was insignificant. While the banks had links with the nascent modern sector of the country, they functioned overwhelmingly in the port cities, which were only loosely tied to the economy of the vast hinterland; the 'domination of the modern sector, if it could be achieved by outsiders, or even by insiders, hardly constituted control of China' (Feuerwerker, 1983, p. 199).

Western firms also possessed a lion's share of the transport by ship of imports and exports. In the first two decades of the twentieth century, 85 to 90 per cent of the total value of China's foreign trade was carried by foreign-flag vessels. Western-owned ships moved two-thirds of the coastal trade among the open and treaty ports (Feuerwerker, 1983). The steamer trade to or among other ports was also dominated by foreign ships.[2]

Overall, for most of the 100 years up to 1949, Chinese trading organizations played only a secondary role in China's foreign trade. 'There is scarcely a Chinese firm of any importance engaged directly in China's export and import business,' stated a report in 1935 (Moser, 1935, p. 44). 'Virtually all the great import and export houses are foreign firms, although the bulk of the commodity collection and distribution outside of the treaty ports is in Chinese hands.'

The treaty system deprived China of tariff autonomy. This furthered the direct interests of the Western powers in weakening the Chinese authority over customs. Moreover, foreign nationals, not Chinese, were in charge of customs until 1928. Although nominally subordinate to Chinese authority, the Maritime Customs Service of China, which also administered the Post Office, was highly autonomous and was under the management of Westerners.[3]

For many years, all customs revenues were used to pay off war indemnities and foreign loans. The war indemnities were imposed by treaty as a result of China's repeated defeats by Western powers. Foreign loans were negotiated by the Qing government so as to finance the suppression of the many domestic insurrections, including some directly targeting Westerners, such as the Boxer Rebellion in the late 1880s and early 1890s. The Chinese customs service was a *de facto* debt-collection agency for Western bondholders, and its administration by Westerners represented a further assurance that this task would be accomplished.

On the one hand, the customs service made sure that tariffs were kept at the low, fixed level that China's trading partners had imposed by treaty. Import–export duties were set at about 5 per cent *ad valorem* from 1842, the year of the Treaty of Nanking, until 1928–30, when tariff autonomy was partially recovered. Sometimes the rate was even lower. Thus, for example, it was 3.2 per cent in 1902 and 3.6 per cent in 1919 (Feuerwerker, 1983, p. 180).

On the other hand, the customs service guaranteed tariff collection so as to secure a source for the loan and indemnity payments. Because virtually all customs revenue went to cover loans and indemnities, there was no customs-revenue surplus until around 1920.

The control of the customs service by Western administrators formally ended after the consolidation of the GMD government (1928–37). Pressed by a rising wave of nationalism, the GMD government attempted to regain the sovereignty of the country by revoking Western municipal concessions and, especially, by abolishing the fixed tariff.[4] The tariff was changed from a fixed rate of 5 per cent to a differential rate, which ranged from 7.5 per cent to as high as 27.5 per cent. As a result, tariff revenues increased substantially. They had accounted for 21 per cent of total public revenue in 1913. From 1927 to 1937, they represented 48 per cent of total public revenue (Zong, 1992, p. 97). The restitution of all China's lost rights was not completed until 1943. However, residual problems in tariff autonomy persisted until 1949, and Westerners continued to be involved in customs administration until that time.

Under the treaty-port system, although Western traders conducted their business mainly within the ports, the trade routes naturally had to reach beyond the ports. Merchants therefore demanded – and were eventually granted – more privileges, including access to the interior for foreign steamers, railways and mining enterprises, the abolition of transit taxes, permission for foreigners to reside anywhere, and so on. This fostered the proper conditions for the greater mobility of goods, capital and labour. Through trade, domestic trading organizations were linked to foreign trading organizations.

The institutional framework through which trade occurred took the form of chains in a hierarchy. The chains were composed of trading companies at the top and producers at the bottom. The middlemen were the domestic agents, especially the local agents who bought from the producers. The companies continued to be called *hong* ('business firms'). The *hong* were the *de facto* 'foreign market' for the output of the domestic producers. Because the *hong* monopolized the commerce with overseas buyers, they were well situated among the various links in the chain to make the most profit.

The Chinese compradors working in the *hong* were the agents who actually executed the orders of the *taban* (*hong* 'general manager') through dealings with the domestic trade chains. As had been common even previously, the various links in the chains were bound together by a sort of credit relationship, through which the compradors would make loans to the Chinese merchants, but receive cash when they sold to the *hong*.

Many large, well-known Western trading companies, while establishing branches in a number of ports, gradually extended business beyond their traditional areas of activity. In addition to imports and exports, Western companies often came to operate shipping, insurance and even production mills. However, most Western companies operating in China began as trading companies handling imports and exports.

Up to the late 1920s, *laissez-faire* was the watchword in the foreign-trade market in the sense that the role of the government was almost nonexistent. After the Opium War, the collapse of the *hong* system, which had exercised a quasi-state monopoly over foreign trade, ended the government's direct control over the import and export business, and the emergence of the treaty-port trading system made it impossible for the government to implement a state trade policy even if it had wanted to. During the period of the Westernization movement, the Qing government succeeded, to a degree, in establishing a state presence in certain areas of the domestic modern sector, such as mining, textiles and shipping, but no effort was made to do so in foreign trade. The import and export business was left to private merchants.

Private Chinese merchants were in an obviously disadvantageous position *vis-à-vis* their powerful Western competitors. They lacked capital, access to world markets, information and expertise, and the backing of their government. Given this environment, foreign dominance over China's foreign trade was nothing if not inevitable. The change from a quasi-state monopoly to a 'no-interference' orientation seemed especially acute in Guangdong Province, which had the longest history in foreign trade among the trading centres in China (Liao, 1990, pp. 77–83). In a word, the Qing government and its immediate successor were unable to take on the leadership role in commerce, in business law and in international trade law which governments were performing in the industrial countries.

Only when it had consolidated its power in the late 1920s did the GMD government begin to adopt some sort of state trade policy.[5] The policy was rather protectionist in that the intention was to encourage the development of domestic industries. Moreover, having partially recovered tariff autonomy, the government began to use tariffs as a tool to provide limited protection for the domestic market. This affected most noticeably the agricultural market. Import taxes on wheat, flour and some other grains were imposed in late 1932. Meanwhile, agricultural exports were encouraged through government measures, such as the reduction or elimination of export and transfer (*zhuan kou*) taxes on sesame and soybeans. Accompanied by other social, economic and technological initiatives to promote agricultural production and, most importantly, because of good harvests, these measures helped cut agricultural imports. Between 1933 and 1937, rice imports dropped from 1.3 million tons to 300000 tons, wheat from 1.4 million tons to 70000 tons and cotton from 100000 tons to 15000 tons (Zong, 1992, p. 99). By the mid-1930s, exports were growing relatively quickly, whereas imports were falling off. These favourable developments in agriculture, especially the decline in the level of imports, contributed to an improvement in the balance of trade, which had been negative for so long and now began to turn positive.[6]

The sudden surge in foreign trade that was typical in other regions being incorporated into the capitalist world economy did not occur in China until about 20 years after the country had been forced to open up to free trade in the early 1840s. During this period, China's major exports were silk and tea, and its major imports were cotton textile and opium. Great Britain continued to be the dominant partner, accounting for about 80 per cent of China's foreign trade in the 1860s. Trade grew very slowly and in some years even stagnated. From 1842 to 1845, nursing high hopes of a trade boom, British merchants more than doubled their textile exports to China. However, they were soon disappointed by the sluggish sale of these goods, which continued to clog the Chinese market throughout the 1840s and 1850s. Up to the end of the 1870s, British textile exports to China rarely exceeded the level of 1845. On the other hand, the exportation and smuggling of opium to China were growing more rapidly than they had done before the Opium War, and the volume of the opium trade doubled between 1842 and 1860. In Shanghai, which replaced Guangzhou as the largest port in the early 1850s, annual opium imports sometimes outstripped by a factor of more than two all other imports combined (He, 1995, pp. 46–7; Wang Fangzhong, 1982, pp. 106–15; Yao, 1963, pp. 1595–8).

From 1870 to 1911, the value of China's imports jumped from 64 million taels silver to 472 million, while the value of exports climbed from

55 million to 377 million. The total volume of trade mounted by more than a factor of seven (Feuerwerker, 1980, pp. 45–7).

Tea continued to be the key export product during the mid-to-late nineteenth century. Tea exports, which had reached their highest level in terms of volume by the 1870s, having come to represent over half the total value of all exports, had begun to decline by the 1890s. The tea trade fell even more sharply after the turn of the century, largely because of intense competition from tea producers such as India and Ceylon, which were British colonies. The tea exported from the Indian subcontinent was grown on large plantations, was standardized and exported duty free, whereas the production of tea in China continued to be based on the small-scale household economy, and the tea was taxed both in transit and upon export.

Silk surpassed tea as the number one export at the turn of the century, accounting at that time for about one-quarter of total exports. However, faced with increasing competition from Japan, Italy and France, China's silk, the most well known product of the country, began to suffer a decline similar to that of tea. The share of silk in total exports fell steadily, although not as dramatically as the export share of tea.

In the early-twentieth century, China's exports shifted from tea and silk – the two had accounted for nearly 90 per cent of total exports in the 1870s – to other products, such as other agricultural goods, minerals, cotton yarns and other cotton products. China's exports in the 1920s and 1930s included raw silk; tea; wood-oil (tung-oil); hides, skins and furs; beans and bean products; raw cotton; bristles; sausage casings; peanuts and peanut oil; walnuts; oilseeds and their byproducts; wool and carpets; embroideries and lace; straw and fibre hats; hair nets; tungsten; antimony and tin (Table 2.1; see also Moser, 1935, pp. 30–42).

Table 2.1 China's major exports, 1871–1936 (in percentages of total exports)

	Tea	Silk and products	Beans and bean cake	Seeds and oil	Minerals and metals	Cotton and products	Other
1871–73	52.7	34.5	0.1	–	–	–	12.7
1891–93	26.9	24.6	1.2	–	–	–	47.3
1913	8.4	25.3	12.0	7.8	3.3	0.6	42.6
1920	1.6	18.6	13.0	9.1	3.2	1.4	53.1
1931	3.6	13.4	21.4	8.4	1.6	4.1	47.5
1936	4.3	7.8	1.3	18.7	7.7	3.0	57.2

Sources: Xu and Wu, 1990, p. 83; Zheng, 1984, p. 43.

During the same period, the growth of imports was more rapid than that of exports. Opium continued as the most important imported product up to the 1890s. According to the stipulations of the treaty settlement of 1858–60 following the defeat of China in the second Opium War, opium imports were legalized and began to be taxed. Opium imports reached a peak of 87 000 chests in 1879, but declined thereafter. The dropoff was due mainly to expansion in the domestic production of opium that to a certain degree took the place of imported opium.

In terms of the structure of imports, cotton and cotton products had risen considerably in significance by the turn of the century. Around 1920, imports began to become more diversified and now included industrial materials and industrial products, as well as tobacco and a variety of grains. Among the major imported items were electrical equipment; aircraft and aircraft accessories; railway materials and railway sleepers; automobiles, trucks and buses; tyres and innertubes; chemicals, chemical compounds and medicinal preparations; dyes, inks, paints and varnishes; petroleum products; liquid fuel and lubricating oils; leather and leather goods; paper, including newsprint; timber and wood; photographic materials; cigarettes and leaf tobacco, and wheat, wheat flour and cereals (Table 2.2).

Table 2.2   China's major imports, 1871–1936 (in percentages of total imports)

					Columns						
	(1)	(2)	(3)	(4)	(5)	(6)	(7)	(8)	(9)	(10)	(11)
1871–73	37.7	30.2	2.8	3.8	–	0.9	0.9	–	–	–	23.7
1891–93	20.5	20.5	14.6	0.9	3.7	2.7	1.8	0.5	–	–	34.8
1913	–	19.3	12.7	0.5	4.5	6.4	5.3	1.4	5.6	–	44.3
1920	–	21.8	10.6	2.4	7.1	5.2	8.3	3.2	6.4	0.8	34.2
1931	–	7.6	0.3	12.6	4.5	6.0	6.2	3.1	8.0	2.6	49.1
1936	–	1.5	0.2	3.8	4.2	2.2	13.2	6.4	10.8	2.3	55.4

Columns: (1) Opium   (7) Iron and steel
          (2) Cloth   (8) Machinery
          (3) Cotton yarn   (9) Chemicals
          (4) Cotton   (10) Transportation equipment
          (5) Kerosene   (11) Other
          (6) Sugar

Sources: Xu and Wu, 1990, p. 83; Zheng, 1984, p. 41.

Great Britain remained the most important trading partner up until World War I. In 1899, the trade with Britain still had a commanding share of more than 60 per cent of the total China trade. In 1913, nearly 30 per cent of China's imports came from Hong Kong, of which the bulk was of British or European origin. In addition, 16.5 per cent of China's imports came directly from Great Britain. At that time, Japan was the next most important trading partner, accounting for about 20 per cent of total imports (Moser, 1935, p. 28). Meanwhile, the country's trade was growing rapidly with the US, which was poised to overtake Britain as the hegemon of the world economy. World War I cut China off from European markets and left a vacuum that the US and Japan were only too eager to fill. After World War I, the trade with the US and Japan exceeded that with Great Britain and dwarfed all others. By 1934, the trade with the US represented more than one-quarter of China's foreign trade, was equal to China's combined trade with Japan and Great Britain and was three times greater than the trade with Germany (Table 2.3). The dominant position of the US in the Western commerce with China continued until 1949.

The development of China's foreign trade was by no means linear. In the late-nineteenth century, the trade was affected by the worldwide

Table 2.3   The share of principal countries in China's foreign trade (in percentages)

	1929	*1931*	*1932*	*1933*	*1934*
Imports					
United States	18.02	22.19	25.43	21.86	26.16
Japan	25.22	20.04	13.95	9.71	12.21
Germany	5.23	5.77	6.75	7.95	8.99
Great Britain	9.30	8.29	11.20	11.33	12.00
Hong Kong	16.74	15.33	5.71	3.55	2.86
France	1.42	1.49	1.46	1.75	2.16
Exports					
United States	13.37	13.01	12.17	18.48	17.60
Japan	24.87	26.97	21.80	15.65	15.16
Germany	2.18	2.50	6.05	3.40	3.58
Great Britain	7.21	6.98	7.62	7.96	9.30
Hong Kong	16.83	16.05	15.35	19.75	18.85
France	5.46	3.69	4.63	5.26	3.95

Source: Moser, 1935, p. 29.

drop in the price of silver, as silver output rose and many countries shifted to the gold standard and demonetized silver holdings. Because silver continued to be used as a currency in China until the late 1920s, the fall in the price of silver had a negative impact on the country's balance of trade. Coupled with the more rapid growth of imports relative to exports, it was no surprise that, except for only four or five years, the entire late Qing period was characterized by trade deficits, with the worst deficit coming in 1905. This unfavourable pattern continued until the mid-1930s, with imports almost invariably exceeding exports. The cash remittances from Chinese living overseas and the spending of foreign legations, missionaries and others helped to relieve the imbalances to a considerable degree and thus enabled trade to go on.[7]

After peaking in 1931, the trade with Western countries began a steady decline. In 1933–34, exports dropped by 12.4 per cent and imports plunged by 24 per cent (Moser, 1935, p. 29). The change has been attributed to various factors, including the high and uncertain silver–currency exchange rate which was especially evident throughout 1934. This tended to reduce the price of imports and raise the price of exports. Another important factor was the worldwide depression and the collapse of world trade in the 1930s. The annexation of the Northeastern provinces by Japan in 1931 and the domestic social instability generated by the increasing intensity in the rivalry between Nationalists and Communists added socioeconomic constraints on growth in trade.

However, the fact that imports dropped more sharply than did exports and that the country's total trade continued to decline even when other nations were recovering suggests that something more may have been at work. The structure of the Chinese economy and the way the country was evolving during the process of integration into the world economy may have been the deeper causes of the problems.

Despite the rapid growth in foreign trade since the 1860s, China had not lived up to the expectations of the West. It had failed to provide the anticipated outlet for Western products. It was almost a cliché that entrepreneurs in Western industrial countries fantasized over the opportunities represented by the Chinese market. On the eve of the Opium War, the British were sure that China, with its huge population, would be able to keep the entire British textile industry healthy and happy. This turned out to be an illusion, but one which touched many. With only a slight alteration, an American saying might just as easily have been spoken by a British trader: 'A foot added to the length of the China man's shirt would bring prosperity to all the cotton mills in the United States' (Moser, 1935, p. 3). Yet, in 1890, the total value of the China trade, both imports and exports, was still less than that of many much smaller countries. Even in 1936, the per capita value of the foreign trade of China, including the Northeastern provinces, was less than that of any other independent country in the world (Feuerwerker, 1983, p. 197).

It has been estimated that by the late 1920s foreign trade represented about 10 per cent of gross national product (Table 2.4). Given China's size and level of economic development, this trade ratio was not considered abnormally low relative to that of other large countries. However, the figures for this period may be exaggerated. For one thing, China was overwhelmingly an agrarian society in which a great portion of the economy was not calculated in money terms. Perkins (1969) has estimated that exports accounted for only about 1 per cent of total agricultural output in the 1890s, 2 per cent in the first decade of the twentieth century and 3 per cent in the 1920s and 1930s. The exports of major agricultural goods and agricultural sideline goods were almost exclusively the output of traditional small-scale production. Of the major agricultural export goods such as tea, silk, vegetable oil and oil products, egg products, and hides, skins and bristles, virtually none were produced on foreign-owned plantations as they would have been in some other periphery countries.

If, as the above data show and as some have argued (for instance, Dernberger, 1975), neither China's trade ratio, nor its per capita foreign trade could be considered 'abnormally' low for a developing country of China's size, and with China's resources, the structure of the trade tells a slightly different story. On the export side, China was largely a producer of special agricultural and mineral goods, the demand for which on

Table 2.4   China's imports, exports and total trade, 1871–1929

	Exports	Imports	Total trade	Per capita	% of world trade	Exports as % of GDP
1871–84	102.5	106.2	208.7	0.58	1.3	2.5
1885–1900	110.2	143.5	253.7	0.66	1.3	–
1901–14	201.0	293.8	494.8	1.19	1.5	–
1915–19	521.2	570.8	1092.0	2.47	–	–
1920–29	619.6	799.0	1418.6	3.01	2.4	7.3

Note: Commodity trade only, annual averages in millions of current dollars.
Source: Dernberger, 1975, p. 27.

foreign markets did not tend to generate an additional demand for other Chinese products. On the import side, the foreign goods went mainly to satisfy end-users, and the demand for foreign goods by traditional economic sectors was very limited. It is true that the percentage of producer goods in total imports was rising: the share in total imports of producer goods such as machinery, iron, steel and other metals, chemicals, dyes and pigments, and transportation equipment increased from 6 per cent in 1880 and 5 per cent in 1900 to 8 per cent in 1913 and 17 per cent in 1928 (Cheng, 1956, cited in Dernberger, 1975, p. 35). Yet, China's emerging modern sector, which was the major user of producer goods, was too small to be significant in the overall economy. Moreover, a considerable portion of the imported producer goods went to the foreign sector operating in China, that is, the goods were used in projects either financed, or owned and operated by foreigners. Thus, imports in general did not introduce substantial foreign capital or raw material inputs into Chinese production. As a result, given the foreign–domestic, modern–traditional divisions in the structure of the economy, the importation of producer goods had less impact on China's industrial development than it might otherwise have had.

The difficulty of expanding the Chinese demand for foreign consumer goods remained an old, unsolved problem. The aggressive marketing of kerosene in China by US companies was an exceptional success story.[8] Aside from a few other exceptions, such as the marketing of cigarettes and cotton-piece goods, imports were not very important in China's economy. For foreign traders who came to China in the hope of big money, the slow pace of the market expansion for foreign goods was beyond comprehension. British merchants ascribed it to a mandarin conspiracy. Thus, for example, many of them viewed the transit tax as a means to prevent the market from being opened up. For some, the gap between the potential size of the market – around 450 million 'consumers' at the time – and their actual market share was simply too large to be accepted as rational. The repeated complaints suggest that there was a stubborn belief that population size was the same as market size and that a taste for Western goods in such a huge 'traditional' society should simply spring up because the goods were available.

When China was opened up to 'free' trade and even during the twentieth century, foreign trade played only a relatively small role in the economy. It was not just that most of the economy remained beyond the reach of the foreigner. Over time there was indeed a shift from the exchange of 'rare' goods, such as the tea exports and the opium imports, to that of bulk goods, but the volume of the exchange was too slight to have an effect on the productive output and the daily lives of the majority of the people living in the countryside.

During the 'century of integration', the chief reasons behind the difficulties foreigners faced in expanding trade in China to the level they expected were found by many to be China's poverty, self-sufficiency and conservatism, factors which, ironically, characterized in similar fashion the period of autarchy before 1840. The attempt to transform China into a well-functioning periphery country of the Western core was not successful because it was blocked by a 'Chinese wall' of poverty, which in fact became even higher by international comparison during the course of the nineteenth century. The growing poverty was, of course, not a direct result of foreign trade. Rather, it was rooted in the country's evolving economic structure. While the opening up to foreign trade and investment contributed to the slow transformation of China's economy of self-sufficiency, the economic structure it helped to create also demonstrated the limitations of the peripheralization of the country.

3 The Dual Structure of the Economy

Foreign investment followed in the footsteps of foreign trade. At first, the involvement of foreign capital in China took the form of bank loans. Between 1861 and 1894, the Qing government borrowed money to meet military needs, pay war indemnities and cover government spending on projects such as palace construction and river conservation. Before the Sino–Japanese War in 1894, government borrowing was on a limited scale, and direct foreign investment remained officially illegal. The Treaty of Shimonoseki, signed by the Japanese and Chinese governments in 1895 after the war, granted Japanese nationals the right to establish factories and engage in manufacturing in China.[1] The right acquired by the Japanese to establish factories was automatically extended to all other treaty powers in accordance with the most-favoured-nation clause, a step that formally legalized foreign direct investment in China.

In practice, foreign direct investment had been occurring even before it had been legalized. In 1845, long before the appearance of Chinese-financed factories, a British subject had established a dockyard in Canton for the maintenance and repair of foreign vessels.[2] Before the Sino–Japanese War, there were already 80 foreign enterprises with a total capital of $14 million and 19 foreign shipping companies representing a total investment of $13 million (Xu and Wu, 1990). That foreign enterprises were able to operate without the legal right to do so was made possible partly by the ambiguity in the Chinese legal system. Administratively, the Chinese government usually turned a blind eye towards these activities. As a result, foreign capital operated in a legal 'grey area' long before it was officially allowed.

The new legal status of foreign direct investment provided a favourable opportunity for the Western powers, including Japan, to expand activities in China's modern economy. On a far larger scale and at a greater speed, Western countries now intensified efforts at economic penetration. They constructed railways, opened mines, established factories, and set up banks and other financial institutions. Foreign loans and investment increased sharply at this stage. During the 20 years immediately after the Sino–Japanese War, from 1894 to 1914, foreign investment in enterprises jumped by nearly nine times, from $109 million to $962 million.

As a result of the rapid growth in foreign investment, more than 90 per cent of China's 9568 kilometres of railways had come under the direct or indirect control of the Western powers by the end of 1914, even though foreign involvement in the railroads had been initiated only after 1895. Western countries owned and operated 12 cotton textile enterprises, accounting for 47 per cent of China's cotton-yarn spindles. In 1913 foreign concerns and joint ventures were responsible for 93 per cent of China's total output of machine-produced coal. In other areas, such as shipbuilding, flour processing, tobacco, oil processing, and public utilities, including electricity, water and gas, and trolley transportation, foreign capital similarly overwhelmed domestic capital (Wang Fangzhong, 1993, pp. 21–2). Enjoying distinct advantages in terms of capital, technology, expertise, and socioeconomic privileges, Western investors were quick to achieve the upper hand over their Chinese counterparts in the country's nascent modern industries.

Estimates of the amount of foreign direct investment between 1902 and 1930 range from around $1.5 billion (1975 US dollars) to nearly $2 billion, while the foreign loans negotiated by the Chinese government between 1861 and 1937 totalled $1.25 billion (Dernberger, 1975, pp. 28–9). The number of foreign-funded enterprises stood at 166 in 1913 and had grown to over 820 by 1936 (Zhu Cishou, 1987, pp. 52–6). Many of the Western-funded enterprises were large and possessed monopolistic power over domestic industries. In some cases, the contrast was stunning. An American-owned electricity company in Shanghai produced as much electricity as all the domestic electricity companies combined; the output of one of the British tobacco companies surpassed that of all the domestic tobacco companies; and the soap production of one British company was over half that of the domestic soap companies (Zhu Cishou, 1987, pp. 52–6).

The expansion of foreign capital also involved control over domestic enterprises through merger or outright acquisition. Many domestic industries were dependent on loans from Western financial institutions to finance their operations. They easily fell victim to foreign capital when difficulties arose.

The domestic capital shortage was a severe barrier to the successful launch of China's modern industries, which, besides other social and economic constraints, had to struggle for survival under the constant threat of being swallowed up by more powerful foreign companies. Foreign investment was concentrated almost exclusively in the foreign concessions in the treaty ports. Shanghai, the largest port city, absorbed nearly half the total foreign investment, mainly from Great Britain and Japan.

China's Northeastern provinces took more than one-third, mainly from Japan and Russia (Remer, 1967, cited in Dernberger, 1975).

Of the total foreign capital in China in 1931, 15 per cent was accounted for by real estate holdings acquired by foreigners, 20 per cent by the inventories of foreign businessmen involved in foreign trade, 10 per cent by banking and financial assets consisting of physical facilities, the net silver holdings of foreigners, and outstanding loans to the Chinese sector of the economy, 5 per cent by utilities, especially the electric power and light provided to foreign residents in the treaty ports, about 25 per cent by transportation, mainly in the financing and operation of railroads, about 17 per cent by manufacturing, and a small share by mining (Remer, 1967, cited in Dernberger, 1975). Overall, half the total foreign investment was linked directly to the business activities and housing of foreigners in the treaty ports. Of the less than 20 per cent of foreign investment that was tied up in manufacturing, the majority went to the consumer goods sector for products such as textiles and tobacco, and very little went for producer goods. This suggests that in the early 1930s, although foreign capital had a significant share in the total output of China's modern industries, most of it was concentrated in the tertiary industry. The apparently strong presence of foreign capital in the modern manufacturing sector was but another reflection of the regrettably much weaker position of domestic capital in this sector.

The major foreign countries which were investing in China at the turn of the century were Great Britain and Japan, followed by Russia and the US. Of the 636 foreign firms operating in China by 1897, more than half – 374 – were British. This corresponded to the development pattern in other parts of the world. Great Britain, being the hegemonic power, was leading the capital expansion in the capitalist world economy.

Some experts (for example, Hou, 1965) believe that foreign investment in China was not large relative to that in other underdeveloped countries. Others (such as Dernberger, 1975) argue that, if one measures foreign investment not on a per capita basis, as Hou does, but as a percentage of national income and of gross domestic capital formation and if one also takes into consideration the development level and social environment of China at the time, foreign capital investment, though not large in aggregate terms and though certainly geographically limited, was far more significant than the opposite opinion suggests.

For a proper assessment of the volume and significance of foreign investment in China, it is important to situate the country in the world context. Worldwide capital flows into developing countries were insubstantial compared with the flows into developed countries. According to Kuznets (1966, cited in Dernberger, 1975), between 1921 and 1938, the developed countries received 79 per cent of the total flow of foreign capital, and, if Argentina is included in the group, the figure rises to 93 per cent. This means that developing countries (excluding Argentina) shared less than 10 per cent of the total. Among large developing countries, such as India, Indonesia, Argentina, Brazil, and Mexico, the total foreign investment in China in 1913 was greater only than that in Indonesia, while the per capita figure for China – $3.72 – was the lowest, followed by India at $6.91, Indonesia at $12.47, Brazil at $81.66, Mexico at $113.55, and Argentina at $409.80 (Maddison, 1989, p. 45). Although foreign investment in China was growing rapidly at the turn of the century, China's overall share in world capital flows appears to have been negligible, and this share was also small relative to the shares of other, comparable developing countries.

None the less, although foreign capital flows to China may have been limited in volume, they were concentrated in key sectors and in large-scale enterprises. The domination of foreign capital in a number of key modern sectors, such as banking, foreign trade, shipping, railroads, mining, and energy, was well established, which meant that foreign capital had effective control over the strategic areas of the Chinese economy.

Foreign investment soared by 95 per cent between 1920 and 1936 (Xu and Wu, 1993, pp. 37–41). The increase was most noticeable in the 1920s, slowing in the 1930s at least in part because of the world economic recession. Meanwhile, in both relative and absolute terms, investments of domestic capital in the modern sector gradually rose, and Chinese began to participate and boost their role in the capital formation linked to the country's industrial development. This led to some realignment between foreign and domestic capital in the ownership structure of the modern industrial sector. However, overall, foreign capital maintained its dominant position up until 1949.

In 1937, more than three-fifths of the national output of coal came from Western establishments, as did 86 per cent of the iron ore, 80 per cent of the pig iron, 88 per cent of the steel, and 76 per cent of the electric power. Western investors owned 54 per cent of the spindles and 44 per cent of the looms in the textile industry, 68 per cent of the power-generating capacity, 73 per cent of the shipping tonnage, and the bulk of the public utilities. Over half the output in shipbuilding and in a variety of light industries, such as woodworking, tanning, cigarette-making, and soda production, was due to Western establishments (Riskin, 1987, pp. 19–20).[3]

The share of foreign investment in total capital formation in China was 60.7 per cent in 1894, 80.3 per cent in 1913 and 78.4 per cent during World War I. On the eve of the Communist take-over in 1949, national capital accounted for only 13.6 per cent of all accumulated capital, while the rest was shared by state monopolistic capital (so-called 'bureaucrat capital') and foreign capital (Wang Xiang, 1993, p. 10). However, the penetration of foreign investment into the economy was not as deep as these figures may suggest. Foreign economic activities were confined to the modern sector, which was relatively small. At the peak of its pre-revolutionary expansion in 1936, the modern sector accounted for only 8 per cent of total national output (Yu Heping, 1993, p. 401). Because it was concentrated in the treaty ports, foreign economic engagement was geographically and structurally separated from the vast countryside. A great part of the Chinese economy and society remained beyond the direct reach of foreign capital.

Yet, the impact of Western economic expansion went beyond the volume or geographical location of foreign trade and capital investment. The role of foreign economic activities in China has been analysed from various points of view, including, for instance, the development of modern industry and capitalist development.[4] Such assessments, of course, cannot be based simply on physical indicators like output share. An important aspect of foreign investment was its role in shaping the socioeconomic structure of modern China. The domination of Western capital in the modern sector and the concentration of foreign capital in port cities clearly contributed to the formation of a dual economy in China, that is, the emergence of modern industries in big cities and of a combination of traditional farming and handicrafts elsewhere.

In terms of regional differences in economic activities and lifestyles, the city and the countryside were further polarized following the Western economic expansion into China. A few coastal cities quickly became metropolitan centres. Shanghai, a fairly small city with a quarter of a million residents in 1840, had become one of the country's largest cities within three decades of the 'opening of the door'. In 1870, Shanghai was already handling 63 per cent of all the foreign trade of the country (Zheng, 1984, p. 29). In Wuhan, another major open-port city, foreign trade swelled fiftyfold between 1867 and 1933 (Zhang Keming, 1935). Some of the port cities became economically very dynamic, and the ways of life among the port-city dwellers increasingly assumed a Western character.

However, these ports remained economic enclaves surrounded by vast rural areas which experienced few 'forward' or 'backward' linkages.

The countryside continued to be a world apart, where economic and social change took place very slowly. Although agricultural production was mounting, labour productivity was falling because labour input was growing more rapidly than was agricultural output. Per capita income stagnated, despite some improvement in production technology and production methods. This pattern of development – called 'involution' or 'growth without development' by Philip Huang – altered little despite the more energetic dynamics of the urban economies. 'Like the earlier commercialization, the accelerated commercialization that accompanied international capitalism brought not transformative change but further involution of the peasant economy,' Huang (1990, p. 15) has written.

Investments of foreign capital in port cities had only a limited impact on the mode of production and the ways of life in rural areas. The industrial and commercial activities in the treaty ports were oriented essentially towards urban needs. For example, in the mid-1930s, of the 21 major industries in Nanjing, which was a treaty port and the capital of the GMD government from 1927 to 1937, more than 16 were producing goods almost exclusively for urban consumption. Not one single factory was producing farm tools or fertilizers. While the city's industries, especially the processing industries, did draw raw materials largely from the surrounding rural areas (at extremely low prices), the city itself offered little in return (Tang and Lin, 1987).

Alongside the city–countryside dichotomy, there was also a dichotomy within manufacturing between the modern industrial sector and the handicraft sector. Together with farming, handicraft industries had been the backbone of the Chinese economy for centuries. While it is evident that traditional handicrafts were very resilient and were able to coexist with the emerging modern industrial sector throughout this period, it is also certain that the presence of a foreign-dominated modern sector had an important influence on them, although the exact nature of this influence is still being debated. According to one theory, modern industrial development stimulated not only handicrafts, but also the rural economy as a whole because it provided employment opportunities and created demand for agricultural and handicraft products. The opposite theory argues that the appearance of the modern sector destroyed peasant handicrafts because of the intense competition represented by the higher productivity of modern enterprises and because of the political and economic privileges which Western capital enjoyed in China.

China's economy remained highly self-sufficient and changed only marginally until the first half of the twentieth century. Handicrafts were an integral part of the overall rural economy in which the peasants themselves produced almost everything they needed. Of course, self-sufficiency did not preclude exchange linkages at the household, local and regional levels. Indeed, many small-farm families depended on the household production of handicrafts for cash income. It has been estimated that, in the early decades of the twentieth century, between 30 per cent and 70 per cent of rural households, depending on the scale of and the available labour force for family farming activities, were engaged in the production of handicrafts for additional income. The handicraft industry accounted for about 70 per cent of total industrial output in terms of both quantity and value.

There were good reasons for the persistence of the handicraft industry. Most notably, the unfavourable ratio between the amount of available land and the size of the labour force meant that there was a large amount of surplus labour seeking opportunities for additional work. In order not to disrupt agricultural production, peasants usually engaged in handicrafts whenever their farm duties permitted. For a long time, most of China's exports were the output of cheap labour based on small farms, not of plantations or factories. It was a characteristic of this economic structure that the prices of the handicrafts produced by households could be kept low because the labour was cheap and often not even counted or not fully counted into the cost. Historically, the Chinese were used to meeting all their own demands through the products of their own labour. In international trade before the coming of the Europeans, China had been an exporter of manufactured goods.

In a country with a tradition of manufacturing that may go back further than that of any other nation, self-sufficiency based on a combination of farming and handicrafts was a way of life. If a Westerner wished to sell manufactured goods which were not produced locally, he had to create the demand, and, if he wished to market manufactured goods which were already being produced locally, he had to set a competitive price. Given that China produced virtually everything it needed, factory-produced goods had to compete with handicraft goods in price and quality.

The result of this long-term competition was mixed. On the one hand, for Westerners, the Chinese market turned out to be more of a disappointment than a windfall. The only foreign commodities that can be said to have carved out a genuine market in China were opium and, later, kerosene. On the other hand, some handicrafts waned or went into oblivion; others survived by retaining a market niche, and still others were transformed on the model of the modern factory and met the competition in this way.

Thus, for example, by the 1930s, in the face of the influx of foreign goods and the increase in manufacturing in the modern industrial sector within China, some traditional areas of production in handicrafts, such as agricultural processing, had eroded. Flour milling and the extraction of oil from soybeans and rapeseed were among the most seriously affected agricultural processing activities. Flour milling had been a very important rural industry in the North. Mounting imports of foreign flour and the marketing of machine-milled flour in the larger cities caused flour milling as a village industry to decline. The home extraction of vegetable oils also diminished in the face of the competition of kerosene oil from the US, the Dutch East Indies and the USSR. Papermaking, one of China's greatest inventions and earliest industries, although still common enough in places where raw materials such as bamboo and rice stalks were in abundant supply, also fell off because of the rising imports of cheaper papers from abroad. Hand-fashioned and hand-fired pottery, another traditional handicraft industry, likewise suffered because modern machine-made pottery possessed advantages in utility or price. The same was true of the small-shop production of glass. According to a study in the 1930s, the only traditional handicraft products in this area that stood up well despite the availability of foreign-made substitutes were bricks and tiles. Because of the higher freight costs tied to the imported bricks and tiles, local production could meet the competition (Fong, 1932, cited in Moser, 1935, p. 6).

No handicrafts were more profoundly affected by the imports and the modern industrial sector than cotton textiles. This has been documented in detail in numerous studies, for cotton spinning and cotton weaving was the factory industry which had been organized the earliest and which had become the largest in China (see Chao, 1975; Feuerwerker, 1970; Myers, 1965; Yan, 1955). Cotton production, mainly in the Yangtze Valley, had been by far the most important handicraft industry. Imports competed with the handicraft cotton industry for market share, and the cheaper cotton yarn from abroad was crippling the native spinning industry. However, by 1925, the growth of domestic factory production, generally carried out on a small scale and with little machinery, had gained the upper hand not only over handicraft production, but also over the imports.[5] Gradually, a kind of division of labour appeared between the foreign factories and the Chinese factories. The finer and more valuable yarns, once imported, came to be produced in the foreign-owned mills, while the Chinese-owned factories specialized in the less-expensive, low-count yarns which had previously been made by peasants. Thus, while foreign production within China may have taken the place of the imports of particular types of cotton yarns, the Chinese-owned factories largely replaced the domestic cotton-textile handicraft industry.

However, the emergence of the modern textile sector affected the handicraft industry differently at the various stages of production from material inputs to finished goods. While the modern sector largely took over the cotton spinning operations, thus contributing to the gradual dropoff in handicraft cotton-textile production, weaving continued to be dominated by peasants working on household hand-looms. Thus, when local spinning began to decline under the weight of the competition from imports and domestic factories, handicraft weaving was able to survive and may even have expanded. Statistics show that, of a total yarn consumption of 961 million pounds (437 million kilogrammes) in 1930, power looms accounted for only 207 million pounds (94 million kilogrammes) and hand-looms for 754 million pounds (343 million kilogrammes). The ratio of power production to hand production in terms of yarn consumption was almost 1 to 4 (Moser, 1935, p. 5).

The situation varied in other handicrafts. Perkins (1975, p. 121), assessing the impact of imports and the modern sector on handicrafts, concludes that 'other handicrafts could not have been badly hurt by importers and probably were not much hurt by domestic modern factories either.' He points out that, of China's total imports in 1923, for example, only half (51 per cent) could in any way be considered to have been competitive with handicrafts. The remaining 49 per cent consisted of such items as machinery, fuel oil, metals, and unprocessed foods. Of those products that were competitive, 60 per cent (31 per cent of total imports) were cotton textiles. In addition, according to Perkins, total imports in the 1930s represented only 2 or 3 per cent of GDP. Hence, the imports which were even potentially competitive with handicrafts (exclusive of textiles) accounted for less than 0.5 per cent of GDP. In contrast, the output of domestic handicrafts in the 1930s was over 10 per cent of GDP. Perkins suggests that the effect of domestic modern industries on handicrafts should not be exaggerated, given that no more than an estimated 5 or 6 per cent of farm output was processed in modern factories during the 1930s, or less than half the percentage increase in farm output between the 1910s and 1930s.

According to one study (Wu, 1991), the import of foreign goods beginning in the 1840s devastated eight traditional handicrafts, but, with the exception of hand spinning, these were not considered essential. Up until 1920, most handicrafts continued to flourish, as did the total output of the handicraft sector. Even during the period of the rapid expansion of modern industries, handicraft production registered high growth rates. Indeed, handicrafts possessed a rising share in the national economy up until 1949, although this share did not climb as quickly as that of the modern sector. The shares of the modern sector and handicrafts in the national economy were, respectively, 4.9 per cent and 10.8 per cent in 1920, 10.8 per cent and 20.5 per cent in 1936, and 17 per cent and 23.1 per cent in 1949 (Wang Xiang, 1993). In the midst of relative decline, handicrafts remained preponderant in total manufacturing output, accounting for 82.8 per cent in 1920 and 69.4 per cent in 1936, while the modern sector was responsible for the rest (Wu, 1991).

In the 1920s and 1930s, largely in response to Western economic expansion, the Chinese began to use modern equipment to produce a large number of products which had formerly been imported from the West. By the mid-1930s, the emerging domestic machine-based textile industry was generally rendering unnecessary the importation of cotton yarn and, to a lesser degree, foreign cloth. It was proving difficult for foreign goods to compete for market share with domestic handicrafts. Even more important, the development of a domestic modern industrial sector meant that there was potential for local industry to compete with foreign imports for domestic market share in manufactured goods.[6]

The question is not whether handicrafts were destroyed by the Western competition and the modern industrial sector, since this did not in fact happen. Rather, one wonders why this did not happen, given the 100 years of privilege enjoyed by the Western powers in their economic penetration of China.

It is undeniable that foreign capital competed 'unfairly' on China's markets, since it operated under favourable conditions unavailable to Chinese producers. The privileges included extra-territorial status and artificially low tariffs in China and, at home, the highly developed industrial economies and the political backing from the Western governments, which were, moreover, siphoning indemnity and loan payments from China. In addition, as the Chinese government surrendered to the demands of the West and then came to depend on foreign support to remain in power, foreign businesses in China were not confronted by political barriers or by economic restrictions.

Yet, despite all these conditions and despite the fact that foreign capital managed to dominate modern industry in China, foreign economic expansion did not lead to a revolutionary transformation of the Chinese economy. Likewise, factory-made goods rarely reached the wider rural market. The peasant economy continued to rely on handcrafted goods without becoming significantly monetized. Thus, for instance, despite the widespread habit of male smoking in the countryside, as late as 1935, less than 20 per cent of all farm families ever purchased tobacco of any kind (Perkins, 1975, p. 200). While the Chinese-owned segment of the modern sector began to grow moderately, handicraft industries continued to rule in the non-farm economy outside urban centres. This phenomenon does not seem to reflect entirely the classic Marxist theory which suggests that the emergence of machine industries will disrupt the handicrafts in the farm economy of a backward country and thereby transform this economy into a modern one. Nor does it reflect the modernization theory which holds that all countries experience a similar sequence of steps in the process of economic modernization.

In light of the incorporation process in other parts of the world, the experience of China may not appear to be very different in that the development of the modern sector was accompanied by the underdevelopment of the rest of the economy. In fully colonized countries, the incorporation process often led to the restructuring of the local economy so as to meet the needs of worldwide capital accumulation. This usually meant that the local economy became a supplier of raw materials and cheap labour at the low end of the world commodity chain. To 'modernize' the local economy was never the concern of the colonizers or the foreign investors. Indeed, if the existing indigenous production system was useful or at least not harmful to capital accumulation at the core, the foreign investors had no interest in destroying it. This tendency partly explains the dual economic structure in periphery countries. Moreover, if profitable, there was little economic or moral barrier against the application, during the process of capitalist worldwide expansion, of the so-called 'pre-capitalist method of surplus extraction' such as the use of slave labour on plantations in Latin American colonies.

The fact that the attempt to incorporate China in the world economy did not involve full colonization was less a result of the unwillingness of the Western powers to colonize the country than of the inability of any single Western power to do so, given the intense competition among them all. The semi-colonial status of China proved to be well suited to the collective interests and needs of the capitalist core countries, in that, while relieving the administrative burden of each individual Western power, it gave them all virtually every economic privilege which a colonizer might have enjoyed.

What mattered most to the Western powers was the aim of making the country a venue for profitable economic activities. For urban-centred foreign capital to operate profitably in China, the support of the rest of the economy was necessary. Such support was not built on direct linkages between urban industries and rural handicrafts and agriculture. Rather, the growth of foreign economic influence, while it required that the competition from Chinese handicrafts and the emerging Chinese modern sector be overcome, also depended on the survival of the self-sufficient production system, which helped keep labour costs low, raw materials cheap, and the market for finished goods open on howsoever limited a scale. Thus, in the case of cotton textiles, because handicraft weavers represented the largest available market for machine-produced cotton yarn, the destruction of the handicraft sector, even if it had been possible (which is unlikely, since only rapid industrialization could have provided a replacement for the handicraft industries), was never the goal nor in the best interests of foreign capital.

The maintenance and continued growth of traditional handicrafts were favourable to the process of incorporation. The coexistence of a modern industrial sector and the traditional handicraft sector, despite the differences in their paths to development and in their functions in the capital accumulation process, did not constitute a barrier to the practical pursuit of the incorporation of China into the modern world economy. Thus, the dual economy was both a result and a precondition of the successful incorporation of China.

The argument that the expansion of foreign economic activities did not require and did not actually lead to the transformation of China in the image of the capitalist West does not mean that the West was totally responsible for the lack of 'modernization' in China. The lack of fundamental structural change was due mainly to the failure of China to undertake domestic reform, especially land reform. None the less, foreign capital had little interest in fostering fundamental structural change. It was active in a sector which was quite detached from the vast rural economy. Moreover, foreign capital was nurturing and collaborating with social groups and political forces within the government whose interests were deeply tied to those of the existing propertied classes, including the landed class. This mode of foreign economic expansion enhanced the tendency to maintain, rather than disturb, the actual socioeconomic order.

Yet, the dominance of foreign capital within the modern sector and the lack of government support did not prevent a Chinese national industry from taking root and eventually carving out a place in the economy. Although modern Chinese-owned manufacturing plants were mostly small and operated at a low capital–labour ratio relative to foreign manufacturing, the Chinese modern industrial sector had a much greater forward- and backward-linkage effect on the domestic economy because of its diversity and its dispersion throughout the country. The vertical linkages between rural handicrafts and the Chinese-owned cotton textile industry proved to be beneficial to both. In other areas, such as flour milling, match-making, knitting, machine-tool manufacturing, and consumer chemical products, the domestic industries were able to boost their market share by combining production based on modern, often imported, machinery, production based on the adaptation of traditional methods and tools, and handicraft production (Wu, 1991).

Overall, the development of the domestic modern sector was an extremely difficult process subject to frequent ups and downs. It was vulnerable to changes in the world market because of its heavy dependence on foreign capital, machinery and technology, and domestic industries faced competition from imports, foreign manufacturing in China and the local handicraft industries. The government provided little protection for the weak and struggling Chinese modern industrial sector. Indeed, under the Qing Dynasty and then up to the late 1920s, the various governments offered no preferential treatment for domestic enterprises, but 'dealt with Chinese and foreign businesses equally in terms of taxation' (Wang Fangzhong, 1993, p. 98). The difficult but remarkable birth and development of the Chinese modern sector were, therefore, largely due to the long history of China's traditional handicrafts that nurtured the entrepreneurial spirit of the first generation of Chinese industrialists.

For some, the emergence of a national modern industrial sector was the first step in China's full-scale duplication of the Western model (Dernberger, 1975). However, given the pressures of peripheralization, this may exaggerate the development possibilities open to the country. The repeated failures in China's attempt to modernize seem to suggest the opposite. Foreign capital was not particularly interested in helping China duplicate a Western model. Indeed, while the growth of modern Chinese-owned industries may have accelerated in response to foreign capital expansion, there is plenty of historical evidence indicating that foreign economic forces, with the support of foreign governments, made every effort to block this growth. Moreover, successive Chinese governments were unwilling or unable to take positive action in support of modern national industries. This assisted Western capital in exploiting fully its financial, technological and political advantages.

The consequences of the economic incorporation of China into the world economy were, of course, not limited to the economic or production spheres. More than the extent of foreign trade and investment can reveal, the incorporation process after the 1840s exerted a critical influence on the overall course of the recent history of today's China.

4 Falling Behind: The Lessons

The incorporation of China represented an important step in the final stage of the geographic expansion of the world economy. After China, there was no other 'external arena', and the world economy can be said to have encompassed the entire world, for no country or region remained that was able to operate independently of the world market and world capital.

The incorporation of China turned out to be easier than may have been thought. China's resistance to the British military during the Opium War was unsuccessful. This encounter exposed the profound internal weaknesses and the decay of this ancient and seemingly powerful empire. The British victory demonstrated to other Western countries that the giant had feet of clay and could be brought to its knees by Western gunboats. The West learned too well that, if it could not wring concessions from China by diplomatic manoeuvre or naked threat, war would never fail to achieve the goal. China was a fruit ripe for the picking. Virtually no important economic, territorial or political demand made by the Western powers was left unfulfilled. Because there were no more internal obstacles to the free entry of the West, China became 'open' to the outside world.

Yet, for the West, China was a disappointment. It proved not to be a vast market able to absorb unlimited amounts of Western goods. Besides their poor standard of living, the Chinese were, in the eyes of Westerners, too 'primitive'; they 'had not yet acquired a taste for the products of our modern civilization' (Moser, 1935, p. 28).

None the less, the West undertook every effort to peripheralize the country, for China remained attractive as an abundant source of cheap labour, a virgin market to be developed and a fertile ground for a local modern sector owned by the West. Indeed, some Western companies amassed huge fortunes in China.[1]

An extensive literature exists on a wide-ranging debate among scholars over the impact of Western capitalism on the Chinese economy and Chinese society. One of the major issues is whether the influence of Western capitalism was positive or negative in terms of the modernization of the country, whether the Western economic expansion into China represented a catalyst or an obstacle for the development of Chinese capitalism. For those who believe that the effects were essentially both positive and negative, the problem has been to determine the significance of each type of impact.[2]

For the purposes of this study, these questions are relevant, even crucial, but they are not the final concern. Rather, the discussion here is focused narrowly on China's economic performance. It attempts to explore the economic aftermath of the country's incorporation, that is, the changes in the country's overall economic strength during this period, and to analyse key factors responsible for these changes.

Historically, incorporation was critical to socioeconomic processes within China after the early-nineteenth century, and strong reactions in one form or another from the Chinese side were unavoidable. The government's half-hearted attempt to Westernize was a defensive gesture rather than a genuine, conscious effort to catch up to the West. None the less, this can be seen as the beginning of the long process of catching up. The relative performance of the Chinese economy can thus serve as an important gauge of the consequences not only of the Western economic expansion within China, but also of the responses of the Chinese themselves, that is, whether and to what degree the Chinese succeeded or failed in their attempt to face up to the challenge of incorporation at this stage.

It needs to be emphasized that China had been in the throes of a long-term economic decline before the arrival of the Western powers. This decline was not, however, a direct result of the rise of the West, since these two phenomena had been occurring in relative geographical isolation at least up to the early-nineteenth century.

For most of recorded history before the sixteenth century, China had been the world's largest economy.[3] According to figures assembled by Maddison (1991), China had the highest income per head until around 1500 and was still the biggest economy on earth until this position was taken by Great Britain after 1820. A study by Bairoch (1982) suggests that the 'Third World' (principally China and India) accounted for 73 per cent of world manufacturing output in 1750, and as late as 1830 the share was still over 60 per cent, with China accounting for 30 per cent of the world total. By 1913, the share of the Third World had plummeted to just 8 per cent, mainly because China and India had fallen far behind the level of industrialization in Europe. Meanwhile, the share of world manufacturing output produced by the rich industrial countries had jumped from about 30 per cent in the early-nineteenth century to almost 80 per cent by 1913. The eclipse of China was dramatic. After the mid-nineteenth century China had not only disappeared from the list of world powers, but the aggregated size of its economy had been surpassed by several European countries, each with a population less than one tenth that of China (Kennedy 1988, pp. 198–202). While China's long-term economic decline began long before the country's incorporation into the world economy, it clearly accelerated after the incorporation.

To demonstrate the change in the share of China in the world's wealth, a more credible measure is per capita income. Table 4.1 provides a rough comparison between China and the Western core countries, and shows that, while per capita income in China was stagnating up to the nineteenth century and declined slightly thereafter, the West was experiencing rapid economic growth. As a result, China fell behind, and the gap between it and the West began to widen sharply in the nineteenth century. While the per capita income of China was the highest in the world in 1500, it fell to half that of the West over the next three centuries, and, within only one century after the onset of the country's incorporation into the world economy, per capita income in China had shrunk to less than one-tenth of that in the West. Population growth cannot take all the blame for such a dramatic drop, since China's population declined relative to the population of the West.

During the first half of the twentieth century, the economic performance of China contrasted sharply with that of the Western countries, but it may also have been inferior even to that of other large countries outside the capitalist core (Table 4.2). In comparison to the West, all

Table 4.1 Comparative performance of Western Europe and China in per capita GDP, 1400–1950

	GDP per capita (dollars, 1985 prices)		Population (millions)	
	Western Europe	*China*	*Western Europe*	*China*
1400	430	500	43	74
1820	1,034	500	122	342
1950	4,902	454	412	547

Source: Maddison, 1991, p. 10. The per capita income figures for China and 'Western Europe' (including also Australia, Canada and the US) have been derived from the assessments of long-term economic performance presented in a number of studies. Independently, both Perkins (1969) and Philip Huang (1990) offer evidence for the stagnation in per capita income in China from 1400 to 1950.

Table 4.2 Per capita GDP in advanced capitalist countries and
other selected countries, 1900–50 (dollars, 1985 prices)

	1900	1913	1950
Average, 16 advanced countries*	2374	2937	4693
China	539	498	454
Argentina	1724	2377	3121
Brazil	586	700	1441
Mexico	872	1104	1570
India	508	536	482
Indonesia	670	710	650

Source: Maddison, 1991, pp. 24, 197.
*Australia, Austria, Belgium, Canada, Denmark, Finland, France,
Germany, Italy, Japan, the Netherlands, Norway, Sweden, Switzer-
land, the UK, and the US.

large developing economies in America and Asia seem to have been
falling further behind. However, the pace varied. The per capita
income in Latin American countries such as Argentina, Brazil and
Mexico was growing sufficiently to allow these countries to maintain a
stable relative income gap with the West (even though the difference
was becoming larger in absolute terms). Big Asian countries were doing
worse, as can be seen in the case of China, India and Indonesia, where
per capita income was declining even in absolute terms. This tendency
appears to have been more pronounced in China, where the decline
was deeper than it was in India or Indonesia. These figures may be subject to error, and one should be cautious in drawing firm conclusions.
None the less, in terms of economic performance, China probably
ranked among the worst, if not the worst, of all large developing countries of Asia and Latin America during the first half of the twentieth
century.

Because of its long-term economic decline, China had become one of
the poorest countries in the world by the first half of the twentieth century. In 1929, GDP per capita in China was nearly one-quarter less than
the Asian average,[4] and the purchasing power of the Chinese people is
believed to have been less than that of the people of any other big country. A field-survey in China by an American scholar (Buck, 1930, cited
in Moser, 1935) in the late 1920s found that earnings among the families of farmers or urban or rural workers ranged from 100 to 400 yuan
per year. Assuming that the average annual income per family was
200 yuan and that the average family consisted of 5.94 individuals, then

the average per capita income of the majority of the population was less than 35 yuan per year. This represented about $9 at the exchange rate in 1933, or about $7 on the old gold rate. At this low level of income, food shortages were the most persistent problem in the daily lives of the overwhelming majority of people. It has been estimated that at least 80 per cent of the population lived their entire lives practically from hand to mouth and never far from complete destitution (see Moser, 1935).

While China's fall from advanced economy to backward economy may have taken no more than 200 years, it seemed unstoppable (Boltho *et al.*, 1994). The expansion of the capitalist world economy into China occurred in parallel with the accelerated decline of the country. The Westernization movement and collaboration with the Western powers failed to reverse the trend. Yet, the reasons for this failure are not as apparent as the failure itself.

It can be argued, as many have done (Deckers, 1994; Lin, 1995), that the lack of industrialization was the key factor in China's economic backwardness. From this point of view, it was the Industrial Revolution that enabled the Western countries to forge ahead of the rest of the world, and it was the absence of an industrial revolution in the rest of the world that resulted in the growing gap between rich and poor. This explanation of China's economic backwardness is not only widely shared, but also seems to be well founded, since China remained largely a rural society, with an overwhelmingly rural population and a dominant share for agriculture in the national product.

However, there is no consensus on why China was unable to achieve industrialization. For some, an internal failure within China was responsible. In particular, the Westernization movement is said to have been unsuccessful because of the nature of Chinese society (Fairbank *et al.*, 1965, pp. 404–7). Social inertia, which was deeply embedded in China's traditional economy, culture, psychology, and social institutions, rendered the Westernization movement superficial and, indeed, 'Westernization' virtually impossible, whether through a formal movement or otherwise. Chinese society was both so massive in size and so inflexible in organization that it could not rapidly shift to Western models of organization, and thus China was bound to remain backward.

This explanation is sociological and institutional and undoubtedly possesses a great deal of truth. However, by focusing exclusively on China's internal social structure, the argument seems to lose sight of the historical options available to China, given the constraints imposed by the Western powers during the process of incorporation.

Moreover, the argument does not question the rationale behind the Westernization movement, as if the problem of China's economic development in the nineteenth and early-twentieth centuries depended solely on the need and the ability of the country to do as the West had done.

An important corollary of this argument is the view that a modern China could not be built until many of the decaying structures of the old society had been torn down. The country required a very strong shake-up, a sweeping revolution, in order to cast off its historical inertia. Drastic change represented the only opportunity for development. And the drastic change came in 1911. Yet, shake-ups and revolution proved insufficient to achieve industrialization. For nearly 40 years following the 1911 Revolution, the economic decline continued, even though the GMD regime did more than any of its predecessors to 'Westernize' the country. Evidently, more than just revolution or even the passage of time was required to adapt institutions and society in general so that successful industrialization would be possible.

Another popular explanation of why China was unable to achieve industrialization revolves around the interactions between Chinese society and the world system. According to this explanation, Western imperialism set back the country's industrialization in its embryonic stage. This explanation relies on several lines of thought. Some argue that, without the interference of outside forces, China would have moved towards industrialization on its own and perhaps would have achieved it more quickly. Had it not been for the presence of Western capital in China, different and perhaps healthier economic structures and regional patterns of development would have emerged. All agree that the protracted wars and social upheavals which were either directly caused by or in one way or another associated with the Western powers, were extremely detrimental to China's industrialization.

Beginning with the Opium War in 1840, modern China slipped into a long period of upheaval that did not end until the mid-twentieth century. In the late 1840s, widespread social disorder in the South culminated in peasant rebellions which swept through much of the rest of the country after 1850 and continued for the greater part of two decades, including the Taiping rebellion. In 1856–60, British and French troops invaded China, leading to the outbreak of the second Opium War. In the mid-1870s, the Chinese government faced yet another crisis when the Russians and the British sought control over the Northwest and a Muslim rebellion erupted. Then there were the Sino–French War in 1885 and the Sino–Japanese War in 1894. In 1900, the allied forces of eight

Western powers advanced into China's capital to compel the Qing court to wipe out the Boxer movement.

In response to the deepening crisis within society, as well as the foreign menace, the Revolution of 1911, after years of preparation and several defeats, succeeded in overthrowing the Qing Dynasty and establishing the Republic. The Revolution, however, did not bring peace, and China entered another turbulent period. Between 1916 and 1928 and in some places even longer, the country was divided up among competing warlords. The armed struggle of the Chinese Communist Party against the GMD regime took many years and was successful only in 1949. In the meantime, Japan annexed the Northeastern provinces in 1931 and undertook a full-fledged military invasion of China in 1937. The war with Japan lasted eight years. Then there was a four-year Civil War, at the end of which peace finally came to the country, and the mainland was unified under the government led by the Chinese Communist Party.

The repeated aggressive wars launched by foreign powers not only deprived China of the peaceful environment necessary for the pursuit of economic development. They also placed China under constant political and financial pressure, since, as the losing party in these wars, it was required to meet the constantly mounting demands of the victorious Western powers.

While social upheavals were also common during the industrialization of the Western countries, these countries were able to continue their overseas military and economic expansion and plunder the resources of other nations as part of the capitalist process of 'primitive accumulation'. In contrast, China's economic development was constantly held hostage by war and military threats. China's political and economic weaknesses made it an easy target for invasion, which, in turn, hampered the country's ability to industrialize. Under such circumstances, it is doubtful that any amount of 'Westernization' could have generated successful industrialization.

A comparison is sometimes made between the failure of China and the success of Japan in the pursuit of independence and industrialization. Factors such as government policy may have made the difference. However, one should not lose sight of the close (if not directly causal) relationship between the development processes in the two countries. The rise of Japan and the peripheralization of China were two sides of the same coin.

Like many people in other Asian countries, Chinese often looked to Japan for inspiration during the early-twentieth century. Japan became a major destination for Chinese studying abroad. None the less, it is clear that China's attempt to Westernize was not inspired by the Japanese experience, since the two processes started virtually at the same time. In the nineteenth century, both China and Japan were burdened with treaties that impaired their sovereignty and threatened their independence. However, after the Meiji Restoration, Japan managed to narrow the gap between it and the Western world between 1868 and 1912. By defeating a major world power, Russia, in 1905, Japan was able to join the West in aggressive overseas expansion. Japan's success more than anything else highlighted China's failure, for the rise of Japan not only contrasted sharply with China's difficulties in industrialization, but, more importantly, it created a new obstacle and a serious threat to China's national survival. It should not be forgotten that China's defeat by Japan in 1894 had marked the collapse of China's initial attempts at industrialization.[5]

Up to around the 1860s, China and Japan were each pursuing a relatively separate course towards national development.[6] In both cases, the effort was undertaken to Westernize so as to fend off economic and military aggression. However, the steady and rapid rise of Japan was fostered by its own aggression against weaker neighbours in Asia, particularly China. Japan became one of the most ferocious imperialist powers involved in the dismemberment of the Sino-centric order in East and Southeast Asia and in threatening China's territorial integrity. Thus, for instance, Russia occupied Ili in China's Northwest, and France annexed Vietnam, a long-time tributary state of China, after the Sino–French War in 1884–85, but Japan had occupied Taiwan in 1871–74; then Korea, a leading tributary state of China during the Ming and Qing Dynasties, fell into the Japanese sphere in 1876, and the Japanese annexed Liuqiu Island, another tributary state of China, in 1879. Overall, Japan took the leading role in restructuring East Asian geopolitics by replacing China at the centre of power.

The brief period of economic growth in China after the 1910s was likewise disrupted by Japanese aggression. As a result of the annexation of the Northeastern provinces by Japan in 1931, China lost 30 per cent of its coal output, 71 per cent of its iron production, 99 per cent of its oil, 26 per cent of its electricity, and 47 per cent of its cement production (Zhu Cishou, 1987). Within only about 50 years, from the late-nineteenth century to the end of World War II, Japan may have inflicted more damage on China than all the other Western powers had done in over 100 years. Japanese actions against China, including its murderous wars, its annexation of large amounts of land and its grab for control of many resources, went a long way towards destroying China's prospects for industrialization during the first half of the twentieth century.

The imperialist invasions occurred in parallel with protracted domestic social disorder which was widespread throughout the country. Much of the country's political, organizational and material resources were squandered in disputes among social forces over the issue of state power, and economic development was further sidetracked. The few steps successive governments did take to promote industrial development, including the early Westernization movement and the measures adopted by the GMD government after the 1920s, were too limited to alter the long-term economic decline.

In reviewing the failure of these early efforts, historians and other observers of the process of the modernization of China have strongly criticized a popular idea that appeared in support of these efforts: 'Let the wisdom of China serve as substance and the learning of the West serve in practice'. The criticism rightly points out that no amount of Chinese wisdom could have regenerated the decaying regime. The Qing government fiercely resisted radical institutional, social and political change. Although China became a republic after the fall of the Qing Dynasty, the fundamental characteristics of the social relationships were left virtually intact. The landed class continued to represent the social foundation of the government. Detached from the vast majority of the peasant population and relying on the landed and propertied classes which were only interested in maintaining the status quo, the GMD government, like the Qing Dynasty, was unable to take the lead in transforming society, although this was a necessary condition for any genuine attempt to achieve industrialization. The emerging national bourgeoisie, on the other hand, remained too weak to play a significant political role, and its efforts to develop local industries were not very fruitful, because the government offered no protection from the onslaughts of foreign capital.

However, the debate over the merits of this idea is far from over. The idea itself carries great weight even today and represents a dilemma for Chinese political leaders and modernization practitioners. The problems for which it may offer a solution are still very real. For development latecomers such as China, industrialization must involve a process of learning from the more advanced nations. Yet, one must be careful to avoid a situation in which 'learning' from the West comes to mean 'subordination' to the West. This would run counter to the motives for industrialization. The failure of China's initial attempts to industrialize through 'Westernization' should not be taken to signify that it is not necessary to learn from the West. It merely proves that the particular approach adopted was seriously flawed. In the late-nineteenth and early-twentieth centuries, after all, the 'wisdom' of China was being applied to save unsavable regimes, and 'Western learning' was being used by a country which had neither the strength to block foreign military and economic encroachment, nor the ability to mobilize its own resources.

The explanation for the failure to industrialize is also to be found in the fact that potentially useful policies were sometimes adopted under the wrong conditions. In the 1980s and 1990s, the free-market doctrine has once more become fashionable, and mainstream thinking is emphasizing the positive relationship between economic liberalization and openness on the one hand and economic growth on the other. However, this correlation did not exist in China in the late-nineteenth and early-twentieth centuries, when the country was experiencing an accelerated economic decline in the midst of 'liberalized' markets and economic 'openness'. Trendy economic thought in the 1990s has been strongly in favour of free trade, promoting it as an indispensable (though not sufficient) condition for economic growth. Yet, as measured according to tariff levels, China during the first half of the twentieth century had already become a 'free trader' (Table 4.3).

Table 4.3   Average tariff levels, 1913–25

	1913	1925
Free traders		
United Kingdom	0.0	3.0
Netherlands	2.5	4.0
China	4.0	8.5
India	3.5	13.5
Indonesia	5.5	9.0
Thailand	3.0	3.0
Mild protectionists		
Germany	12.0	13.5
Japan	12.0	–
France	16.0	10.5
Chile	10.0	16.0
Heavy protectionists		
United States	32.5	27.5
Philippines*	32.5	27.5
Argentina	26.0	26.0
Brazil	34.2	21.4
Mexico	31.5	25.5
Peru	23.0	17.0

Source: Maddison, 1989, p. 47.
*The Philippines was incorporated within the US tariff system in 1909.

The degree of free trade and the relative position of each country in the world economy are telling. Among the free traders were two distinct groups of countries in terms of economic wealth: the richest countries and the poorest countries. The first group was composed of the Netherlands and the UK, which were among the richest nations in the world at the time and which were also successive hegemonic powers in the capitalist world economy. The UK had long ago surpassed the Netherlands as a leading world power, although its own hegemonic position was being challenged.[7] The second group among the free traders consisted of the poorest countries. Both groups belonged to the category of free traders, but their situations in terms of economic performance were entirely different. In light of the experiences of the two groups among the free traders, it is clear that the issue which needs to be addressed is not the theoretical merits of free trade, but the significance of the historical conditions that determined trade policies and the subsequent economic results.

A comparison of China and other big Asian countries with Latin American countries in the area of trade and economic performance is also quite illuminating. Unlike the Asian countries that remained under colonial or semi-colonial rule, the Latin American countries gained political independence in the 1820s, and this enabled their governments to pursue economic policies more freely with the aim of furthering the perceived national interest. Is it not true that their protectionist orientation towards trade contributed to their better economic performance relative to the Asian countries in the first half of the twentieth century?

Protectionism is not necessarily more desirable than free trade, nor is economic autarchy in all cases better than economic openness. In brief, protectionism can serve and indeed has served as a tool to foster the process of industrialization and help a country catch up to economic leaders. It may even be the case that, after China was forced open, its industrial development was hindered not by too little free trade, but by the lack of protectionism. However, this was not a matter of choice. To pursue protectionism was simply beyond the ability of a weak country like China while the imperialist powers were making every effort to keep the country open to free trade.

In any discussion about the openness of China to the world economy, it is hard not to mention the American 'Open Door' policy, which seems to bring easily to mind the similarly named reform policy in China in the late 1970s. After US Secretary of State John Hay issued two diplomatic notes on the 'Open Door', the American policy towards China became publicly known. The first note was delivered to Great Britain, Germany, Russia, France, Italy, and Japan in September 1899. It reflected the interest of the US, as a latecomer, in the maintenance of the original principle of the treaty system in China: the equal taxation of foreign trade in all treaty ports, inside as well as outside the new 'spheres of influence' of the Western powers.[8] The second note, in 1900, extended the scope of the policy to include the preservation of Chinese territorial and administrative integrity. All the major Western powers agreed with the first note. Because the second note was merely a statement of intention, it did not solicit an answer from the other powers. None the less, the American Open Door policy was accepted as the balancing principle among the interests of the Western powers in China.

The Open Door policy did not open China, since China had already been 'opened' in the sense that it had already surrendered its autonomous control over customs tariffs to the Western treaty powers. The Open Door policy was aimed at the preservation of equal access to trade and commercial opportunities among the Western powers in China in order to prevent self-defeating conflicts, while protecting the vested interests of each power. The American action was prompted by the wild scramble among the old and emerging Western powers to partition China. It was not a surprise that the US played the leading role in formulating the policy. The US was an ascending hegemonic power, and it was on the road to taking the lead in further overseas expansion after the Spanish–American War and the annexation of the Philippines. The other Western powers accepted the Open Door policy not so much for the purpose of preserving China as a state and certainly not because they respected the American call, but because they 'feared rivalry and conflict among themselves' (Hsu, 1980, p. 115). It was the equilibrium or stalemate among the Western powers that saved China from immediate breakup. Given the size of China and the difficulties any single colonizer would have faced in administering it, the Open Door policy was the most logical and most clearly elaborated policy the Westerners were able to devise.

Because of the *de facto* division of the country among the major Western powers, China's international position plummeted. It was rendered dependent not on a single foreign power as was the case with India, the Southeast Asian countries (except Thailand) and most of Africa, but on the whole West. 'A moderately progressive and prosperous but weak China, dependent on foreign advice, good will, trade, and aid, would be much more to the interest of the West than a completely independent and assertive China,' historians have observed in describing the Western view (Fairbank and Reischauer, 1984, p. 449). Thus, the Western powers felt that 'China must not be allowed to modernize too far and acquire the strength to repel the West.'

By the end of this period, China's economic and social weaknesses indicated that the West had won the battle. A modern economic sector had slowly appeared and even made some slight progress. However, Westernization – whether the formal movement under the Qing Dynasty or the attempt of the GMD government to turn towards Western models – was not leading to industrialization and development. 'Westernization' in the sense of the attainment of Western standards of living remained even more remote, if not hopeless. On the eve of the 1949 Revolution, China was one of the poorest countries in the world, with an average life expectancy among the population of only 36 years, a little more than half the average in the most developed countries.

Moreover, Westernization had produced little change in the way China was treated by the West. The protracted and brutal demonstration of power by the Western countries up to the end of this period left a deep scar on China's social psyche. Once the West had forced its way in, China was never treated as an equal among nations. The pride and self-respect of the Chinese people were shattered. The scar was felt the more keenly because China had once been the self-proclaimed 'centre of the world'. This profoundly influenced the attitude of the Chinese towards the West, a mix of disdain, suspicion and hostility with admiration and fear.

As they witnessed the hopeless struggle for industrialization under heavy foreign pressure, many Chinese Marxists, modernization practitioners and intellectuals reached the same conclusion: 'in modern China, without the elimination of the forces of imperialist aggression and feudalism, industrialization is but an illusion' (Wu, 1991, p. 67). They turned to revolution as the only hope in the effort to chart a new course for the nation. The Communist-led Revolution and the Communist rise to power in 1949 were, most of all, a response to this popular call for national revitalization. It is not surprising that, when Mao Zedong, leader of the Chinese Communist Party, declared victory on the day of the establishment of the People's Republic, the message sounded rather more nationalistic than Marxist. It was: 'The Chinese people have finally stood up.'

Part II: Delinking and Self-reliance (1949–78)

PART II: DELINKING AND SELF-RELIANCE (1949–78)

Today, delinking and self-reliance are generally perceived to embody an extreme nationalistic development strategy which is irrational and detrimental from the point of view of economic efficiency. It is taken for granted in the mainstream economics literature that the international division of labour and trade among nations contributes to greater productivity in all countries engaged in the process. Moreover, in reviews of postwar experiences, it is commonly accepted that, without openness to world trade, no country can succeed in economic development.

Attempts to modernize through various forms of delinking from the capitalist world economy such as those in the USSR after 1917, in India and the nations of Eastern Europe during the postwar period and in Latin America in the 1960s and 1970s proved unsuccessful. Those countries which have succeeded in catching up, notably the newly industrialized economies of East Asia, have all been implementing policies to promote export-orientation and openness.

The delinking approach, however, has been followed by too many countries in circumstances which are too diverse to be labelled as merely a historical mistake. Calling it irrational does not help to understand its origins, nor to understand why it has been so widespread. Like revolutions, delinking has not been undertaken without a reason. In the case of China, the failure of the Westernization movement under the Qing government and of the liberalization policies of the GMD period created the proper conditions for the emergence of an alternative development path.

Economic autarchy, the extreme form of delinking, cannot be justified, much less recommended, as a development model in today's increasingly economically integrated world. Yet, given the historical circumstances, delinking and self-reliance appeared to be nothing but rational to the Chinese, which led to a turning point in the country's development.

5 The Formation of a Strategy for Catching Up

After a protracted period of war and social turmoil, China found itself, at the end of the 1940s, mired in economic backwardness. Living standards were extremely low, and poverty was everywhere. Mao Zedong once described this poor China, bare of modern industry and material wealth, as 'a clean sheet of paper'. However, for him, this condition of naked poverty was not entirely negative. He actually considered it a good thing because it could be a source of strength and inspiration. Determination, extreme effort and innovative action were required to change it. On this clean piece of paper, he insisted, the most modern and beautiful essays could be written, and the most modern and beautiful pictures could be painted.[1]

Mao's optimism about the immediate future of a strong China may have been lavish, but the vision was widely shared, and the confidence was not totally groundless. Never before in China's modern history had the possibility of mobilizing the country as a single nation been so real and a government been so determined to pursue the possibility. The establishment of the People's Republic had restored national unity (with the exception of Hong Kong, Macao and Taiwan); it had freed China from the semi-colonial rule of the Western powers, and it had brought in leaders with the will and the ability to take the steps necessary to revitalize the nation. China had travelled a long way to reach this stage. From a historical perspective, the Communist-led Revolution represented a genuine turning point. The establishment of the new government was not merely a changing of the guard among ruling elites. It marked a radical departure from earlier revolutions in that it heralded an era of fundamental social transformation which set China on a new course in the effort to reposition itself in the modern world economy.

The revitalization of China, however, would not be an easy task. Politically, there was no precedent for a modern form of governance. The Communist-led government was only the second central authority since the end of the dynasty less than four decades earlier. While the Chinese Communist Party had acquired considerable organizational experience before coming to power, there were hardly any modern centralized political institutions upon which it could rely. Much of the strength of the CCP was drawn from the support of people who were inspired by the clear goal of a strong China in the 'inter-state' world system.[2] Now, it was up to the leadership of the new and inexperienced government to deliver on its promises.

Economically, the new government had inherited a crisis. The country was in ruins after 12 years of full-fledged war. Invasion and war had not only devastated the already long-stagnant agricultural sector and destroyed most of the existing yet already inadequate infrastructure, but they had also ravaged the tiny modern industrial sector, which was even less developed than India's (Meisner, 1977, p. 59). Shortly after the Revolution, the government was confronted with a level of inflation and monetary breakdown rarely seen in world history, a legacy of the GMD regime.

Social chaos had been the order of the day before the Communists came to power. During most of its modern history, the country had been repeatedly assaulted by Western invaders and had been badly administered by corrupt bureaucrats, warlords, local elites, and ruthless property owners. Sun Yat-sen once compared China to sand, lamenting the lack of national cohesiveness which, for example, had played an important role during the modernization process in Japan. The rural communities in China were largely self-contained and were isolated not only from urban centres, but also from other communities distant only a few score miles. Neighbouring villages were linked to market towns mainly through petty trading activities at country fairs (Skinner, 1964). The authority of the state rarely reached beyond the county level.

The new leadership, however, was confident. A crucial element was the fact that, fresh from its victory, the CCP had earned authority and credentials its predecessors had never acquired. In three decades of struggle on its road to power, the CCP had gained considerable experience, strength and popular support.

The leadership of the CCP was institutionalized soon after the Revolution. The post-1949 state apparatus was based on a tripartite power structure: the Communist Party, the government administration and the army, each constituting a separate layer, but all tied together by the Communist leadership. In order to protect the centralized leadership, the system did not permit any political opposition to challenge the authority of the CCP. One of the CCP's most valuable assets was its organizational ability, which had grown out of its long experience with grassroots mobilization. Relying on this and other advantages, such as the highly charismatic central leadership and the large number of devoted party members and cadres, the state quickly established a sophisticated nationwide administrative and organizational framework which permitted it to reach from township to village in ways that had never been possible under previous governments (Schurmann, 1966). The CCP, moreover, had successfully accomplished a comprehensive land reform within a few years after the Revolution, something the GMD regime had never been able to do. Sweeping land reform strengthened the social foundations of the CCP. It won the support of landless peasants and set the groundwork for a nationwide drive towards industrialization.

In general, the CCP had been pursuing a class-based strategy of reliance on people without property to overturn the propertied class. This gave it at least two advantages. First, the CCP-led government was able to act in the name of the vast majority of the people, that is, poor peasants and city workers. Second, the CCP had struggled against the propertied class for decades, and this enabled the new government to have a free hand in its dealings with important property owners, who had mostly affiliated themselves with the GMD regime or the foreign establishment within the country. The state confiscated the assets of those people who, under the patronage of the ousted regime or the Western countries, had appropriated property (known as 'bureaucrat monopoly capital' and 'comprador capital'). Within a few years of the Revolution, nationalization had been achieved, and the state controlled all major industries and the natural resources of the country.

A triumphant army under the absolute leadership of the CCP was a guarantor of the new government. The Communist Revolution had been won through a protracted armed struggle, during which the Red Army had grown into a large and highly disciplined force. The army played a crucial role in the establishment of order and of the administrative apparatus during the first years of the People's Republic. Thereafter, at each moment of crisis, the army has never failed to carry out the will of the government. Given the country's numerous military defeats and general defencelessness during the previous 100 years, the presence of a powerful army after 1949 was welcome because it provided a sense of national security.

The CCP-led government made the difference in the effort to reshape China's image. Within three years of the Revolution, in 1952, the state had an administrative network in place down to the village level and had consolidated its power over all the provinces on the mainland. A serious financial crisis was quickly solved, and the economy was restored to its highest prewar level.[3] It appeared that the country would now have a real chance to pursue the goal of becoming a strong nation within the world system. Although few outside China thought at the time that the revolutionary government would succeed, it is a common view 50 years on that the historical importance of the 1949 Revolution to China, as well as to Asia and the world at large, cannot be overemphasized.[4]

To sum up: the consequences of the 1949 Revolution were unprecedented in China's modern history. First, the country was finally unified under a single government. Second, internal wars and military conflicts were brought to an end; relative security returned to the country. Third, mechanisms were established for the centralized allocation of natural and human resources for the comprehensive development of the national economy. Fourth, the national defence force was relatively strong. Fifth, conditions were favourable for more independent foreign policies.

From the perspective of national development, the goals of the new government may not seem to have differed essentially from those of the GMD regime, since both claimed to pursue national unification, independence and wealth. However, the government of the People's Republic was different from its predecessor not only because it actually succeeded in achieving national unification and independence and because it was more determined to pursue 'wealth and power' (*fu qiang*). The CCP-led government was also qualitatively different because it had an even more significant goal. It intended to transform China into a wealthy and powerful country, but one that would be socialist.

The major features of the Chinese version of socialism would include the dictatorship of the proletariat, public ownership of the means of production and income distribution according to labour. Socialism, it was perceived, would be but an initial step towards communism. One of the major differences between the two was the insufficient development of productivity in the former. Therefore, for China, which claimed to have embarked on the road to socialism after the 1949 Revolution, the pursuit of 'wealth and power' assumed a new significance. The aim was to achieve national revival, but also to become an active part of the joint efforts necessary to accomplish a far more grand and nobler goal of human kind, that is, to assure the future of socialism. The emphasis on the 'socialist' character of the Chinese approach was not merely a matter of Communist ideology. National revival and socialism also served the purpose of guaranteeing the legitimacy of the Revolution and of the Communist state.

However, the pursuit of the simultaneous goals of national wealth and socialism was not without contradiction. Theoretically, the first goal implies the acceptance of the ideology of the nation-state, while the second goal is by nature 'inter-national'. The goal of strengthening China's position in the world by accumulating national wealth was based on the assumption that it is possible for individual countries to become 'upwardly mobile' within the world economy. The only question was, how to do this. On the other hand, the goal of establishing socialism meant, by definition, the pursuit of a different logic of economic and social development that would require the transformation of the existing structure of the world economy, a task which was beyond the reach of any individual country. In other words, it was highly questionable that the accumulation of national wealth within the framework of the capitalist world system would lead to socialism in China or anywhere else. This dilemma, although at the time it did not seem to trouble the government leadership as it sought to implement a national development strategy, later proved to be an important factor in the emergence of policy inconsistencies, as well as in shifts in development orientation.

The development approach and main policy orientation of the People's Republic that took shape in the 1950s and continued to be followed until the late 1970s can be described as a 'delinking' from the capitalist world economy in the midst of a pursuit of self-reliance.[5]

Delinking can be readily identified with autarchy. However, Amin (1990, p. 62) makes a distinction between autarchy and delinking. For him, 'autarchy' is 'withdrawal from external commercial, financial and technological exchanges', while 'delinking' is the 'pursuit of a system of rational criteria for economic options founded on a law of value on a national basis with popular relevance, independent of such criteria of economic rationality as flow from the dominance of the capitalist law of value operating on a world scale.' Of course, both autarchy and delinking represent a rejection of active participation in the single-world division of labour, and therefore the two are not without similarities. Judged on the criteria defined by Amin, the general position that China took in its relationship with the world economy was delinking, not autarchy. The adoption of delinking as part of a development strategy, however, was not a premeditated decision. It was the result of the mutual influence of the official ideology of the government, the general development orientation of the country, social and political feasibility at the time, and the international context.

It took the government several years to complete the formulation of the new development strategy. The short period of preparation, known as the 'new democratic stage', was not aimed at wiping out capitalism in general, the upper petty bourgeoisie or the middle bourgeoisie. This was because, given China's economic backwardness, the 'capitalist sector will still be an indispensable part of the whole national economy' (Mao, 1967, p. 168).

The essence of the economic strategy under the new democratic state 'was to permit private capitalism some leeway and motivation to encourage its productive potential, but to harness it to the goals and priorities of the new state' (Riskin, 1987, p. 39). This strategy was endorsed in the 'Common Programme', which was adopted at the first Chinese People's Political Consultative Conference in September 1949, as a national policy guideline during the entire period of 'new democratic development'. In this document, delinking was not set forth as the official position in China's relationship with the capitalist world economy. Rather, the document explained that China would restore and develop relations of commerce with governments and peoples on the basis of equality and mutual benefit. However, this was only the principle. The actual strategies adopted were determined by unfolding events.

One of the major events that influenced the government was the outbreak of the Korean War in June 1950. China entered the war in October to assist North Korea, and the US was on the side of South Korea. The Korean War and its aftermath had a great impact on China's domestic socioeconomic development, but they clearly also had an impact on the Cold War world order in which China's position was to be defined.

On the domestic front, the increasing and heavy government demands for war-related goods provided an incentive for the growth of the urban economy. At the same time, this growth exposed the residual power of the private business sector *vis-à-vis* the state, which encountered difficulties in acquiring from the private sector goods at the desired price, of the desired quality and in the desired quantity. In order to establish effective control over supply, the state therefore took measures to restrict the private economy and to accelerate the transition towards public ownership. As a result of nationalization, the merger of private business and the state sector through state–private joint ventures, and the cooperative movement in the countryside, by 1956 the predominance of public ownership had been essentially established in the economy.

The Korean War took place at a time when the newly established People's Republic had already begun to reposition itself in its relations with other countries, including Western countries. The involvement of China and the US in alliances on opposite sides in the Korean War significantly limited China's choices. If the war had not broken out, China would still have had several options in its response to the post-World War II world order. It might have become part of the Soviet-led bloc; it might have joined the American-led bloc (although less likely), or it might have stayed out of either bloc and stood on its own. Probably out of a desire to keep its options open, the Communist government had left the property of the US, Great Britain, France, and other Western countries intact immediately after the Revolution.[6]

At the end of 1950, less than three weeks after China had entered the Korean War, the US administration imposed a total embargo on all trade and payment transactions with China and froze bank accounts and other assets in the US that were owned by China or its nationals. In retaliation, the government of the People's Republic froze US assets in China. The embargo and other economically punitive measures taken by the West, combined with Chinese countermeasures, crippled the activities of foreign enterprises in China and eventually put an end to the possibility of economic exchanges between China and the Western-controlled world market. China's access to trade with Western countries was essentially blocked. In five years, from 1950 to 1955, China's trade with Western industrial countries plunged from 36 per cent of the country's total trade to less than 8 per cent. Under the influence of the US-led embargo, the share of trade with many other nations also fell. For example, trade with Japan dropped from 4.3 per cent to 2.6 per cent of China's total trade, that with Hong Kong from 13.3 per cent to 6 per cent, and that with ASEAN countries from 6.5 per cent to 1.4 per cent. In 1950, China had imported large amounts of rubber from Malaya. After the US embargoed all trade in so-called 'strategic' goods with China, Malaya suspended rubber exports to China (Yu Yong-ding, 1989, p. 177).

Hostilities between China and the US were fuelled by other developments as well. The deployment of the US Seventh Fleet in the Taiwan Straits paralysed the effort of the Chinese government to take over Taiwan. Publicly, the US made China a major target of its strategy of global containment. As part of this strategy, the US formed alliances with South Korea and Taiwan and financed an anti-Communist, pro-Western 'frontline' in Asia with the clear purpose of overthrowing the Communist-led government. These actions were viewed by the Chinese government and people not only as a gross offence against the country's sense of nationalism, but, more importantly, as a revival or a continuation of the historical aggression of the West against China. For its part, the US did not conceal its hostility or its intention to contain China.[7]

Under such circumstances, it became impossible for China to develop 'normal' economic relations with the West in general or with the US in particular. Even if China had been willing to participate in the capitalist world economy, the political and economic initiatives undertaken by the US and its allies, such as the trade embargo, effectively delinked China from it.

The delinkage from the capitalist world economy was also a result of the Chinese policy of 'leaning to one side', that is, towards the socialist bloc. This policy was not prompted entirely by China's difficult relationship with the West. In addition to similar ideology, China and the socialist bloc shared a common desire for a different economic relationship among nations. The willingness of the socialist bloc to provide support was in sharp contrast with the Western hostility. In February 1950, Mao and Stalin signed a 30-year Sino–Soviet treaty of alliance. A powerful ally afforded the newly established People's Republic a degree of security. By declaring their position in the socialist camp, the Chinese also gave new meaning to their revived nationalist sentiments, which seemed to merge with socialism in the worldwide struggle against imperialist power.

However, it was not long before China had to face the failure of its policy of 'leaning to one side'. Mao had believed that an alliance with Moscow would help China to become secure and eventually stronger. The Soviet Union, for its part, did provide important political, moral and material support in the early stages of the existence of the People's Republic. The share of China's trade with the USSR and with Eastern Europe more than doubled between 1950 and 1955, rising from 32 per cent to 72 per cent (Yu Yong-ding, 1989, p. 177). By the late 1950s and early 1960s, however, the alliance was falling apart. The split between China and the Soviet Union had a number of causes. The main one was the fear felt by Mao that the acceptance of Soviet leadership and of various Soviet demands would lead to national dependence (Mao, 1977, p. 102).

In the late 1950s, neither the West, nor the East seemed friendly, and China found itself even more isolated. Over the next two decades, although the government continued to cultivate trade relations with foreign countries, the economy became in large measure inward-looking in the sense that economic development depended overwhelmingly – if not exclusively – on the mobilization of domestic resources. This development approach became known as 'self-reliance'. The final push that had caused China to adopt this approach had come from the government's disillusionment in regard to the Soviet Union. Mao later claimed that the social imperialism of the USSR was not so different from Western imperialism in terms of the desire for expansion at the expense of weaker states.

Although self-reliance and delinking are closely related, they are not entirely identical. The term 'self-reliance' has been used differently by different political forces in China (Oksenberg and Goldstein, 1974).[8] 'For Mao, self-reliance meant controlling one's own future to the greatest extent possible and preventing powerful outside forces from establishing structural control over the productive life of one's country' (Van Ness and Barney, 1989, p. 263).

As many have pointed out, self-reliance does not necessarily connote autarchy, nor is it synonymous with 'self-sufficiency' (Amin, 1990; Deckers, 1994; Riskin, 1987). At root, self-reliance suggests that the main resources for development should be found within the entity concerned. External relations are not ruled out, but are limited to a subsidiary role.

For the Chinese leadership, 'delinking' was not meant to be long term. It was adopted partly because of the lack of other options. Therefore, it could be modified, and even a radical shift was not inconceivable once alternatives became feasible. 'Self-reliance', on the other hand, was more than an expedient measure or a short-term solution. It was also an idea and an ideal based on the belief that the future of China ultimately depended on no one so much as the Chinese themselves. This ideal had been nurtured by China's experiences with foreign powers. Historically, the Western powers had rarely presented themselves as forces friendly to China, and the antagonistic international environment dominated by these powers following World War II had only served to confirm the impression of Western hostility.

China was not alone in opting for delinking and self-reliance. They had been taken up by Prussia in the nineteenth century. Deckers (1994) has pointed out that, when the much weaker German states had been confronted by Great Britain, a more advanced industrial country in ascendance in 1800, the economist Friedrich List proposed a strategy of selective self-reliance so as to develop productive power through internally based industrialization and eventually gain a place of equality in international trade. By following this approach, some relatively weak European countries have actually succeeded in joining the rich core of the world economy.

Selective self-reliance and delinking have not been available to many underdeveloped economies. As it turns out, the formulation and actual implementation of these approaches require a relatively strong state. China attained this ability only after the 1949 Revolution. One may say that delinking is a weapon of countries with relatively weak economies, but ones which have relatively strong governments.

Amin (1990) and Frank (1969, 1978) have suggested that delinking was used by backward countries during periods of world capital contraction. According to Amin, delinking enabled these countries to reintegrate into the world economy in stronger positions later, following periods of world capital expansion. Since this also occurred before the twentieth century, it is argued that delinking is not an invention of this century. Certainly, rich countries do not normally need to rely on such a strategy, since, as Amin has pointed out, they are the masters of their external relations, and this distinguishes them from the weaker economies.

The delinking which followed the socialist revolution in China has been seen by some commentators as voluntary and positive, although it was embraced to counter the pressure of imperialism and failed in the long run. Moreover, it was associated with profound social and ideological changes which were not without long-term significance, even if some of these changes were tied to the myths of 'socialist construction', the 'new classless society', the 'cultural revolution', and the new 'social mode of production'.

Many of the arguments in favour of delinking and self-reliance have not been based on pure economic rationales. They have taken a much broader perspective according to which the overall strategy is affiliated with economic and social transition external to capitalism. The strategy embodies the attempt to pursue development independent of the powerful forces of the capitalist world economy that have always sought to incorporate weak economies into the lower echelon of the world division of labour. From this point of view, uncertainty about the immediate outcome of the strategy is not necessarily a significant factor, since the transition is a long-term process.

In the case of China, criticism of the strategy has been frequent. Some regard the adoption of the strategy as an outright mistake by the Chinese revolutionary government. According to these critics, the government itself was ultimately to blame, because its decision to enter the Korean War created the situation in which the country had to become isolationist. This view is echoed particularly in neoclassical economics, which favours nearly unconditional free trade and considers the world economy neutral in that all countries can benefit as long as they play by the rules. Even in the world-system approach, despite its powerful and effective critique of the capitalist world economy, there is a strong vein of scepticism about the existence of viable options for nation-states which pursue national goals independent of the established order of the world economy.

What concerns us here is not so much the arguments over the rationale of the Chinese strategy. Rather, we are interested in evaluating the actual Chinese experience, since, for China, self-reliance and delinking were not academic issues, but a historical process. In addition to answering the question of why China opted for the strategy, we want also to understand the conditions which made the implementation of the strategy appear feasible. Moreover, in order to appreciate its significance, it is important to examine what the strategy contributed in terms of China's efforts to industrialize and catch up to the core countries during this period, as well as the implications for China during the subsequent stage of development.

While international pressure pushed the government to resort to delinking and self-reliance, the strategy was viable, even though it may not have been ideal. China was already highly self-sufficient not only because of its large size, diverse and plentiful natural resources, immense labour force, and enormous market potential, but also because the Chinese people had a long history of subsistence through a combination of agriculture and handicrafts. Western economic expansion in China before 1949 had not fundamentally changed this economic reality.

Other, non-economic factors also favoured delinking and self-reliance. In the 1950s, with the victory of the Revolution still fresh, the spirit of independence and self-confidence among the people was palpable. National unification under a strong government had generated a powerful sense of nationalism. This fostered popular support for resistance to foreign pressure. Measures associated with the elimination of Western influence, such as the establishment of mechanisms for the central control of foreign trade and the adoption of policies emphasizing self-reliance, corresponded not only to Communist ideology, but also to the general sentiment of the nation. To a certain degree, opening the Chinese market to the West rather than closing it might have been more difficult at the time. Thus, the government was easily able to nurture and channel the feeling of nationalism and mobilize support for the implementation of the strategy of delinking and self-reliance.

Ideology and the economic thinking fashionable in the early 1950s provided a solid theoretical foundation for delinking and self-reliance. The Communist government accepted the Marxist criticism of free market doctrine and believed that the market economy was a source of social polarization. In a country in which competitive markets had never dominated either in ideology or in reality, the Communist rejection reinforced the traditional pragmatic attitude of the Chinese in adapting whichever development approaches were thought to be effective for achieving goals. Moreover, the Japanese postwar economic 'miracle' and the export-led growth of the Asian tigers had not yet occurred. The relative advantages of an open economy for the developing countries had yet to be demonstrated. This was important in that it enabled delinking and self-reliance to be embraced more readily by the nation and to be carried out without hesitation.

In practice, the strategy of delinking and self-reliance highlighted a number of characteristics of the country. Thus, for instance, because there was little expectation of foreign aid, industrialization had to be based entirely on domestic resources. Since China was poor and largely rural, its most valuable assets were the labour and skills of the people. In this context, Mao considered China's large population a positive factor, a strength rather than a liability. To tap this resource, the government formulated a policy of providing full employment. This was essentially achieved through the expansion of urban industries led by the state sector and through the mobilization of rural labour in the collective farming system.

In the early years of the People's Republic, the most urgent problem facing China was the accumulation of the capital needed for industrialization. However, unlike the Western countries during their early stages of industrialization, China in the mid-twentieth century was in no position to count on overseas markets for primitive accumulation. The assistance available from outside the country was limited and problematic, as the dealings with 'the friendly ally' had shown. It quickly became clear that China had to depend on its own resources.

China therefore relied upon domestic savings to finance capital accumulation for industrialization. The lack of capital had been one of the most important reasons industrialization had previously failed. The savings rate, which had only been around 5 per cent or even lower before 1949, reached about 10 per cent shortly after the Revolution and nearly 25 per cent during the First Five-Year Plan (1953–57). During much of the time thereafter, it was kept at around 30 per cent or higher (Dong, 1982, pp. 88–9; Perkins, 1997, p. 27). The sharp increase in the savings rate was achieved principally by the expansion of production, the central resource-allocation mechanism and a more equal distribution of income, although forced savings due to, for example, the insufficient supply of consumer goods also played a role.

Self-reliance aimed at the establishment of a comprehensive national industrial system. However, the principle of self-reliance was also applied at times and to various degrees at the regional level. The government required that the regions should create regional economies which would not be dependent on other regions for essential needs. For this purpose, individual provinces and even counties were urged to establish independent economic systems and rely on their own resources, capital and labour for survival and economic development. Regional self-reliance was to a large extent prompted by the fear of foreign military attack, and the international situation in the 1950s and 1960s did not offer China much assurance that there was no such threat. As an important part of the programme of comprehensive industrialization, delinking and self-reliance thus also aimed at the establishment of an independent military capability to defend home territory.

In both theoretical and practical terms, delinking and self-reliance did not mean a rejection of foreign trade or a rejection of the use of foreign technology. However, foreign trade was to be permitted only in so far as it met domestic needs and fostered domestic economic development, but not so much that it became either the driving force of economic growth, or a channel for the further integration of the economy in world markets. There was to be no indiscriminate imitation of foreign methods to the detriment of the accumulation of indigenous experience suited to conditions in China. The strategies thereby placed a premium on internally generated development.[9]

Likewise, self-reliance did not mean that foreign borrowing was forbidden. However, in practice, the role of foreign funds was reduced to a negligible level. China had no access to loans or investment capital from Western countries. Nor did it encourage the search for foreign funds. The main source of foreign funds was the Soviet Union, from which China borrowed limited amounts shortly after 1949. From 1949 to 1959, foreign loans, mainly from the Soviet bloc, accounted for only 2 per cent of total state revenue (Dong, 1982, p. 82). After the China–Soviet split, China relied entirely on domestic financial resources.

In order to act consistently and coherently as a nation in the international market, all business with foreign partners was conducted by state organizations under the centrally planned system. The state export companies exercised a monopoly over foreign trade and other international economic activities. Producers, including large state-owned enterprises, had no direct involvement in such matters on their own.

One should not lose sight of the overall objectives which delinking and self-reliance were supposed to achieve. The goal of the Chinese government under the leadership of Mao was clearly stated in 'The General Guidelines of Socialist Construction' (*shehuizhuyi jianshe zongluxian*), which was formulated in the late 1950s. According to these guidelines the country should 'take an unusual path and adopt advanced technology as much as possible in order to transform China into a powerful socialist country in a relatively short time.'

In May 1958, during the second session of the eighth CCP conference, a target for catching up with the West was announced, as follows: 'to catch up with and surpass Great Britain in five years or a bit longer and to catch up with and surpass the US in 15 years or a bit longer.'

While this target proved far too ambitious and overoptimistic, at the time it was taken seriously and, indeed, was the central concept behind subsequent social and political campaigns initiated by the government, such as the Great Leap Forward. As a public slogan, the target of 'catching up' with the most economically advanced countries within a specified time period was eventually dropped, but catching up with the West remained a goal none the less. It was again explicitly proclaimed during the modernization campaign of the mid-1970s, a few years before the onset of the economic reforms in 1978.

6 Industrialization

Industrialization was a dream of generations of Chinese who wished to see a powerful China rise again and witness an end to the country's 'humiliation' at the hands of the industrialized world. For the post-1949 government, industrialization was viewed as a central concern in the planning for the nation's long-term development, as well as a task of considerable urgency, given the confrontational atmosphere of the Cold War. Thus, the goal became not simply to industrialize, but to industrialize within the shortest possible time. Rapid industrialization seemed to be the key both to meeting the immediate need of defending national independence and to narrowing the huge gap with the advanced countries. Aware of the success of Soviet industrialization, the Chinese leadership was convinced that an economically backward country like China could industrialize rapidly if the proper methods were chosen.

Based on a consensus among the top leaders over the necessity of finding a shortcut, the government issued a guideline for accelerated industrialization: agriculture would represent the foundation; industry would be the principal area of development, and the expansion of heavy industry would be the priority. The state was to play a leading role. Several considerations were at work in the decision to focus on heavy industry. First, from the point of view of economic structure, heavy industry was believed to be the keystone among all industries in supporting the expansion of production. Second, from the point of view of national security, heavy industry was thought to be indispensable for national defence. Third, an industrial strategy centred on heavy industry seemed to fit in with the goal of independent development. It was seen that the economic superiority of the most advanced capitalist countries lay in a stout heavy industrial sector. By the same token, the backwardness of China was manifest in the frailty of the country's heavy industry. While China had acquired the ability to produce manufactured goods, it lacked the heavy industry to upgrade from handicraft production to machine-based production. This was felt to be the Achilles' heel of China's economy, the reason the country had been unable to stand up to the Western challenge in the past and an impediment to the entire process of economic development.

While the success in the Soviet Union of a strategy of industrialization founded on heavy industry provided considerable encouragement for the Chinese approach, the country faced enormous difficulties in realizing the approach. One of the most serious problems was the lack of capital. While capital accumulation is a major challenge in any attempt to industrialize, the challenge is even more acute in the case of development led by heavy industry.

In the early 1950s, China was poor and largely rural, with nearly 90 per cent of the population living in the countryside. The share of industry in the net material product was 30 per cent, and the share of heavy industry was less than 8 per cent. Living standards were low. This meant that the demand for manufactured goods was very limited, though, admittedly, the lack of market demand was a more serious barrier to the expansion of light industry, since the expansion of heavy industry was more self-sustaining and less dependent on the consumer market. However, the low income levels were a serious constraint on the nation's ability to accumulate capital.

Therefore, the state took every necessary step to secure sources of investment capital for heavy industry, most notably, via macroeconomic policies, institutional restructuring, microeconomic management, and income distribution mechanisms. At the macroeconomic level, the government began in the early 1950s to implement low interest rates, low exchange rates, low prices for energy, raw materials and agricultural products, and low wages (Lin *et al.*, 1994, pp. 29–35). These steps were attempts to keep the costs of capital investment relatively low, thereby reducing the development costs for heavy industry.

However, in a vast rural society, such macroeconomic policies could not be effective without a suitable institutional framework. The effort to deal with the problem of capital accumulation therefore tended to accelerate the so-called 'socialist transformation'. A central planning system was established, and levels of production, consumption and capital accumulation were brought under the control of the state planning mechanism. Thus, the state replaced the market as the agency of resource allocation. Central planning was based on the strength of the state sector in the national economy. The dominance of the state sector gave the state great leverage in determining the behaviour of enterprises and the allocation of profits, as well as prices and the level of wages. The private sector was gradually eliminated, and all urban wage-earners were placed under the unified state wage system established in 1956. In this system, job rank, the criteria for promotion, and wage-rate increases were all determined at the central level. Until 1978, the general wage rate of industrial workers was kept low, so that labour costs would not impede the development of heavy industry.

The policy of low wages, on the other hand, inevitably limited the purchasing power of urban wage-earners. To assure the means of subsistence of industrial workers, the state implemented a policy of low prices for subsistence goods and services, such as food, housing, other daily necessities, medical care, and education. This was supported by the basic social welfare system. The tradeoff among low wages, guaranteed employment and basic welfare provision functioned well under the central planning system and helped maintain social stability.

However, the wage system was confined to urban areas. After land reform had been successfully carried out, the rural economy became based on the household production of owner-cultivators. Because agriculture had not been nationalized, it was still, strictly speaking, outside the state sector. While the state was able to determine the prices of manufactured goods because of state ownership and control, it was difficult for the state to maintain low prices for agricultural products without a direct controlling mechanism. In the early 1950s, the state purchasing agencies failed to procure sufficient grain because of the competition of private agencies which were offering higher prices for agricultural produce. Largely though not solely for this reason, an agricultural collectivization campaign was initiated in the mid-1950s. This quickly transformed the countryside into a commune system. The commune system guaranteed that the state could purchase agricultural goods at the prices and volumes which it had set. Because the highest administrative level in the system – the commune – was also the lowest level in the state administration, it was both convenient and efficient for the commune system to meet the state purchasing plans. Through the scissors price-mechanism between industrial goods and agricultural products and with the help of the state purchasing system, rural surpluses were transferred to the urban industrial sector. Thus, the rural economy was able to play an important role in the capital accumulation necessary for the development of heavy industry (Selden, 1979, 1993; see also Liu Fuyuan, 1990, for a different assessment).

Because of the two patterns in ownership, the urban and rural systems for income distribution and welfare provision were distinct. Rural residents were not entitled to the low-priced subsistence goods and services offered by the state to their urban counterparts. This, according to Lin *et al.* (1994), served as another means of savings for the benefit of heavy industry. On the other hand, the commune system was made responsible for meeting the subsistence needs of rural residents. Like urban wage-earners, though at a lower level, the rural population had access to guaranteed employment, basic welfare and relatively equal distribution of income.

In the early 1950s, an apparatus was set up within the government to implement state plans, including the formulation, supervision, management, and fulfilment of plans at central, local and sectoral levels. Modifications and adjustments were made in subsequent years, but the main features of the institutional framework remained. Relying on this framework, a central system for the allocation of resources, including capital, raw materials and labour, was established. This system substantially limited the function of the market. Increasingly, state planning rather than the market shaped the behaviour of enterprises and other economic agents.

The establishment of a central planning system and the related institutions changed the role of producers. In urban areas, the purpose of enterprises was no longer to make profits, but to achieve planning targets. Profits were remitted to the government, and the government in turn supplied the enterprises with the capital and raw materials necessary for production. The expansion of the production of existing enterprises and the creation of new enterprises were also undertaken according to state plans.

In the financial sector, the nationalization of banks and other financial institutions led to the establishment of a comprehensive state banking system centred on the People's Bank of China. Through local branches and state banks operating in specific sectors, such as the People's Construction Bank, the Agricultural Bank and the Bank of China, the state was able to control firmly the allocation of capital so as to fulfil key industrial priorities and implement state financial policies.

For the purposes of central planning, the control of the exchange rate alone was not sufficient to prevent domestic producers from importing producer goods. Therefore, in the mid-1950s, the state sector monopolized foreign trade, and beginning in 1958 foreign-trade operations were handled exclusively by state foreign-trade organizations responsible to the Ministry of Foreign Trade.

In 1953, the State Planning Commission began to take charge of the central allocation of raw materials and industrial goods. Raw materials and industrial goods were classified into three categories: those allocated by the central government administration (that is, through the State Planning Commission), those allocated by government ministries and those allocated by local administrations. Subsequently, changes in the share of total allocations among the three categories became an important indicator of the degree of centralization in the country. In the 1950s, in parallel with the formation of the central planning system, the trend was towards increased centralization. Between 1953 and 1957, the number of types of raw materials and industrial goods allocated directly by the State Planning Commission rose by a factor of three and came to account for around 60 per cent of total industrial output (Liu Guo-guang, 1988, p. 238). Direct producers could no longer purchase raw materials on the market, but had to obtain them through the state planning allocation system. This enabled the state to assure the supply of raw materials for economic sectors of national priority.

During the initial phase of the operation of the central planning system the economy began to experience rapid growth. By 1957, industry was expanding more rapidly in China than it was in other developing Asian countries. This raised the confidence of the government in the planning system to such an extent that, in 1958, it took the overambitious and extreme step of attempting to accelerate growth even further through the Great Leap Forward. The disastrous failure of this experiment resulted in considerable economic problems and human loss, forcing the government to enter a period of economic adjustment, consolidation and improvement in order to repair the damage. By 1963, the economy had recovered.

Then, through the Cultural Revolution from 1966 to 1976, experiments were carried out at the microeconomic level to improve efficiency, mainly by fostering the initiative of factory workers.[1] However, during these ten years, economic issues, including any significant efforts to modify the central planning system, were sidetracked by vigorous and protracted political campaigns.

Despite the setbacks and false starts, China's economy witnessed considerable change under the central planning system. A comprehensive industrial base was gradually formed through the extremely rapid expansion of heavy industry. This was largely the result of resource allocations through the central planning mechanism that were highly biased in favour of heavy industry (Table 6.1). During the First Five-Year Plan

Table 6.1   The structure of investment in capital construction, 1952–78
(in percentage shares of total)

	Agriculture	Light industry	Heavy industry	Other
1st Five-Year Plan	7.1	6.4	36.2	50.3
2nd Five-Year Plan	11.3	6.4	54.0	28.3
1963–65	17.6	3.9	45.9	32.6
3rd Five-Year Plan	10.7	4.4	51.1	33.8
4th Five-Year Plan	9.8	5.8	49.6	34.8
1976–78	10.8	5.9	49.6	33.7

Sources: SSB, 1992, pp. 149, 158; SSB, 1987, p. 97; Lin *et al.*, 1994, p. 62. See also the slightly different data in Liang Wensen, 1982, p. 62.

(1953–57), investments in heavy industry accounted for 85 per cent of total investments in industrial capital construction and 73 per cent of total investments in industrial and agricultural capital construction (SSB, 1992, p. 158). This biased investment pattern was followed in subsequent plans.

The focused injection of capital led to rapid growth in industry generally, but especially in heavy industry, which outstripped all other economic sectors. While the average annual growth rate of agriculture was 3.2 per cent, commerce 4.2 per cent, and industry 11 per cent from 1951 to 1980, the growth rate of heavy industry was 15.3 per cent between 1949 and 1981. From 1953 to 1979, the growth rate of heavy industry was almost 1.5 times that of light industry (Lin *et al.*, 1994, pp. 60–1). Data on the labour force indicate a similar trend in heavy industry. The share of the labour force in industry rose *vis-à-vis* that in agriculture, and the rise was due mainly to the considerable increase in the labour force in heavy industry (Table 6.2).

The extraordinary expansion in the industrial sector generated a fundamental change in the economic structure of the country. Within three decades, industry had replaced agriculture to become the largest sector in the economy. Between 1949 and 1978, the share of industry in total national income jumped from 12.6 per cent to 46.8 per cent, while the share of agriculture dropped from 68.4 per cent to 35.4 per cent (Lin *et al.*, 1994, p. 57). Between 1949 and 1980, the share of agriculture in net material product fell from 70 per cent to 24.6 per cent, that of light industry increased from 22.1 per cent to 35.4 per cent and that of heavy industry went up by the largest margin, from 7.9 per cent to

Table 6.2 Employment structure of the labour force, 1952–78 (in percentages)

	Agriculture	Industry			Other
		Total	Light	Heavy	
1952	83.5	6.0	4.2	1.8	10.5
1957	81.2	5.9	3.6	2.3	12.9
1965	81.6	6.4	3.0	3.4	12.0
1978	73.3	12.5	4.6	7.9	14.2

Sources: Ma and Sun, 1981, p. 104; SSB, 1992, p. 97; Lin *et al.*, 1994, p. 64.

40.4 per cent (Liang Wensen, 1982, p. 56). By the end of the 1970s, the industrial sector was able to satisfy the demand for major producer goods in the domestic economy, to equip the national defence force with domestically produced arms and to supply agriculture with domestically produced farm machinery, chemical fertilizers and pesticides.

Yet, the economic achievement did not come without high cost. Poor production efficiency was one of the most serious problems. It was associated with factors such as the inadequate incentive mechanism, the lack of operational autonomy among enterprises and the management rigidity in the planning system. While the efficiency problem was common in other economies with central planning, the particular features of the focus in China on heavy industry meant that the country's most abundant resource, the labour force, was significantly underutilized.

Partly as a result of bad planning, there was a chronic shortage of almost all resources, including capital, raw materials, technology and expertise. But labour was an exception. Despite the change in the basis of the economy from agriculture to industry, urbanization was proceeding very slowly. At the end of the 1970s, 80 per cent of the population was still living in the countryside simply because industrial development had failed to transform a greater portion of the rural labour force into an industrial labour force.

The speed of industrial expansion had been very high even by international comparison, which, theoretically, should have led to rapid transformation of rural labour force into industrial labour force. The reason that this did not happen was the emerging structure of industry. Heavy industry is capital intensive and, relative to light industry, has a low capacity for employment creation. Because of the slower growth of labour intensive light industry and services, the industrial expansion driven by heavy industry had not generated substantial demand for labour. Moreover, the central planning system severely limited labour mobility. Employment in the industrial sector was tightly controlled through state planning; the rural population was tied to the land under the commune system, and urban-bound migration was greatly restricted through an official residence registration scheme. The central planning system did not leave much room for job creation outside the state sector and the collectives. This narrowed the scope for productive labour use.

Over time, with the state and the collectives as the only sources of employment, the lack of alternative non-farmwork opportunities resulted in a decline in labour productivity in agriculture, and the living standards of the population, particularly the rural population, improved rather slowly.

During the post-1949 industrialization process, the role of foreign trade remained secondary. For the central planners, the importation of selected foreign goods was valid as a means to reduce serious domestic shortages and help strengthen domestic production capacity. However, domestic exports were expected to finance the imports.

Many developing countries engage in trade involving the exportation of natural resources and primary goods which are in abundant supply and available at low cost. They use the foreign exchange earnings to import goods, mostly manufactured goods, which are in short supply and which cost more to produce at home. During the industrialization process, China exported mostly primary goods in exchange for what it was not able to produce domestically. However, from the very beginning it was made clear that the purpose of foreign trade was neither to accumulate foreign exchange, nor to take comparative advantage of the farm-based economy. Rather, imports had to contribute to the establishment of China's own manufacturing capability and the development of its own technology.

That trade can also be an engine of growth – a central idea behind the shift in orientation towards exports that became popular after the 1970s – did not occur to the planners. In addition to practical obstacles to China's expansion in foreign trade, such as the US-led trade embargo, the fear of becoming dependent was an important factor in the adoption of the strategy of delinking and self-reliance. This official approach guided China's trade policies for more than two decades after 1949.

The process of industrialization highlighted the fact that the state was playing a leading role. The government was assuming full responsibility, from planning to implementation, for an industrialization drive that was based on highly centralized decision-making and a firm government control over the country's economic resources. In the modern history of China, the state had never before had such a pervasive role. For the government, industrialization was not merely an economic process. It was perceived also as involving a profound social transformation through which a new society, a socialist China, would emerge. While planning economic changes, the party-state initiated a number of nationwide political campaigns to eliminate the resistance which was believed to exist within the CCP itself, as well as in society at large, to the socio-economic transformation.

The culmination of the campaigns was the Cultural Revolution, between 1966 and 1976. Social and economic life became highly politicized. On the one hand, this served to consolidate the absolute leadership of the Communist state. On the other, it rallied national support for the Maoist strategy of delinking in an attempt to offset the isolationist implications. To put politics, or revolutionary ideology, in command, political mobilization was also constantly employed to take the place of material incentives in the effort to boost production.

The road to economic development during the first decades after the Revolution was travelled in the company of delinking, self-reliance, central planning, industrialization led by heavy industry, and political doctrine in command. This was a group of unusual measures. There seems to be no single theory within which each of these elements presupposes the rest. For example, self-reliance and delinking do not necessarily appear to require the existence of central planning as a precondition. In practice, however, these elements worked as an organic whole, each reinforcing the other. Heavy industry was given priority because it was considered the most important in terms of economic development and national independence, and national independence was viewed as one of the most important goals in the effort to catch up. In pursuing industrialization led by heavy industry, a central planning system was established to assure that priorities were followed in resource allocation. Central planning was used to discipline the conduct of domestic economic agents in foreign trade so as to avoid a situation in which the world market became a force in conflict with state planning, thereby leading to a derailment of industrialization. The high savings and investment rates required by the development of heavy industry were achieved partly at the cost of the suppression of consumption. To fend off opposition to this strategy, political doctrine was put in command. This also inspired morally positive initiatives in production that helped offset the lack of profitmaking opportunities for enterprises and personal material gain for individuals. Delinking and self-reliance, despite their limitations and their flaws, provided the country with a high degree of economic and political autonomy for domestic resource allocation, while significantly enhancing the power of the state.

Overall, this development strategy was China's response to the domestic and the world situation in the 1950s and 1960s. It may not have been the best answer in terms of economic potential and development possibilities, but it was a logical product of ideology and national sentiment during the Cold War. It was an attempt to resist being locked into a peripheral position in the world division of labour.

The approach composed of these elements led to a development path never before seen in China's history. Some measures were pushed by the leadership to an extreme that appears today to have been neither necessary, nor desirable, and the consequences were negative. Political events, such as the Cultural Revolution and the split with the USSR, sometimes helped turn delinking almost into autarchy and self-reliance almost into regional isolationism. This inevitably resulted in economic inefficiency.

In the mid-1960s, in preparation for a possible outbreak of war, the government formulated the policy of 'the third line'. According to this policy, the distribution of industrial plants was to be 'mountainous, scattered and concealed'. Defence-related, high-tech industries were to be moved to mountain areas, scattered throughout the country, but especially away from the coasts, and be located in caves if necessary in order to be concealed from foreign military attack. This large-scale industrial relocation, although tending also to redress the regional imbalance in economic development, was costly in terms of economic efficiency and the wastage of resources.

Three decades of development gave rise to certain distinctive features in post-1949 Chinese society. Through rapid industrial expansion, China emerged as a highly egalitarian society in terms of income distribution, with a relatively low incidence of poverty compared to countries at a similar economic level (Drèze and Sen, 1989; Griffin and Zhao, 1993; UNDP, 1994). Without foreign capital and with limited commodity exchanges on the world market, domestic social linkages were influenced in only a limited fashion by the process of capital accumulation taking place in the world economy. The government depended on an alliance of workers and peasants for political support and to carry out the strategy of rapid industrialization. One of the most distinctive consequences of the entire process was the fact that the wealth accumulated through economic growth did not enrich a small group within the country, nor was it extracted by foreign capital. It was controlled by the state, thereby giving the state enormous leverage in planning future economic change. However, this pattern of development left an important issue unresolved: Can equality be achieved only on the basis of a generally low standard of living? This question led to another: At what point do the losses in efficiency offset the gains in social equality? As it turned out, despite the great achievements of the process of rapid industrialization, increasing popular dissatisfaction with the slow improvement in living standards became an important element in a social consensus that eventually led to a new development path.

7 Trade and Trade Performance

From 1949 to the early 1970s, China's participation in the world market was conditioned by certain fundamental constraints. Not long after the establishment of the People's Republic, the US-led capitalist West broke 'normal' trade relations with China. These were not taken up again until around two decades later. Partly in response, China adopted the strategy of delinking and self-reliance. In retrospect, the Chinese government may appear to have overreacted. Yet, the West certainly did not welcome the victory of the Communists in mainland China, and its apprehension quickly escalated into an openly confrontational stance. The US sent the Seventh Fleet to 'neutralize' the Taiwan Straits, and China's territorial unification was left incomplete.[1] China's entry into the Korean War checked the US 'march to the Yalu'. Political and military conflict led to economic blockade, and China, called a 'hostile nation' by the US government, was banned from the markets of the major Western countries. China's trade with nations allied with the West, though still possible, became extremely restricted.

The limitations on trade under the US-led embargo represented a remarkable reversal in the historical pattern in trade relations between the West and China. A century earlier it had been the West that had forced China to open up to trade, and now the West was taking the initiative in excluding China from the world market. This reinforced the scepticism of the Chinese about 'free' trade, which was perceived at this time as a tool to make nations subservient to the capitalist political and economic world order. Depriving China of access to the world market was clearly aimed at inflicting damage on China's economy. The assumption seemed to be that the West could survive without China, but China's new regime could not survive without the West, since China's backward economy would certainly collapse without Western markets.

This assumption turned out to be a miscalculation for a number of reasons. First, although the pre-1949 China had been incorporated into the world economy, its peripheralization had not progressed sufficiently to render the country's economic structure dependent on world trade. The restrictions on trade might create difficulty, but the economy was able to survive. Second, by implementing the strategy of delinking and self-reliance, the government was able to carry out socioeconomic policies which exploited and strengthened the ability of China to be self-sufficient. Third, for the first time in its modern history, China was becoming a powerful modern nation-state with a strong sense of national purpose. Foreign threats and hostilities did more to solidify popular national support for the government than to weaken it. Indeed, Chinese nationalism was considerably boosted by the outcome of the Korean War, during which, for the first time in over 100 years, the Chinese army had been able to fight a major Western military power to a stalemate. Despite the huge human and material losses, this military achievement, which contrasted sharply with the long series of humiliating defeats by Western powers until then, served to stimulate nationalist feelings and popular confidence in the new state leadership. The fact that China was now a nation to be reckoned with in the international arena underlined the fear felt by the capitalist West, which had reacted with excessive and hostile economic measures. On the other hand, the experience of the early 1950s lent a more authoritarian cast to the new regime, as well as a harsher character to the delinking and self-reliance strategy than might otherwise have been the case.

Under these conditions, China essentially followed the path of import-substitution up to the early 1970s. Foreign trade continued to be pursued, but in such a way that it did not disturb the internal economic order or serve as a catalyst of economic growth. Imports were used to strengthen weak points and overcome bottlenecks in the domestic economy, thereby contributing to self-reliance. Exports were used to earn foreign exchange in order to pay for imports. In general, foreign trade was expected to play a supplementary role, that is, to help balance surpluses and shortages and to fill gaps in domestic supply. The centre of gravity of economic activities was in domestic production. It was believed that the development of productive power would lead to a drop in the number of gaps in the economy that would have to be filled by imports, and China would become even less dependent on international markets.

Specific trade patterns changed during the two decades of import-substitution.[2] China's practice was guided by government trade policies which went through a number of adjustments, mainly in response to changes in the world political situation and to domestic socioeconomic events.

In the early years of the People's Republic, China was faced with the enormous task of economic recovery through an ambitious effort to industrialize. The differences between the tasks to be accomplished and the ability of the country to accomplish them were numerous. This provided an incentive to develop trade and to seek outside economic aid.

However, because of the US-led embargo, China's trade with the West (excluding Japan) declined sharply both in absolute volume and as a share of the country's total trade. In the meantime, the Soviet Union and Eastern Europe became China's major trading partners (Yu Yong-ding, 1989, p. 177).

Until the late 1950s, the Soviet bloc was China's source of foreign trade, aid and technology. The Soviet government supplied 156 large industrial plants to China during the First Five-Year Plan (1953–57) and, together with Eastern European countries, provided technological assistance and training. The relationship with the Soviet bloc was very important, not least because of the political implications. From an economic point of view, however, Soviet assistance remained less substantial than the Chinese government had hoped. Over two-thirds of the cost of the 156 industrial plants supplied by the Soviets was borne by China (Meisner, 1977, p. 123). Overall, Soviet financial aid accounted for just 3 per cent of the total Chinese state investment in economic development during these years.

'Leaning to one side', of course, held an intrinsic danger. China ran a huge trade deficit from 1950 to 1955, reflecting the dominant role of Soviet loans and the Soviet trade (Sung, 1994, p. 111). The overdependence in economic relations on the Soviet Union posed the sort of threat that the strategy of self-reliance was meant to reduce. The Chinese government appears to have been aware of the problem. Well before the China–Soviet split, the government had nourished trade relations with non-socialist countries in order to have a multiplicity of trading partners. During the period of the Western trade embargo, it encouraged trade with countries with which China had no formal diplomatic ties. In 1952 China signed its first nongovernmental trade agreement with Japan. Trade relations with ASEAN countries were especially sought after. As a result, Sino–Japanese trade and Sino–ASEAN trade expanded at a respectable pace through nongovernmental channels. From 1950 to 1958, Sino–Japanese trade grew on average about 7 per cent per year, while trade with ASEAN countries increased by around 12 per cent annually (Yu Yong-ding, 1989).

The Sino–Soviet political split resulted in the withdrawal of Soviet assistance in 1960, ending the period of 'leaning to one side'. The policy had helped keep China's foreign trade alive during a critical stage. From 1950 to 1959, trade actually rose more quickly than did national output. The volume of trade in 1959 was almost four times that in 1950 and more than twice that in 1951. However, 1950 was not a 'normal' year since the Civil War had just ended. Moreover, the growth in trade was mainly driven by imports from the Soviet Union during the first half of the decade, and the trade balance did not turn in China's favour until after 1955.

Entering the 1960s, foreign trade was greatly affected by numerous events, including the drop in domestic production as a result of the Great Leap Forward (1958–60) and the related adjustment period (1961–63), the Sino–Soviet split (late 1950s and early 1960s), the onset of the Cultural Revolution in 1966, and the intensification of the conflict between China and the US during the Vietnam War. Foreign trade slowly recovered to the 1959 level only in the mid-1960s, though it remained stagnant throughout the rest of the decade.

In the 1960s, the ideological orientation in domestic politics was unfavourable to the development of foreign trade. During the Cultural Revolution, there were political factions within the government which advocated self-reliance to such a degree that their position almost resembled autarchy. These factions occasionally gained authority over the conduct of foreign economic relations, which sometimes became a highly politicized issue. In extreme cases, promoting foreign trade and acquiring foreign technology were labelled unpatriotic or the product of a slavish mentality which worshipped things foreign. Overall, however, the rationale of import-substitution continued to prevail, and the idea that foreign trade should supplement domestic needs guided trade relations. After the split with the USSR, China increasingly turned to Japan. China and Japan signed the Liao Chengzhi–Takasaki Tatsuno-suke Memorandum in 1960. As a result, the 'nongovernmental' trade between the two nations accelerated. China began to import entire plants from Japan. Japan became the number one trading partner, accounting for 13 per cent of China's total foreign trade. Meanwhile, China's trade with Hong Kong became far more significant. From 1959 to 1966, the China–Hong Kong trade grew at an annual rate of nearly 16 per cent, several times the annual average of 3.5 per cent during the previous decade (Yu Yong-ding, 1989, pp. 177–8). In the mid-1960s, China's trade relations with the Asian-Pacific economies also improved. The expanding trade with these countries more than offset the loss of trade with the Soviet bloc.

China was deeply absorbed in domestic political struggles from 1966 to 1972. Extremists advocated a total end to foreign trade, while the supporters of trade tried to stick to the original concept of self-reliance and oppose policies leading to autarchy. The political stalemate between these two groups resulted in a stagnation in foreign trade. Foreign trade was neither abandoned altogether, nor actively promoted. The total value of foreign trade rose by an average 5.3 per cent per year from 1966 to 1972, that is, at about the same level as the national economy, which advanced at an annual average 5.1 per cent. Trade with Japan, some ASEAN countries, mainly Malaysia and Singapore, and Hong Kong increased at a higher rate than that of overall trade.

The turning point in China's foreign trade relations occurred after the China–US détente in the early 1970s. On 15 July 1971, the US announced a dramatic change in American policy towards China by revealing that high-ranking US officials had gone to China and that the US president, Nixon, planned a trip there. Nixon's visit took place in February 1972. Shortly before that, in October 1971, China had been admitted to the UN. The US economic embargo of China was lifted after the Nixon visit, in 1972.

The so-called 'Nixon shock' was a major breakthrough in the policies of the West towards China. The containment and isolation of China had been one of the cornerstones of the postwar foreign policy of US administrations until Nixon's. The processes that prompted the shift in US policy were related, first of all, to the changing geopolitical situation. Japan was becoming an economic rival of the US, and the mounting tension in Sino–Soviet relations was seen as an opportunity to advance US global interests. There were also internal political considerations in the US that pushed the American government to take the action. More generally, the current cycle of economic expansion of the world economy was about over, and there was, to a certain degree, a recognition that the US could no longer be the 'policeman of the world'.

Yet, the China–US détente was also connected to the progress China had made through 20 years of effort to develop the economy while maintaining national independence. Instead of collapsing under international pressure, China had emerged a stronger nation and a nuclear power. The US action demonstrated a recognition of China's newly acquired status. The purely coercive measures of imperialism were no longer as effective as they had been prior to the 1949 Revolution.

Containment, embargoes and trade restrictions against China proved to be a mistake on the part of the West.[3] This ill-considered policy contributed to the rise of nationalism and to the continued use of the strategy of self-reliance, which in turn meant that the Communist leadership refrained from market-oriented reforms. Under détente and the expansion of economic contacts between the West and China in the 1970s, it became more difficult for Chinese leaders to maintain rigid central planning. The expansion of trade and investment created a more favourable opportunity to 'engage' China within the framework of the world economy.

For China, the relaxation of tensions in its relations with the US was welcome. It was considered a victory of the strategy of delinking and self-reliance. It seemed to the leadership that China had obtained what the strategy had been designed to produce: China was accepted among the nations of the world not as a weak and dependent state, but as a respected power with an honoured status. The Sino-American détente also marked the beginning of China's re-entry into the world market. One of the immediate economic consequences was an enormous boost in China's foreign trade, especially trade with the US, with which China established full diplomatic relations in 1979.

Trade with the US soon acquired great significance in China's overall trade (Table 7.1). From the US, China purchased aircraft, scientific equipment and chemical, industrial and agricultural products which were very important for the modernization of the economy.[4] The US gained considerably from the growing Sino–American trade, which helped it reduce its negative balance of payments. China's demand for Western goods now turned out to be rather huge. The ongoing industrialization of the country created a substantial market for American technology and scientific and agricultural products. Meanwhile, the US market for Chinese goods remained rather limited. Major Chinese exports to the US included small quantities of tin and tin alloys, hog bristles, silk, vegetable oil, and art objects. As a result, there was a growing imbalance in trade that heavily favoured the US.

It could be argued that the 'Nixon shock' marked not so much China's opening to the world economy, but the opening of the world economy to China (Table 7.2). Without publicly casting off self-reliance, the government seized this opportunity to expand trading activities on the world market, although various trade barriers still existed and although there was still opposition from within the government to the growth in trade.

Table 7.1 The China–US trade, 1972–80 (dollars, millions)

	US exports to China	Chinese exports to US	US surplus
1972	66	32	34
1975	304	156	148
1980	3755	1059	2696

Source: Hsu, 1990, p. 732.

Table 7.2   China's foreign trade, 1971–78 (dollars, millions)

	Exports	Imports	Total	% change	Balance of trade
1971	2636	2205	4841	–	431
1972	3443	2858	6301	30.2	585
1973	5819	5157	10976	74.2	662
1974	6949	7619	14568	32.7	–670
1975	7264	7487	14751	1.3	–223
1976	6855	6578	13433	–8.9	277
1977	7590	7214	14804	10.2	376
1978	9745	10893	20638	39.4	–1148

Source: Sung, 1994, p. 111.

The impact of the sudden access to the world market was immediate and enormous on the performance of the trade sector. The total value of imports and exports rose by 30 per cent in 1972 and then by 74 per cent in 1973. From 1972 to 1978, the average annual growth rate of China's foreign trade was about 22 per cent, many times higher than the average annual growth rate of national income over the same period (5.9 per cent). During these years, trade with Japan increased annually by nearly 30 per cent, that with ASEAN countries by 26 per cent and that with Hong Kong by 20 per cent. The record of growth in trade during these years was even better than that later during the reform era of the 1980s and early 1990s. Although the annual growth rate was not steady, foreign trade undoubtedly took a great step forward after 1972, and the momentum has since been maintained.

China's major trading partners also changed during this period. The Soviet Union and Eastern Europe had been the major partners in the 1950s. In the 1960s China had begun to cultivate trade relations with other countries such as Japan and ASEAN countries. However, international political barriers limited China's options. In the 1970s, while China expanded its trade relations with a large number of countries (said to number 174 countries and regions by the end of the decade), there was a clear shift in trade towards the West (Table 7.3).

In a sense China was returning, after a brief break in the 1950s, to its main trading partners of the pre-1949 period, that is, to the Western market. This is shown by data on 1934 (Table 7.4). China's experience indicates that, given the difference in level of wealth between China and the Western countries, it was difficult for China to alter drastically the particular structure and pattern of its trade regardless of the Revolution

Table 7.3 Shares in China's imports and exports, 1979
(in percentages of the total)

	Exports	Imports
Hong Kong* and Macao	28	–
Japan	20.2	25.2
European Economic Community	12.6	21.3
US	4.4	11.9

Source: Teng, 1982, pp. 169–70.
*The trade with Hong Kong was largely an entrepôt trade in that Hong Kong re-exported Chinese goods to other countries, mainly to the West.

Table 7.4 Shares in China's imports and exports, 1934
(in percentages of the total)

	Exports	Imports
Hong Kong	18.9	2.9
Japan	15.2	12.2
Germany, Great Britain and France	16.8	13.2
US	17.6	26.2

Source: Moser, 1935, p. 29.

or the adoption of radical domestic development strategies. The impact of events driven by political considerations – such as the US trade embargo, China's alliance with the Soviet Union, or China's relentless domestic political campaigns – on the pattern of China's economic relations with the world economy was rather limited and temporary.

However, development strategies which combine vision with practical possibilities can make and, indeed, did make a difference in the long run. One of the greatest accomplishments of the post-1949 development strategies was the improvement in the industrial base of the economy. This in turn led to a gradual change in the structure of China's commodity exports on the world market. In the early years after the 1949 Revolution, China's major foreign market shifted from Western countries to the East bloc, yet this did not have any real impact on the structure of China's trade. The major export commodities continued to be the same traditional agricultural and mineral products, including silk, tea, hog bristles, and tungsten ore, that China had been exporting to the West. After the initial industrialization drive in the 1950s and 1960s, the share of manufactured goods in total exports, most notably textiles, handicrafts and chemical products, began to climb. By the end of the 1970s, the share of primary commodities in total exports had dropped from over half to less than one-quarter, while that of manufactured goods had risen proportionately. China also began to export machinery and transport equipment, which together accounted for about 15 per cent of total exports in the 1970s (World Bank, 1994a, pp. 188, 190).

Unlike the situation in exports, most imports both before and after the Revolution were manufactured goods. Between 1953 and 1979, manufactured goods represented 60 per cent to 80 per cent of total imports, with the highest share, 84 per cent, occurring in 1953–55, and the lowest, 60 per cent, in 1962–64 (Sung, 1994, p. 113). However, there was a clear difference in the composition of these imports before and after 1949. Before the Revolution, the imported manufactured goods were mainly consumer goods, while the bulk of the imported manufactured goods after 1949 were capital goods, such as entire production plants, transportation and communication equipment, petroleum refinery installations, and electric power plants, as well as raw materials and other production materials not available on the domestic market or in short supply for industrial use. These imports were used to reduce bottlenecks and to enhance domestic production capacity. The structure of imports after 1949 thus reflected a key concept in the country's development strategy. The priority in imports was assigned to producer goods. During the first three decades after the Revolution, imports of producer goods accounted for about 80 per cent of total imports. The remaining 20 per cent of imports consisted of consumer goods, mainly grain, sugar, edible oil, and watches, most of which were bulk food items used to supplement domestic food supplies (Teng, 1982, pp. 170–1).

In the context of China's central planning system, in which shortages were a 'normal' phenomenon and in which there was no direct link between exports and the earnings of individual producers, the incentive for producers to export was weak. The options in terms of the volume and composition of exports remained rather limited.

Like other developing countries which were exporters mainly of primary goods and other unfinished products, China also suffered from unequal exchanges in the world market under adverse terms of trade. However, unlike many other exporters of primary goods, China was able to exercise a high level of control over exports, as well as imports, through central planning mechanisms. It employed this ability to favour the allocation of resources in order to fulfil the primary goal of industrialization. In this sense, foreign trade was not conducted entirely on terms set by others. While there were economic inefficiencies and the irrational utilization of resources, these were the price to be paid not so much for the application of particular trade policies, but for the overall central planning system. Moreover, this approach allowed the country a higher degree of autonomy in determining the tempo and pattern of industrialization.

The state exercised control over foreign trade through central planning. The general levels of exports and imports were decided by the central government within the framework of state plans. Direct trade, both exports and imports, was carried out exclusively by about a dozen state trade corporations – each in charge of a specific set of commodities – under the authority of the Ministry of Foreign Trade. In effect, this meant that there was no competition among Chinese trade agencies.

The task of mobilizing domestic goods for export fell to various local and regional trade organizations, which usually also supervised related matters such as the supply of raw materials for the production of export goods. The most active and important trade organizations at the provincial level were located in the trade ports, most of which had once been treaty ports. The state trade organizations monopolized the intermediate functions in foreign trade, so that the 'foreign market' for the producers of export goods was, in practical terms, the state trade organizations. Likewise, the distribution of imported goods, as well as the allocation of foreign exchange, was determined in state plans and executed by state administrative bodies. The central control over foreign trade enabled the state to protect the domestic market and concentrate resources in priority areas.

Under national plans, the expansion of foreign trade in large measure followed industrial expansion. Despite the unfavourable conditions, foreign trade increased considerably. By 1977, the volume of foreign trade was nearly seven times what it had been in 1950, and by 1979 the figure had risen nearly ten times (Teng, 1982, p. 168). As mentioned earlier, there were a few years during which the growth in foreign trade actually outpaced that in national product. In 1971–73, after Western markets had opened to China, foreign trade surged by more than twice the growth rate in GNP. In general, however, the expansion in foreign trade was somewhat slower than industrial expansion.

As a result of this asymmetrical development, the share of foreign trade in domestic production declined. In 1979, exports constituted 4 per cent of the gross value of industrial and agricultural output. China was among the countries with the lowest per capita trade in the world.

From 1952 to 1974, the ratio of foreign-trade turnover (imports plus exports) to GNP was around 6 per cent (Eckstein, 1977, p. 234; Riskin, 1987, p. 207). This was lower than the estimated ratio of about 10 per cent during the 1920s and 1930s. In 1973, merchandise exports represented 1.1 per cent of GDP, not only much lower than the corresponding figure for industrialized capitalist countries, but also lower than the figure for the USSR, as well as for other large developing countries. It was substantially below the world average of 11.2 per cent (Maddison, 1995, p. 38).

China's exports declined as a proportion of total world exports from 1.5 per cent in 1955 to 1.2 per cent in 1965 and, with the exception of only one year, to 0.7–0.8 per cent between 1969 and 1979 (Table 7.5).

China's low trade-dependency ratio reflected the low level of the country's economic integration within the world economy. This was a function of the general development pattern guided by delinking and self-reliance. The international environment was an important determinant of the volume of China's foreign trade, as shown by the sharp increase in trade after the lifting of the trade embargo. Changes in the international environment, however, had only a limited impact on the growth pattern of the domestic economy.

The pursuit of industrialization was persistent, and domestic industries were eventually producing a wide variety of manufactured goods, many of which had never before been produced domestically due to weak industrial capacity. In this respect, import-substitution, which was largely a response to the lack of access to and the uncertainty of the world market, had a positive influence on China's emerging industrial base.

Table 7.5 China's share of world exports, 1950–79
(in percentages)

1950	0.91	1960	1.44	1970	0.72
1951	0.92	1961	1.11	1971	0.75
1952	1.02	1962	1.05	1972	0.83
1953	1.23	1963	1.07	1973	1.01
1954	1.33	1964	1.10	1974	0.83
1955	1.50	1965	1.19	1975	0.83
1956	1.58	1966	1.15	1976	0.69
1957	1.42	1967	0.99	1977	0.67
1958	1.82	1968	0.88	1978	0.75
1959	1.95	1969	0.80	1979	0.83

Source: Sung, 1994, p. 111.

Many have argued that the revolutionary leadership was overcautious in promoting foreign trade and that it was preoccupied with the effort to maintain a balance between economic autarchy at one extreme and free trade at the other. Together with the hostile world political context and the unfavourable economic conditions due to the Cold War, this misstep and the unwillingness to profit from China's comparative advantage in international trade, led the country to become more economically isolated than was either desirable for economic development, or necessary for self-reliance (Oksenberg and Goldstein, 1974). This criticism has also represented the official view of the Chinese government in the period of reform during the 1980s and 1990s.

Indeed, China could have been more aggressive in seeking greater openness in foreign trade and investment, despite the 'inter-state' relations existing at the time. The wider role for foreign trade might then have helped generate a different economic structure. Yet, whether China's overall economy would have performed better in that case is not clear. The development record of other large developing countries before the 1970s does not really provide much evidence. What is clear is that the country's trade policies largely achieved what they were meant to achieve within the central planning system. Export earnings were used to obtain goods which were crucial for industrialization. Thus, foreign trade contributed to the increase in the country's capacity to produce, and precisely this growing capacity to produce eventually allowed China to improve its export structure by boosting manufacturing output. Under central planning, foreign trade was brought into line with the dynamics of national development and therefore served the general goal of industrialization.

It is noteworthy that in this process China relied entirely on domestic resources and did not fall into debt. This was a remarkable accomplishment for a big developing country experiencing rapid industrialization. On the other hand, because of problems in the state plans, the import and export schemes may have contributed to the appearance of certain irrationalities in the emerging economic structure. None the less, despite all the difficulties and shortcomings, at the end of the central planning period the economy of China was far healthier than it had been prior to the 1949 Revolution, when free trade and the free flow of capital had been the order of the day. One might say that China could have adopted a more relaxed trade posture, but then the result in terms of the pursuit of national wealth and power might not have been so positive; one need only look at the experience of many other developing countries and at China's own not-too-distant past.

8 Outcome: A Mixed Package

In assessing the socioeconomic performance of the People's Republic during the first 30 years of its existence, we employ some of the commonly accepted indicators, such as the economic growth rate and the human development index. In doing so, moreover, we evaluate specific development strategies in terms of their success or failure in achieving the goals they were designed to achieve. Catching up to the West, industrialization and national independence were the major objectives of the development strategies in China after 1949. From this perspective, the results appear mixed.

The Chinese government found the progress far from satisfactory. According to the Chinese leadership, a major failure was the fact that China remained underdeveloped and the standard of living in the country remained low. 'In the 20 years from 1958 to 1978, the income of peasants and workers changed very little; living standards were very low, and the development of productivity was insignificant,' Deng Xiaoping said in 1985 (Deng, 1993, p. 115). 'Per capita GNP in 1978 was less than \$250.' Indeed, compared with the developed countries, China suffered from economic backwardness in terms of industrial capacity and national wealth. This also posed a problem for the government in its attempts to justify political and economic practices in the name of socialism, because socialism was supposed to demonstrate its superiority over capitalism through higher levels of productivity and better standards of living.

Others regarded the Chinese development programme as a failure because it did not match the success of South Korea, Taiwan, Hong Kong and Singapore, which achieved substantially greater growth and higher levels of industrialization during the same period. According to some, the four so-called 'East Asian tigers' were able to enjoy so much economic success because they were relying on a strategy of export-orientation. The explicit message was that China's economic performance was actually more a disappointment than an accomplishment and that industrialization through self-reliance and delinking was undoubtedly inferior.

It is true that, following the central planning period, China continued to be a developing country, far behind the rich nations and the newly industrialized economies (NIEs) of East Asia. It is also true that not all the economic policies adopted in China contributed to economic growth and human development; some had disastrous results. One of the most serious failures was the Great Leap Forward, the radical economic and social movement led by the government in the late 1950s that brought the country to the verge of starvation. An estimated 20 million to 30 million people died during the famine in the aftermath of the movement. The human loss was comparable to that in the Soviet Union during collectivization in the early 1930s. The inability to prevent a tragedy of such magnitude marred the record of the government's efforts to improve the general well-being of the population that, for example, had successfully eliminated the chronic famine and starvation which had been so widespread in China before 1949.[1]

By any account, however, it has to be admitted that the state-led, self-reliant industrialization programme was unprecedented in China's history. Previous governments, particularly the GMD regime, had attempted to industrialize the country, and even the Qing government had tried to develop a modern arms industry. Yet, none of these endeavours can be compared to the post-1949 industrialization drive. First, unlike the past, catching up with the Western industrialized countries had been announced publicly as the aim of the drive. Second, the government was fully involved as planner and manager, and it was able to mobilize all the resources available to the nation, including the people. Third, there was no significant foreign participation; foreign trade was limited, and investments of foreign capital were negligible.

This new stage of development should also be assessed according to its meaning in the modern history of China and the Chinese economy. The record of economic performance of the three decades immediately after the Revolution represented a sharp reversal of the long-term economic stagnation of the country. The rate of economic growth was generally high, although growth was very uneven. There were two unfavourable periods: three years associated with the Great Leap Forward and, to a lesser extent, the ten years of the Cultural Revolution.[2] None the less, due to the rapid expansion during most years, over the entire period from 1951 to 1978 the average annual GNP growth rate was a respectable 7 per cent (SSB, 1990; World Bank, 1992). Never before in China's modern history had the economy advanced at such a speed over so many years. One may recall that average annual real GDP growth – if it can be called 'growth' at all – had been 0.8 per cent in 1900–13 and 0.1 per cent in 1913–50.

China's economic performance was also favourable relative to that of most other economies (Table 8.1). Between 1950 and 1973, average annual real GDP growth was higher in China than it was in the OECD

Table 8.1   Annual average real GDP growth in selected countries and
regions, 1900–73 (in percentages, at constant prices)

	1900–13	*1913–50*	*1950–73*
OECD average	2.9	2.0	4.9
Asian average	1.7	1.3	5.4
Latin American average	3.9	3.3	5.2
Developing country average	2.6	2.1	5.3
China	0.8	0.1	5.8
USSR	3.5	2.7	5.0
India	1.0	0.7	3.7
Indonesia	1.8	0.9	4.5
South Korea	–	1.7	7.5
Taiwan	1.8	2.7	9.3
Brazil	3.5	4.2	6.7
Mexico	2.6	2.6	6.4

Source: Maddison, 1989, p. 36, Table 3.3, which provides a definition of each
country group and a description of the method of calculation.

countries, in Asia or Latin America, in developing countries generally,
and in the USSR. This was in sharp contrast to the two periods 1900–13
and 1913–50, when the GDP growth rate in China was the lowest among
all these countries and regional groupings. In the twentieth century, China
has been able to embark on a strong wave of growth only since 1949.

It is true that China's growth rate in the first decades after the Revolution was not the highest in the world. A few economies, including the
'Asian tigers', were able to produce higher growth rates. Yet, one should
examine the issue within the historical context. Thus, compared to China,
the NIEs of East Asia actually grew relatively less during the postwar
period than they had previously. Between 1913 and 1950, the economic
growth rate of Taiwan was 27 times that of China, while the corresponding figure for South Korea was 17 times. Between 1950 and 1973, the
economic growth rate of Taiwan was only 1.6 times that of China, while
the figure for South Korea was only 1.3 times. Judged on these terms,
the economic performance of China after 1949 was a far greater 'miracle' than that of the East Asian NIEs.

Industrialization brought about a substantial qualitative change in the
national economy as well. Within less than 30 years, by the end of the
1970s, China was transformed from an underdeveloped rural society
into a semi-industrialized state. The ratio between industry and agriculture in total material output was reversed from around 3 to 7 to about

8 to 2. A relatively comprehensive industrial structure was established. Perhaps alone in the Third World, China became able to produce industrial goods to meet the material requirements for the expansion of production in all sectors and at various levels of technical complexity. The progress in the development of science and technology was remarkable and culminated in the acquisition by China of a nuclear capability in the early 1960s. The fact that China became one of the five nuclear powers was highly symbolic, considering that the other four were all major industrialized countries, most of which had been aggressive in taking advantage of China's backwardness during the 100 years leading up to the 1949 Revolution.[3]

China's record in human development was also unusually good. The industrialization programme involved the predominance of state and collective property ownership. These types of ownership assured that income distribution was far more equitable than it had been at any other time in the modern history of the country. The policy of guaranteed jobs meant that there was no open unemployment and that everyone was entitled to a basic standard of living and a share in national income. The access of the population to education, health care and other social welfare provisions was established. Life-threatening hunger and famine, which had been rather too common before 1949, were eliminated except in 1959 to 1962.

Economic growth and social policies which focused on equality and the satisfaction of basic needs led to considerable improvement. In 1949, average life expectancy was less than 40 years. One child in four did not reach the age of 1. By 1980, average life expectancy had risen to about 65, while the infant mortality rate had been drastically reduced, to 56 per 1000 live births (Sarker and Gaur, 1994). China's human development record was generally better than that in countries at a similar level of per capita income, showing that a system based on socialist principles can be effective.

Eberstadt and others have argued that, especially before the 1980s, the successes under central planning were overestimated and that the problems were downplayed in Western accounts sympathetic to Maoism (see Deckers, 1994). This may well be the case. Moreover, the achievements should be measured against the costs, which were indeed very high. Taking the huge investments and enormous human sacrifices into consideration, one may decide that the accomplishments were actually quite moderate. Yet, it would be equally wrong to go to the other extreme and belittle them. The precise numbers may be subject to dispute, but the large picture and the relative long-term trend are fairly clear. The

transformation brought about by the state-led industrialization programme was remarkable. This had a great impact on events during the subsequent reform process. While delinking and self-reliance during this period brought China
to the front rank of industrializing countries, they also created the need
for further progress. Thus, despite the admirable socioeconomic advances,
the aim of the strategy, to eliminate the gap with the industrialized world,
remained far from achieved.

A study by Arrighi (1991) shows that, as measured by per capita GNP,
which is perhaps the best available indicator of national wealth, the
income gap between China and the West did not shrink, but actually
widened between 1938 and 1980. However, China was not the only country that did not catch up. As Arrighi demonstrates, the failure of regions
outside the core to catch up was rather the norm than the exception.
The income gap between rich and poor regions was generally broaden-
ing during this period. In fact, China's economic performance was more
successful or less poor than that of many other developing countries.
Arrighi points out that China should not be compared to the NIEs of
East Asia, but to countries in South Asia and Southeast Asia, or to the
'Indonesia and Philippines' aggregate. The income gap between these
regions and the rich core nations increased more than did the gap
between China and the core nations (Table 8.2). During the first half of
the twentieth century, China was among the poorest countries in Asia.
After 1949, China's economy registered a major gain relative to South
Asia and a minor gain (or a minor loss) relative to Southeast Asia.
China had taken a 'great leap forward'. It had been one of the worst
performing economies in the first half of the century, but now it was
among the best performing economies in terms of aggregate GNP growth
and per capita income growth.

At the end of the period of delinking and self-reliance, China was still
not an economic power, but it had become an important political and
military power. This stronger position was due to the fact that China
was now a modern nation-state supported by an expanding industrial
base and a sizeable army. China had proved that, though it had been a
latecomer to industrialization, it could do rather well by following a
development path independent of foreign capital involvement. Despite
the difficult international situation during the postwar era, delinking and
self-reliance appear overall to have been a winning strategy.

This economic performance raised the country's political and military
standing in the world. In particular, it demonstrated China's potential as a
key player in Asia. This was a major factor in prompting the US to change

Table 8.2 Economic performance, 1900–87
(annual average compound growth rates)

	1900–50			1950–87			
	GDP	Population	GDP per capita	GDP	Population	GDP per capita	
China	0.3	0.6	−0.3	6.5	1.8	4.5	(2.9)
India	0.8	0.9	−0.1	3.8	2.1	1.7	(1.6)
Indonesia	1.1	1.2	−0.1	4.9	2.3	2.5	(2.5)
Philippines	2.5	2.0	0.4	4.3	2.9	1.4	(1.8)
South Korea	1.8	1.7	0.1	7.6	2.0	5.5	(5.2)
Taiwan	2.4	2.0	0.4	8.8	2.5	6.1	(6.2)
Asian average	1.4	1.4	0.0	5.5	2.4	3.1	(3.1)
Brazil	4.0	2.1	1.8	6.0	2.7	3.2	(3.8)
Mexico	2.6	1.4	1.2	5.3	3.0	2.3	(3.1)
Latin American average	3.5	1.9	1.6	4.3	2.5	1.9	(2.4)
OECD average	2.2	0.9	1.3	3.9	0.8	3.0	(3.8–4.8)
USSR	2.9	0.8	2.1	3.9	1.2	2.6	(3.4)

Sources: Maddison, 1989, p. 15. The figures in parentheses show GDP per capita in 1950–73 and are taken from Maddison, 1995, pp. 62–3.

its policy towards China from miscommunication to diplomatic recognition. Mistakenly or not, many developing countries began to look up to China for inspiration. China was no longer 'the sick man of Asia' to be ordered around by the more powerful West. It had to be reckoned with.

'Wealth and power' (*fu qiang*) had been pursued by generations of Chinese as the key to the country's independence and proper position in the world of nations. Only after 1949 did this begin to produce tangible results, although China was more successful in pursuing power, while the dream of wealth was more illusive.

Could China have done even better, as so many have suggested? The postwar world order and the structure of the capitalist world economy were beyond the control of any single country, and China could not change this. Yet, there were many areas in which it might have done more by implementing better socioeconomic policies. For example, the overzealous Great Leap Forward campaign in 1958–60 that cost the economy and society so dearly might have been avoided or at least rendered less extreme. In general, political campaigns were too frequent and tended to distract attention from the search for solutions to economic issues. Self-reliance was sometimes pushed too far, so that it became identical with rejecting anything that was not indigenous. The central planning mechanism was employed far too rigidly and the role of the market was ignored far too arbitrarily so that economic efficiency and local and individual initiative were often sacrificed. Last but not least, trade might have been allowed to evolve more in ways that would have favoured economic development.

Theoretically, the strategy followed by the East Asian NIEs may have been superior to Maoist industrialization. However, in China immediately after 1949 it would have been very difficult politically to apply the model of the Asian NIEs even if the West's ferocious policy of containment had not existed. The development model of the Asian NIEs presupposed close economic integration with the Western economies. In China, there was the precedent of close interactions with these economies as well. However, this was associated in people's minds more with humiliation than with prosperity. The strategy of delinking and self-reliance was, in a sense, an inevitable reaction to both the historical pattern and the containment policy of the West. This explains the popular support that was so effectively used by the government to mobilize the nation for independent development.

Moreover, the development pattern achieved through the strategy of delinking and self-reliance has to be taken as a totality. The strategy had intrinsic strengths and weaknesses, to be sure, but the strengths could not have existed without the weaknesses. The measures which were largely responsible for the positive outcomes were usually the same ones which were responsible for the shortcomings.

Great human suffering occurred during the period as the strategy was being carried out. Yet, human cost is evident in any process of industrialization, and the human misery which has accompanied the expansion of the Western-led world economy on a global scale has been colossal. This does not justify the policies in China that generated enormous human and material losses, which are simply unjustifiable. None the less, while industrialization in the Western countries benefited a minority at the expense of the misery of the majority, including the subordination of vast regions on the periphery, industrialization 'Mao style' may have been realized at the expense of popular consumption, but it did not create a small wealthy class, and it rendered China economically and politically more autonomous and stronger than ever before in its modern history.

To the question of whether China could have accomplished more if the economy had remained more open, the study by Arrighi (1991) on long-term and cross-regional economic change provides a useful insight. According to the study, over the 50 years from 1938 to 1988, various development strategies and policies were adopted by countries in order to catch up with the wealth standard set by the West. A handful of countries succeeded. Most failed. After analysing the experiences of countries in the West, South and East, Arrighi comes to the conclusion that overall there was a substantial widening of the already large income gap between rich and poor countries during the 50-year period, and the vast majority of the world's population was falling behind in terms of Western standards of wealth.

'Closure or openness to the global circuits of capital seem to have made little difference in halting, let alone reversing, the overall trend towards an increasingly unequal global distribution of income,' writes Arrighi (1991, p. 56). In fact, as one in the group of countries to practise 'economic closure' during the third quarter of the twentieth century, China actually performed better than many countries with greater economic openness.

The argument that China could have done better if its economy had been more open is mainly based on the experience of the East Asian NIEs. While it is true that the East Asian NIEs have succeeded in narrowing their income gap with the West, they have done so by maintaining an average annual GDP growth rate of about 8 per cent (from 1965 to 1993), nearly three times as high as the rate in Western industrialized countries (ADB, 1994, p. 15). No other region of the developing world has achieved so much economically since World War II. Thus, the Asian NIEs are exceptions, and, as such, they deserve the label of 'economic miracle'.

However, the difficulties China would have had to surmount to become a similar exception were enormous. In any event, the socioeconomic differences between China and the Asian NIEs are so great as to render a comparison largely inappropriate. The total population of all the Asian NIEs is only a tiny portion (about 5 per cent) of China's. It is one thing to improve the standards of living of a tiny fraction of the world population; it would be quite another thing – nothing short of a profound and truly radical revolution – to do the same with one-quarter of humanity.

The initial conditions in the two cases were quite distinct. Before 1949, when China had an 'open' economy, the economic growth rate of China was much lower than that in South Korea and Taiwan. GNP per capita was also much lower in China after 1949 than it was in the Asian

NIEs at their respective 'moments of takeoff'. Yet, the gap in growth rates has narrowed appreciably since then.

More importantly, China and the Asian NIEs were differently situated with respect to the Western-dominated world economy. Indeed, some of the world political and economic conditions which tended to help the Asian NIEs succeed were also closely linked to the political and economic path China took.

'The "original tigers'" biggest growth spurts came during the Cold War,' some Western observers have noticed (*Newsweek*, 1994); 'as bulwarks against Communism, US allies Japan, Taiwan, South Korea and Singapore were amply rewarded with aid and investment,' not to mention the generous access to the markets of the West. The East Asian model is a typical case of what Wallerstein (1979b) called 'development by invitation'. The income structure of the world economy and the experiences of so many other developing economies, large or small, closed or open, have suggested that the rich West was not 'an open "club" that any nation can join by proving its worth through appropriate developmental efforts and policies,' because the wealth enjoyed by the West is 'oligarchic wealth', which cannot be generalized (Arrighi, 1991). The club of rich countries can be joined only by invitation. This is the 'secret' of the success of the East Asian NIEs that cannot be copied by other developing countries and certainly could not have been copied by China during the Cold War.

The delinking and self-reliance strategy became necessary not only because of the Western containment policy and the Maoist determination to maintain national independence. It was also supported by socialist ideology. Internally, socialist ideology favoured the equal distribution of wealth. As a result, the lower social strata in China – the majority of peasants – were better off than their counterparts in other countries at a similar level of economic development. On the world stage, the socialist ideology upheld by the Chinese was at odds with the idea of peaceful competition promoted by the Soviet Union. The Chinese leadership was sceptical of the propriety and usefulness of playing the games of the capitalist West on the world market.

None the less, by the end of the 1970s, the income gap between China and the West was causing trouble for Chinese policymakers, who were now as eager to re-examine their current approach as they had been to adopt it. Could the barriers to an acceleration of economic growth be overcome within the existing policy framework, or was it necessary to change course? This was the question that led to a re-evaluation of the Mao era and to the shift to a different path of development.

Part III: Reintegration (1978 and Beyond)

PART III: REINTEGRATION (1978 AND BEYOND)

At the Third Plenum of the 11th Central Committee of the Chinese Communist Party in late 1978, the decision was taken to initiate economic reforms. The subsequent reform process, together with the changes in other countries of the former socialist bloc beginning in the late 1980s, is now often called a 'transition from plan to market'. However, from the official Chinese point of view, the initial purpose of the reform programme was not to install the market, but to 'modernize' the economy. The aim was to modify certain features of the economic system, but not to alter altogether the existing order.

Yet, reforms which begin with limited measures and limited goals may become much more wide-ranging once the logic of change takes root and grows more persistent. Indeed, an examination of the reform experience in China over the past 20 years reveals that the socioeconomic changes have been far more profound than cosmetic. The step-by-step modification of the central planning system has led to a far-reaching process of transformation of the economy and society of China. There has been no clear blueprint of reform, but a market-oriented economy has emerged as the result of the piecemeal, though steady reform measures.

Still, there has been a great deal of continuity because of the incremental reform approach which China has adopted. The Communist-led government has been playing the key role in guiding the reform process, while state authorities at various levels have exercised enormous power over the evolution of social and economic development. In the midst of the growing non-state economic sector and despite the pressure of privatization, the majority of state-owned enterprises have continued to function.

The Chinese economic reform process has been analysed in many ways in terms of origins, policies, approaches, consequences, significance, and so on. From a historical perspective, the reform period has been merely a new stage in China's long march towards a national objective, that is, to catch up with the advanced West.

Naughton (1996, p. 59) has argued that 'the driving force behind change in 1978–79 was a reorientation of Chinese development strategy.' One might promptly add that the driving force behind the reorientation in development strategy was the desire to accelerate growth so that the nation could acquire 'wealth and power'. The goal of catching up, once used to help justify the establishment of the central planning system, now became a key element in the effort to mobilize national support for the shift away from the central planning system. If transition away from the market in the 1950s and transition back towards the market in the late 1970s are seen as practical options for alternative development strategies, then it was the persistence of the wish to catch up that provided the government with the motivation for initiating the changes.

9 A Different Game

After the ten-year-long Cultural Revolution, the state leadership realized that, despite tremendous effort and heavy cost, the goal of catching up to the West still remained distant. It was, therefore, determined that a fresh attempt had to be made. An endeavour was briefly undertaken after the Cultural Revolution to strengthen the central planning system so as to energize the economy. However, due to the lack of immediate success, the endeavour was quickly abandoned.

The search for a more effective alternative strategy led to the identification of two key components of a state programme: 'reform' and 'openness' (*gaige* and *kaifang*). The former means the transformation of the central economic planning system, and the latter means the opening of China to the world market and the reintegration of China into the world economy. The two components were considered to be intimately related.

The decision to reintegrate China into the world economy represented a big step away from the strategy of delinking. Numerous theories have been put forward to explain the causes of this shift. It has been argued that the opening up of China under Deng Xiaoping was primarily a response to an evolving international security environment. New strategic interests had prompted the West, mainly the US, to abandon its longstanding containment policy towards China. This made it possible for China to open up to a now less hostile outside world.

Many others believe that China opted for economic openness because of the failure of the Maoist strategy of self-reliance. They argue that 'the rise and fall of Chinese autarchy and isolation in the 1960s and early 1970s' reflected 'the rise and fall of radical nativism and utopianism in Chinese domestic affairs' (Harding, 1984, p. 202). For them, the change in course represented evidence that China had declined 'to the point where it will feature in world affairs mainly because of its weakness and fragility' (Drucker, 1989, p. 24).

A few have made the opposite argument (for example, see Deckers, 1994). They reason that the move from self-reliance to openness towards the world market was simply the logical outcome of the overall strategy of industrialization. The aim of the Maoist strategy of self-reliance had essentially been fulfilled in that China had become economically and politically more powerful. Industrialization had succeeded to such a degree that the country could now enter the world market as a relative equal or, at least, with much more acceptable terms of trade. It is further argued that delinking was never meant to last forever. Openness represented the conscious response of a rational government to a changing situation.

To see the reorientation in development strategy during the reform era as evidence of the 'failure' of the Maoist model of state-led, self-reliant industrialization is to be ahistorical. There was no lack of success under Mao-style industrialization. The problem was that, while the Maoist model had represented a viable solution to the economic backwardness of the pre-1949 market economy, it had eventually created new contradictions. In the short run and in a context of extensive growth, these contradictions had not been serious obstacles to economic expansion, but, over a longer period, they had a cumulative effect, and unexpected consequences and negative outcomes were coming to the fore as the economy became more advanced and sophisticated.

The Chinese policymakers who formulated and implemented the reform programme were generally more critical of the recent experience than were the proponents of the strategy of self-reliance. The reform-minded government suggested that, by the mid-1970s, the economy had been on the verge of collapse, and it had been to avoid this disaster in the short run and to accelerate growth in the long run that reform had become a matter of urgency.

In fact, the economic situation was far from being the difficult one faced by the USSR in the late 1980s. The economy was not about to collapse. Indeed, it was still growing. However, among a considerable segment of the reform-minded leadership and among many intellectuals close to the government, sober economic analytical precision was sometimes compromised for the purpose of promoting change. Yet, there were reasonable economic concerns, such as the slowdown in growth and the income gap with the rich countries, that pushed the leadership to seek a new path to development, but, as it turned out, the relatively favourable macroeconomic conditions on the eve of the reforms proved to be an important factor in the initial success of the reforms.

The reforms were not launched with a massive ideological campaign to discredit the central planning system. Instead, the reforms 'grew' out of the plan (Naughton, 1996). Only after the reforms began to produce more rapid and dynamic growth, and especially when the wave of transitions to the market began to sweep the entire socialist bloc in the late 1980s, did the official view become more openly critical of the central planning system and, in some cases, even blame it for the unfulfilled dream of catching up with the West.

However, despite the problems associated with central planning, the argument that it was the failure of the central planning system that led to the reforms is not very convincing. Under the central planning system, China had experienced the most rapid economic and social development in its modern history. Moreover, it is hard to conclude that the full potential of the central planning mechanism had been exhausted in China, since there seemed to be considerable room for adjustment and improvement. In the late 1970s, the central planning in China was yet to reach the level of sophistication that existed in the Soviet economy. Chinese industry was still considerably behind Soviet industry, and investment efficiency was lower in Chinese industry than it was in Soviet industry, which was notoriously inefficient. In addition, the central planning mechanism had rarely functioned under 'normal' conditions during its 30-year existence in China. Large-scale political, social and economic campaigns had been undertaken to assure 'politics in command', and these campaigns had frequently distracted attention from economic issues and disrupted the routine operation of the economy. Thus, an improvement of the central planning system might have been a readily available option. In effect, the government tried this option briefly immediately after the Cultural Revolution. Though not very successful, the attempt did not prove that a strategic shift to the market economy was unavoidable, if only because too little time was invested in adjusting the central planning system to permit any final judgement to be made.

Indeed, as some have pointed out (for instance, see Dernberger, 1986), there was nothing inevitable about the market reforms. Many descriptions of the economic reforms are actually 'post hoc' rather than 'ex ante'. What seems to be clear is that, after the reforms had been initiated and had made some progress, a dynamism emerged that induced changes not fully anticipated in the original concept of reform.

In retrospect, it appears that, although central planning led to rapid growth and the potential of central planning was not fully realized, the system, as it was being employed, was responsible for a number of economic distortions. Under the self-reliance and delinking strategy, growth was achieved by protecting domestic industries and by artificial price-setting, and this meant that production could be inefficient, but the economy could still grow. The growth was real, because real industrial products were being produced, but the cost was higher than necessary. However, the Chinese economy under the less well developed central planning turned out to be rather an advantage during market transition. Unlike in the Soviet Union, the structural distortions generated by the central planning system in China had not become too great to be corrected without substantial losses in production.

The change in the leadership of the country was a factor in the timing of the market reforms. To be sure, new efforts to boost economic growth had been planned long before the onset of the reforms. As early as 1964, and again in 1975, at the third and fourth plenaries of the National People's Congress respectively, then Premier Zhou Enlai called for national attention to be focused on the modernization of the economy. Economic adjustment was proposed. However, both attempts were aborted because, in the first instance, of the upcoming Cultural Revolution (1966–76), and in the second, of the intense power struggle not only within the central government, but also at various administrative levels. Mao and several other members of the core leadership passed away in 1976. Not until the central government had been consolidated under Deng could economic development once again become the focus of national policies. Indeed, Deng quickly guided the work of the government towards economic development and the launch of the reform programme.

Deng and Mao had belonged to the same generation of revolution and perhaps had been inspired in similar fashion by socialism. However, Deng's philosophy and his views on the world and China were not entirely identical with Mao's. Deng was a nationalist like Mao, but he seemed to care about Marxist ideology and socialist ideals much less than Mao had done.

This is illustrated by his well known pragmatic dictum on economic development: 'no matter whether they are black or white, the best cats are the ones that catch mice'. Translated into economic language, this meant that economic and technological mechanisms and methods – market mechanisms included – were not class-conscious, but were neutral and could therefore be used in socialist China so long as they helped produce economic results.

Deng was deeply apprehensive of the country's persistent poverty and backwardness, and, in the late 1970s, he was keenly aware of the world's most quickly developing economies, most of which happened to be China's close neighbours. The adoption of a new development strategy would not have become so attractive if the newly industrialized economies of East Asia had not met with such success. The Chinese could live with the idea that the West was wealthier and more powerful than China, but they had difficulty accepting the fact that small neighbours, most of which were the historical 'peripheries' of China, had surpassed their country. The lesson drawn by Chinese policymakers from an ostensive comparison of economic performance was that market mechanisms and export-orientation, which seemed to be the force behind the East Asian 'miracle', might also work in China.

This view was reinforced by the popular yearning among the people for better living standards. After years of austerity, constrained by ideology, as well as economic shortage, the population was becoming more aware of the differences in living standards between China and the developed countries, particularly the neighbouring Asian tigers. This created pressure on policymakers to turn the economy around and to do it quickly.

External conditions favoured the closer participation of China in the world market. China's stance of independence was being perceived in the West as a force which could be used by the West in its rivalry with the Soviet Union. Following the establishment of diplomatic relations between China and Western countries and the recovery of China's membership in the UN, the capitalist world seemed more interested in contacts with China. Within this immediate context, economic reform gained momentum.

Economic openness was regarded by the reform designers as inseparable from the overall reform programme. To promote greater economic openness, the reformers began to portray the world market as a much-needed source of raw materials, capital goods, advanced technology, and managerial skills and as an outlet for China's products.

None the less, especially in the early stages of reform, the old concern frequently surfaced about the consequences of active participation in the world market and about whether closer integration with the powerful capitalist world economy might not lead to the economic and political subordination of China to the West. This had been a key issue and had buttressed the strategy of self-reliance and delinking. Now, however, Deng assured the nation that the new approach would enable China to enhance its self-reliance. 'If we take protectionism as the major avenue in the development of the national economy,' he said, 'we will certainly isolate ourselves from world economic life. This can temporarily protect national industry and commerce, but it is an unwise move from a long-term point of view.'[1]

Leaving aside a discussion of the relative advantage of various trade policies (not so easy to determine abstractly in any case), the Chinese leadership had a measure of confidence in economic openness because of the socioeconomic foundations laid during the process of industrialization over the previous 30 years. China in the late 1970s was fundamentally different from what it had been before 1949. Now, the country had a strong government, a seat on the five-member UN Security Council, a large standing army with a nuclear capability, and a relatively well-established industrial base. None of this had existed before the World War II. Moreover, although the essential structure of the capitalist world economy had not changed fundamentally, political détente was a characteristic of the 1970s.[2] Direct colonial rule had long ago ceased to appear desirable in the West. An outright threat to China's sovereignty seemed highly unlikely. On balance, joining the world market at this moment seemed a good option.

The government was determined to maintain previous gains by following a fresh strategy, but this did not dispel people's misgivings about the consequences of entering a world market dominated by the West. Many were still worried that, by active involvement in the world market, China might become subjugated to the world division of labour. This hesitation in view of the many possible outcomes of market reform and especially of economic openness must have contributed to the 'gradualist' or 'incrementalist' approach which emerged. None the less, the reform programmes were carried out with a fair amount of faith on the part of the government in its ability to conduct national economic strategy, guide change and correct 'errors' which might occur.

In fact, a shift to a market economy was not a goal on the initial reform agenda. Rather, market forces were to be allowed to function to the extent that they fostered greater efficiency and higher quality in production. Yet, gradually, the external pressure for economic liberalization rose, especially following the events of the late 1980s, with the wholesale market transition in the former Soviet bloc. The internal economic reforms also generated strong market forces. The establishment of a 'socialist market economy' thus became a reform objective.[3] From the very beginning, Chinese economic reform has borne the mark of pragmatism, and, to date, the characteristics of the so-called 'socialist market economy' have yet to be defined.

China was a relative latecomer in the wave of socialist reform. While China was still energetically pursuing socialism during the 1960s and early 1970s, centrally planned economies such as Yugoslavia, Hungary, Poland, and the USSR were already experimenting with reform measures. The attitude of the Chinese government towards the early attempts at reform elsewhere was rather sceptical and critical. The government was worried about the consequences of the reforms and any possible 'deviation' from socialist principles, as defined by the Chinese Communists. The lack of outstanding economic success among the early reformers meant that the Chinese were not tempted to initiate reforms themselves.

However, in the late 1970s, among the centrally planned economies, China took the lead in the introduction of market-oriented reforms. Moreover, the reforms in China were clearly distinct from those undertaken in the Soviet bloc. The difference lay not only in the approach, often called 'gradualism' as opposed to 'shock therapy', but also in the goals and outcomes. China's adoption of a new development strategy drew inspiration not from the socialist bloc, but from the Asian model, mainly Japan and the four tigers.

In weighing the difficulties involved in switching from the exportation primarily of low-wage products to the substantial exportation of high-wage products, Wallerstein (1979b) has observed that there are three basic strategies used by countries to move upwards in the hierarchy of the world economy: the strategy of 'promotion by invitation', the strategy of 'seizing the chance', and the strategy of 'self-reliance'. The success of the Asian NIEs in catching up is a typical case of 'development by invitation'. The reforms in China appear to represent a shift from the strategy of 'self-reliance' to the strategy of 'seizing the chance'.

During periods of world-market contraction, when the terms of trade are worsening for the primary exports of countries on the periphery, the governments of these countries may experience financial difficulties which force them to search for unusual solutions. One solution may be 'import-substitution', but, whatever the solution, it is a matter of 'seizing the chance', since it involves aggressive state action. The expansion of industrial activity in Russia and in Italy in the late-nineteenth century and in Brazil and Mexico in the wake of the Great Depression of 1929 are good examples of seizing the chance. Wallerstein suggests that, as in each of these cases, only relatively strong periphery countries are able to pursue the strategy. In each of these cases, moreover, the country already had an industrial base and was able to expand this base at a favourable moment. 'The capacity to react in the face of ... economic crises depends in large part on the internal composition of the dependent countries. If they possess a very important complementary industrial sector, the latter can profit from the crisis ...' (Dos Santos, cited in Wallerstein, 1979b, p. 77).

By the late 1970s, when China adopted the new development strategy, it had a strong state and a comprehensive industrial base, two of the preconditions for 'seizing the chance'.

In contrast to the strategy of self-reliance, which in China had been accompanied by delinking, the new reform strategy aggressively promoted the expansion of relations with the world market. However, similar to the strategy of self-reliance, in the new strategy the strengthening of

China's industrial capability remained the most important incentive for foreign trade. After the strategic shift, there was an immediate surge in foreign trade, and imports came to exceed exports by a wide margin. China had huge trade deficits from 1978 to 1989 as a result of substantial imports of capital goods. During this 12-year period, there was a trade surplus only during three years, and the cumulative surplus during these three years was less than the average annual trade deficit during the other nine years. Since then, China has gradually become an active exporter of manufactured goods. Thus, the policy of openness, which was first implemented to strengthen and expand domestic production so as to 'fill in the industrial gaps', has now led to export-oriented growth.

'Seizing the chance' also possesses intrinsic problems. The reforms and the outward orientation have accelerated industrial development, but they have also meant that China has had to import from Western countries. This has inevitably increased China's dependence on the West for producer goods and technology.

The development of both internal and external markets has become necessary so as to absorb the output generated by the expansion in domestic industry and the rise in production. The redistribution of wealth and income has been evolving, and access to material and social gains has become more unequal. New social structures and social tensions have also appeared. Yet, as the reform process has advanced, both the flow of events and state policy have continued to push the economy towards outward expansion. Thus, as of the late 1990s, China's economy has come under the mounting influence of the world economy.

By following a fresh strategy and participating actively in the world economy, China has entered a new game with new stakes. The state has established a timetable for narrowing the gap with the West. By the end of the twentieth century, national product is expected to have doubled with respect to 1980. This would mean a per capita income of $800. By the mid-twenty-first century, China is to have become a middle income country, that is, to have income close to that of the rich countries. To realize this goal, the government regards greater economic openness as a necessity.

'It would be absolutely impossible to approach the level of the economically advanced countries within 50 years, if [we] continue to follow the strategy of autarchy instead of opening up,' Deng said in a speech in 1984 (Deng, 1993, p. 90). The initial success of the reforms has enhanced the expectation that catching up with the West is not merely a topic of discussion, but also a goal to be reached. However, whether the new strategy will actually help China catch up, and, more importantly, the nature of the social and economic impact of the reform process on China and on the world economy are two issues which are still unclear.

10 Economic Restructuring

The new wave of modernization in the name of economic reform has introduced significant change in Chinese society and the economy. The move towards an outward-looking, market-driven economy has involved micro- and macroeconomic reform measures, including the decollectivization of agriculture, the decentralization of economic decisionmaking, encouragement for the growth of the non-state sector, enhancement of the incentives for profitmaking among enterprises, and the adoption of liberal economic and fiscal policies. The measures have been implemented in a piecemeal, yet consistent fashion. 'Shock therapy' has not been applied, but new initiatives are constantly being undertaken. The reform process has proved to be protracted: nearly 20 years have passed since the onset of reform. Yet, as has been officially recognized, much remains to be done. The transition from the central planning system has turned out to be much longer than the transition to the central planning system.

Like the industrialization programme under Mao, the modernization drive under Deng was initiated and led by the state. The initial purpose of 'reform and openness' was to revitalize the economy by introducing market elements, while maintaining the basic framework of the central planning system. However, this gradually led to the emergence of an outward-looking, market-oriented economy. Institutions have been restructured; market forces have been reintroduced into economic life, and policies now encourage outward economic orientation. The transformation has been slow, but far-reaching. Little by little, the economic reorientation has involved reform in all economic sectors, and the consequences have been significant.

Since 1979, the government has carried out rural reforms through the 'household responsibility system'. As a result, rural communes were dismantled almost as quickly as they had been established 20 years earlier. In their place, households became the basic units of rural production. The main goal of rural institutional change was to improve the low efficiency of collective agriculture. Inefficiencies had arisen largely because of the 'free-rider effect' associated with the income distribution mechanism used by the communes. The approach has been grounded on the provision of incentives to individual producers. Rural households have re-acquired the right individually to cultivate 'contracted' land. They have also gained economic autonomy, especially in terms of labour allocation.

This has proved to be the key factor in reinvigorating the countryside. The surge in local initiative has been driven by access to personal material gain, but it has been fostered by the rural infrastructure established during the commune era.

Agricultural output rose appreciably for several years immediately after the onset of reform. By the mid-1980s, however, the potential of institutional change seemed to have been exhausted, and agricultural growth slowed. Rural development and growth began to depend on diversification, specialization, the application of science and technology, greater inputs, and the creation of market niches.

Rural reform evolved on the basis of the relatively equal distribution of the land under household cultivation. Land was leased to households for cultivation for a fixed period of time. The formal ownership of the land remained with villages. An agriculture based on household production was thus re-established without the need for privatization. Perhaps the most important advantage of this change in rural economic structure was the additional opportunity for tapping China's most abundant resource: human labour. Drawing on this rich resource, labour-intensive manufacturing began to be carried out in rural areas. This has been the major engine for the continued growth of the rural economy since the mid-1980s.

The monopoly position of the state sector in industry and services has been seriously eroded because of the re-emergence and rapid growth of the officially sanctioned and encouraged non-state sector, including private, collective and foreign-owned enterprises and businesses. The share of state-owned enterprises in industrial output has declined slowly but substantially. In 1978, state-owned enterprises accounted for 80 per cent of industrial output. By the mid-1990s, the share had fallen to less than 50 per cent, while the rest was produced by the non-state sector. According to one report (see *The Economist*, 1997, p. 65), by 1997 the share of state-owned enterprises had dropped further, to one-third of total industrial output. This occurred not because of any stagnation or absolute decline in the production of the state sector, but because of the more rapid growth in the non-state sector. In fact, the state sector has retained a leading position in key industries (the so-called 'commanding heights'), but is no longer dominant in total industrial output or in retail sales.

Before the reforms, resources had been concentrated disproportionally in heavy industry. This meant that the growth rate of heavy industry was quite a bit higher than that of light industry. The situation has been reversed under the reforms. Between 1978 and 1992, the expansion of heavy industry was less than two-thirds that of light industry (Lin *et al*., 1994, p. 166). The overall economic structure began to shift. This shift was not due to stagnation or decline in heavy industry, but to the more rapid growth in light industry and other non-farm sectors, such as construction, transportation, telecommunications, finance and services.

The role of central planning in resource allocation has been reduced. In the mid-1990s, even the operations of state-owned enterprises were being conducted largely on the basis of market principles. State-owned enterprises have been allowed more autonomy in investment, sales, prices, the purchase of goods and raw materials, the retention and allocation of funds, wages and bonuses, employment, technological choices, and so forth. The burgeoning non-state sector is not subject to state planning, and its increasing significance in the national economy has naturally diminished the scope of state planning. Indeed, the non-state industrial sector itself would not have been possible without a relaxation of the control of the state planning system over the allocation of labour, raw materials and capital. The state has sharply cut the raw materials and producer goods allocated by the central planning system. With few exceptions, enterprises can now obtain producer goods and raw materials on the market. Prices are no longer set by the state, but depend on market conditions. In 1993, 95 per cent of the prices in the retail trade, 90 per cent of the prices for agricultural products and 85 per cent of the wholesale prices for production materials were being determined by the market (Lin *et al*., 1994, pp. 145–6).

Because of the rising importance of market forces and the corresponding decline in central planning, income distribution and the structure of employment have become more stratified. In the state sector, the old welfare system still supplies protection and social benefits for employees, but the provision of such benefits has become more closely tied to the performance of the individual enterprise. In the non-state sector, wages, hiring and the distribution of fringe benefits have become largely matters for individual businesses to decide. As the non-state sector has grown and as the economy has become more diversified, new social groups which were mostly nonexistent before the reforms have begun to emerge, including the owners of small shops, private entrepreneurs, temporary employees, and propertied individuals. Income distribution has become more unequal.

One of the main components in economic restructuring has been the outward economic reorientation. While the immediate cause of the shift from an inward-looking to a more open economy has been specific reform measures, the process has been led by the evolution of events. Outward reorientation and marketization have gone hand-in-hand, and jointly they have transformed the overall economic structure of the country. Indeed, the policy of economic openness 'involves not only choices about the allocation of central economic resources, but also, and indeed more importantly, the granting of particular "rights" and "privileges" to selected areas, sectors and social groups' (Howell, 1993, p. 4). The process of the creation of a more open economy has left an unmistakable mark on virtually every aspect of China's economic and social life, from the overall restructuring of the economy and investment decisions to emerging patterns in regional development and income distribution.

The outward economic reorientation has occurred in parallel with the reform of the central planning system that began with a restructuring in foreign trade. Measures were taken to decentralize decision making and management, to encourage the development of foreign trade and to promote profit making as an incentive for improvements in production efficiency. Permission to engage in foreign trade was granted more readily to local authorities and enterprises, and the absolute monopoly of state trading companies was eliminated. Trading companies and enterprises of various types gained greater autonomy in foreign trade. To boost exports, a foreign-earnings retention system was established for exporters, and the earnings retention ratio was gradually raised. The overall trend in the reform of foreign trade has been to favour a trade regime and trade regulations compatible with the emergence of a market economy at home and with trading procedures on the world market.

A crucial step in the process of opening up the economy was the decision to allow foreign direct investment in China. To attract foreign investment, the government first created special economic zones in the South. This was followed by the opening up of 14 coastal cites and areas along the East Coast and eventually more cities in other areas, including China's largest city, Shanghai, where the Pudong New Area was established. These 'open' areas were granted greater autonomy in decision making and management. Authority over preferential policies in foreign trade and investment, as well as certain rights to implement some social policies, was also decentralized. As local governments began to compete for foreign investment, foreign-funded enterprises and joint ventures were encouraged to locate in the 'open' areas, which became widely scattered throughout the country.

The vigorous promotion of foreign trade and investment by the government has produced impressive results. Starting from scratch in 1978, foreign direct investment in China began to take off in the late 1980s.

China and the Global Economy since 1840

By the end of 1997, accumulated foreign direct investment had reached over $200 billion (*People's Daily*, 1997). By the year 2000, based on investment agreements signed in recent years, the accumulated foreign direct investment is expected to double, that is, to reach $400 billion. Every year since 1993, China has been the largest recipient of foreign direct investment after the US. The substantial inflow of foreign capital has been a key factor in the overall economic growth of the country. In particular, foreign-funded enterprises and joint ventures have played a major role in the growth of exports since the early 1990s and are now responsible for more than 40 per cent of total exports.

Foreign trade swelled in 1979 after the onset of reform. The following years witnessed trade expansion by leaps and bounds, with the total volume of exports and imports rising from about $20 billion in 1978 to nearly $300 billion in 1996 (Table 10.1). Yet, the yearly growth rate was uneven. Thus, for example, exports picked up by only 1.5 per cent in 1996, the lowest growth rate in 18 years (ADB, 1997, p. 53).

Table 10.1   China's foreign trade, 1978–95*
(dollars, billions)

	Total	Exports	Imports	Balance
1978	20.6	9.8	10.9	−1.1
1979	29.3	13.7	15.7	−2.0
1980	38.1	18.1	20.0	−1.9
1981	44.0	22.0	22.0	−
1982	41.6	22.3	19.3	3.0
1983	43.6	22.2	21.4	0.8
1984	53.6	26.1	27.4	−1.3
1985	69.6	27.4	42.3	−14.9
1986	73.9	30.9	42.9	−12.0
1987	82.7	39.4	43.2	−3.8
1988	102.8	47.5	55.3	−7.8
1989	111.7	52.5	59.1	−6.6
1990	115.4	62.1	53.4	8.7
1991	135.6	71.8	63.8	8.1
1992	165.5	84.9	80.6	4.4
1993	195.7	91.7	104.0	−12.2
1994	236.6	121.0	115.6	5.4
1995	280.9	148.8	132.1	16.7
1996	289.9	151.1	138.8	12.3

Source: SSB, 1997, p. 127.
* Total trade and the balance of trade may not sum due to rounding.

The balance of trade was not always in China's favour. In fact, only in 1990 did a trend of trade deficits begin to reverse. The balance of trade was in China's favour during all but one year over the next six years. Largely as a result of trade surpluses and the inflow of capital, China's foreign reserves began to exceed those of some of the foreign-reserve 'champions', such as Taiwan, in the mid-1990s.

There is no solid evidence that, at the onset of economic reform, China had already opted for an export-oriented development strategy. The original aim of the government's encouragement for exports was to generate foreign currency in order to finance the importation of advanced technology and equipment. This aim was similar in spirit to the goal of delinking in that the reform of the foreign-trade system was undertaken to help boost domestic production capacity. For this purpose, the central planning constraint on foreign trade was reduced, freer entry to foreign trade was permitted to producers, the autonomy of local governments and producers in foreign-trade operations was enhanced, and the foreign-earnings retention system was established. The nearly constant annual trade deficits during the first years of reform indicate that the demand for imports was exceeding the country's capacity to export. Export capacity caught up only belatedly, after ten years of economic restructuring and active export promotion.

The structure of imports and exports over the reform years reveals more clearly the nuances of the strategy behind foreign trade. From 1980 to 1994, the structure of imports showed the following changes (World Bank, 1996, p. 81). First, the share of foodstuffs in total imports fell considerably due to the rapid growth in agricultural output that came on the heels of rural reform; the decline was from 16 per cent to 4 per cent. Second, the share of intermediate goods and raw materials dropped from 53 per cent to 38 per cent. Third, the share of capital goods, including machinery and transport equipment, steadily increased from 27 per cent to 48 per cent. Fourth, the share of consumer goods doubled from 3 per cent to 6 per cent, though this was still a low level.

This import structure reflects a conscious import strategy, the purpose of which is 'to assure the supply of key raw materials and to acquire embodied technology through the import of capital goods, while imports of consumer goods have been regarded as a residual' (World Bank, 1994b, p. 17). The import pattern stressing capital goods reminds one of the Asian NIEs, but not of large developing countries such as India and Brazil, where capital goods have represented a much smaller share of imports.

More significant changes occurred in the structure of exports. In 1975, exports consisted mostly of food, agricultural raw materials and petroleum, which together accounted for over half of total exports. In the early 1980s, manufactured goods took over the leading position among exports. In the mid-1980s, the exports of manufactured goods began a further rise, reaching more than 80 per cent of total exports by the early 1990s.

Among the exports of manufactured goods, the growth in the exports of electrical machinery was the most rapid in relative terms, mainly because of the extremely low starting point. The lively export expansion was driven overwhelmingly by growth in the production of clothing and footwear, and manufactured exports in general were dominated by labour-intensive production. In 1990, labour-intensive manufacturing accounted for 74 per cent of total exports; unskilled-labour-intensive manufacturing took 51 per cent, while the share of capital-intensive manufacturing was 19 per cent (World Bank, 1994b, pp. 8–9). However, the structure of exports was evolving in the direction of more sophisticated manufacturing. By 1995, machinery and electronics accounted for nearly 30 per cent of total exports. This trend is likely to continue since the government is committed to industrial upgrading, so that Chinese manufacturers will be able to produce goods of higher quality and more value added.

The changes in the structure of exports reflect a conscious state policy. Reform measures, including the decentralization of the foreign-trade system and other incentive policies, have provided strong encouragement for the producers of exports. The use of foreign investment has supplied the manufacturing sector not only with capital, but also with technology and access to the world market. This has also been a result of the long-standing strategy emphasizing the role of foreign trade in helping to establish and upgrade the production capacity of domestic industries.

The rapid expansion of foreign trade and investment has contributed to the emergence of new economic structures by increasing the linkages between China's domestic economy and the world market. Because joint ventures and foreign-funded enterprises benefit from preferential treatment which is not available to state-owned enterprises, the problems of the latter have become even more serious. Distinct labour practices in the state and non-state sectors have augmented the differentiation within the labour force and created new relationships between capital and labour. The growing backward and forward linkages among foreign trade, foreign investment and the domestic economy have meant that the allocation of resources, particularly labour resources, has come under the influence of the world market situation. In other words, the growth of foreign trade and investment in China has been accompanied by the greater participation of the country in the world division of labour.

The outward reorientation of the economy has introduced a new factor in the division of labour within the country. Most obviously, the expansion of trade and foreign investment has played a major role in emerging regional development patterns. As a general rule, sectors and areas which have become extensively involved in foreign trade and investment have advanced more quickly, at least partly by relying on labour and resources from other, less-developed areas. Differences in growth rates and the emerging division of labour have contributed to a widening internal development gap. Foreign investment has been concentrated in about a dozen provinces on the East coast, particularly along the Southern part of the coast and there mainly in two provinces, Guangdong and Fujian, where special economic zones have been established. The highly skewed distribution of foreign investment was especially evident during the early years of reform. From 1979 to 1991, of the total contracted foreign investment in China, the share of coastal areas was 82 per cent and of the South, 53 per cent, while Guangdong Province alone accounted for 43 per cent and Fujian, 9 per cent. The two special economic zones of Shenzhen and Xiamen represented 10 per cent. In 1991, the five special economic zones took in 23 per cent of the total contracted foreign investment (Economic Research Centre, 1994, p. 4). The general pattern of distribution has not changed substantially since then, although it has become somewhat less skewed.

The highly skewed distribution of foreign investment was initially encouraged by the deliberate preferential policies of the government. It was felt that the close geographical proximity and traditional ties of the South to Hong Kong and Taiwan would make the area more attractive to foreign capital, particularly from Hong Kong and Taiwan. Moreover, in case the attempt failed, the negative consequences of the experiment would be limited to the area.

In 1992, efforts began to be taken to channel foreign capital into other areas. These efforts were somewhat successful, and the Northeast improved relative to the Southeast in attracting foreign investment. However, the general pattern of distribution has not been fundamentally altered, and foreign capital investment in non-coastal areas and in the West is still more limited. Export producers have been overwhelmingly concentrated along the East coast as well. In 1988 the East accounted for over 80 per cent of national merchandise trade and almost monopolized manufactured exports. In the mid-1990s, Guangdong Province alone accounted for 40 per cent of exports.

Coastal areas have also registered growth rates above the national average. In the first ten years of reform, from 1979 to 1988, the average annual GNP growth rate was 9.8 per cent nationwide, but 10.5 per cent in coastal areas, and 8.9 per cent in the rest of the country. The differences may have been due largely to the rise in foreign trade. It has been suggested that, if exports are excluded, the differences in growth rates among the East, the Centre and the West would almost disappear (*China Statistics Abstract*, 1990, cited in Ma and Zou, 1991). In any case, the income gap between the coast and the interior has continued to widen.

The outward reorientation in the economy has resulted in two apparently opposing trends in regional development. There are still forces tending to fragment the national economy by resisting integration and maintaining internal boundaries, but there has also been a simultaneous process of integration among regional economies that has tended to strengthen economic linkages across internal boundaries. Many rural areas, especially those close to 'open' cities, have become tied into the division of labour in production for the world market. Rural industries have likewise become involved in international trade and in the use of foreign capital and technology. This phenomenon has been described as the 'internationalization of the countryside' (Zweig, 1991a). The share of township and village enterprises (TVEs) in total exports has ballooned. Between 1988 and 1992, the share of rural industries in the total purchases by all trading companies for exports shot up from 19 per cent to 42 per cent.[1] About 90 per cent of TVE exports were manufactured goods, of which almost half were spread evenly among textiles, clothing, and arts and crafts. The vast majority of TVE export earnings were generated along the East coast.

The rapid economic growth in some areas, especially in the export-driven Southeast, has required large inputs. As investments of domestic and foreign capital have intensified in the more developed areas, these areas have become more dependent on the rest of China for raw materials, labour and markets for finished goods. Guangdong, at the vanguard in economic openness and the number one exporting province in the country, exports one-third of its manufactured goods, consumes another third itself and 'exports' the remaining third to other provinces. Meanwhile, Guangdong draws large amounts of raw materials from other parts of the country. Provinces to the North, such as Hunan, reportedly first reacted by raising barriers to Guangdong, but, having failed to keep Guangdong's products out and to stop their own agricultural goods and raw materials from flowing to Guangdong, they began to open their borders and to enhance their transport links with Guangdong (Lardy, 1994, pp. 26–7). Areas may be developing unevenly, but various areas have also become tied into a commodity chain which is geared particularly towards exports.

Economic integration among regions through capital investments, labour flows and commodity exchanges has fostered the appearance of a unified domestic market. Yet, regions have not become integrated into this emerging domestic market on an equal basis, and the process has not benefited all participants equally. Like nation-states in the world economy, the more developed coastal areas and the less developed inland areas of China are linked in a hierarchy of economic relationships. The coastal areas absorb capital, raw materials and labour from the inland areas and 'export' finished goods back to the latter, as well as to the world market, while enjoying higher profits because of their 'comparative advantage'.

Despite numerous efforts by local governments to maintain them, especially during the early stages of reform, province boundaries no longer serve as serious obstacles against domestic economic integration. Administrative control over the flow of resources has been considerably reduced because of the official abandonment of the central planning system. None the less, the backward linkages between developed and developing areas are much weaker than the forward linkages. This has meant that the less developed areas are handicapped with regard to economic gain.

In the late 1980s, the unequal terms of trade for the less developed inland provinces led to an uproar against 'internal colonialization'. The problem became so serious that the central government took measures to encourage the East to offer economic assistance to the inland provinces, in the form of technology transfers, investment, skill and management training, and joint ventures. These efforts have yet to produce any fundamental reduction in the income disparities among provinces. In fact, it is generally anticipated that the income gap between the rich Eastern provinces and the backward areas will continue to widen in the years to come.

In the nearly 20 years since the onset of reform, strategic reorientation has increasingly rendered China's economy subject to market forces and has tied it more closely to the world market, although a mixed economy has emerged in which private capital is not yet dominant. During China's economic restructuring, growth and development have been sustained by a wide variety of players, including state enterprises, TVEs, joint ventures, foreign companies, and private businesses. It might have been a different story if the state planners had simply been replaced by a small group of big capitalists during the transition to a market-oriented economy.

If the new development strategy can be considered an overall success, it is so less because of what China has done to restructure the economy and more because of what China has accomplished by supporting growth during the restructuring. The market economy or export promotion alone could not have achieved this.

11 The State

Studies of the latecomers to industrialization, especially the Asian NIEs, have emphasized the crucial role of a strong interventionist state (cf. Amsden, 1989; Wade, 1990). Examining the historical decline of China from one of the most advanced countries to one of the poorest countries, Perkins (1997, p. 29) concludes that 'the core problem for China's development was the issue of governance'. If its lack of industrialization, more than anything else, was China's weakness relative to the capitalist West, then the lack of a strong state was the primary reason for China's inability to industrialize. This situation changed drastically following the rise to power of the Communists in 1949. As if to prove the point, the state immediately undertook full-fledged industrialization and made tremendous progress within a relatively short time.

While the strong state may yet prove to be a common feature of successful late industrialization everywhere, the post-revolutionary state in China has been a particularly powerful and pervasive actor in the country's economic development. Under the central planning system, the state acquired a monopoly position in the national economy. State policies and state plans determined the pattern and to a large extent the outcomes of economic development. Because of this overwhelming influence of the state, the Chinese government was responsible not only for the successful start to industrialization, but also for the problems and the disasters in the course of industrialization. The state's responsibility for economic development was almost taken for granted within China and also, perhaps surprisingly, outside China. Evidence for this is the fact that very few questioned the role of the Chinese government in putting China back on the road towards a market-oriented economy in the late 1970s.

The establishment of a market orientation through the reforms was a process which grew out of the central planning system. The economic achievements of the self-reliance strategy formed the groundwork for the rapid growth and industrial upgrading of the reform era, and the Maoist legacy of a strong state has shaped the course of the market transition. Along with the gradual dismantling of the central planning system and the decline in the significance of the state sector, there have also been modifications in the functions of the state. The government no longer manages the economy through the planned allocation of resources. However, it would be wrong to say that the state has no longer played an essential role in the economy. Nearly 20 years after the onset of the reforms, the same Communist-led government is still in control. In the literature of transition, this characteristic is often described as economic reform in the absence of political reform. The experience of China during the market transition is in such sharp contrast to that of most former socialist countries that China appears to be an anomaly.[1]

That the government has continued to perform key functions during economic restructuring has been readily accepted in mainstream thinking in China. According to the CCP's interpretation of the Leninist theory of proletarian revolution, the Chinese Revolution was a first step towards the construction of a socialist society. Because the socialist revolution has not triumphed on a global scale, but has taken place in individual countries, it is considered quite proper that the Chinese leadership should ignore Marx's idea that the state would wither away after the socialist revolution. Instead, the establishment of socialism in one country requires a proletarian state strong enough to defend itself from external threats and able to generate rapid growth so as to overcome the economic backwardness which is considered the major obstacle to the attainment of the next stage in socialism.

According to this logic, the transformation of private property into public property after the Revolution not only reflected a long-term objective of socialism, but was also a necessary step so that the state could carry out effective national planning. Since the revolutionary state considered itself the guarantor of the interests of the overwhelming majority of the people, it naturally acted on behalf of society in owning, controlling and managing property.

This ideology has not been seriously challenged during the reform era. The concept of the role of government in a laissez-faire market economy has had some influence, but the idea has never been embraced wholeheartedly, and it has not deterred the government from strengthening the functions of the state in whatever ways and in whatever areas are deemed necessary during the process of reform.

Traditional Chinese concepts about the relationship between the state and the economy provide strong support for the leading role of the state. During China's long dynastic history, official doctrine held that the emperor 'considers the empire as a single household' and that rule over the empire, though on a much larger scale, was equivalent to the management of a household. The imperial state (and the rulers) might choose not to intervene in economic matters, but the right to do so was considered sacred.

While the history of the market exchange in China is perhaps the oldest in the world, the idea has never taken hold that the state should remain aloof from the market. As late as the nineteenth century, it was considered a prerogative of the imperial court to allow private business, including foreign trade, to be conducted. The notion of the laissez-faire economy has never implied a lesser role for the state, not before 1949 and not even during the short-lived Republic after the fall of the dynasty. Despite its superficial liberal rhetoric and its efforts to copy Western-style economic institutions and management, the GMD regime during the first half of the twentieth century never saw any need to separate the state and the economy. Indeed, the status of the government with respect to the national economy, particularly the modern sector, was strengthened. Before 1945, only its struggle against political and military enemies, mainly the Communists, prevented the GMD government from expanding the state sector and establishing a more pervasive control of the state over the national economy. State finances benefited from a windfall immediately after World War II when the state confiscated the assets of the Axis powers and their Chinese collaborators. The GMD regime instituted a monopoly or at least a dominant position in the modern sector in manufacturing, mining, public utilities, transportation, communications and banking. Thus, for instance, the state-owned textile company possessed 40 per cent of the spindles and 60 per cent of the weaving machines in the country (Xu and Wu, 1993, p. 618).[2]

The leading role of the GMD government – after its retreat to Taiwan in 1949 – in the so-called 'Taiwan miracle' has been convincingly demonstrated in a number of studies (for example, see Li, 1995; Wade, 1990). The major concerns of the Taiwan government have not included the question of whether the state should intervene in the market, since the practice in Taiwan seems to suggest that the government has no doubt that it should intervene. Rather, the government has been concerned with finding ways to strengthen and enforce state policies. The attitude seems to be: Since the state can do a better job, why shouldn't it?

The idea that the state has an incontestable place in the economy is similar in Taiwan and on the mainland, although the two governments have been long-term political foes. The differences are of degree, method and the mode of state intervention, and these have been determined according to the respective socioeconomic systems established in the two parts of China. The parallel is evidence of the influence of China's traditional thinking on contemporary practice in economic affairs.

On the other hand, China's traditions also contain the idea that there ought to be a certain distance between the state and the economy. Confucian thought stresses the importance of a social hierarchy for a stable social order through, for instance, the control exercised over manual labour by mental labour. It is the duty and the privilege of the state to collect wealth, not to create wealth. The latter is considered the task of those who perform manual labour. Modern Chinese governments have departed from this particular tradition.

Yet, neither ideology nor tradition is sufficient grounds for the strong role of the state. It was the actual situation that rendered this role possible and necessary. The CCP learned much about economic management in the base areas before it came to power. After 1949, the CCP government realized only too well that it simply could not afford the luxury of not being involved directly in economic affairs, given the vast changes arising from radical social transformation. It succeeded in eliminating private property through the confiscation of foreign imperialist capital and the GMD state-monopoly capital which had controlled the modern sector. It accomplished this through land reforms which deprived the owners of large-amounts of property of their assets, and transformed small private holdings into collective or cooperative enterprises. This created a working class without capitalists and a proletariat without a bourgeoisie. Official propaganda hailed this as a process by which the working classes became the masters of national property. In practice, it was the state which assumed responsibility for the management of the national economy on behalf of society.

This responsibility became greater following the expansion of the state sector. The incipient state sector was based on the enterprises and businesses which had been owned by the GMD regime at the county, provincial and central government levels, as well as the property of high ranking GMD officials (Xu and Wu, 1993, p. 701). In the early 1950s, the CCP government confiscated 2858 industrial enterprises which employed 1.29 million people and brought major banks, railways, shipping and airline companies, and commercial and trading companies under state control (Xu and Wu, 1993, pp. 703–4). Between 1949 and 1952, the share of state-owned enterprises among all enterprises rose from 35 per cent to 56 per cent, and the share of the wholesale trade controlled by state-owned enterprises climbed from 24 per cent to 64 per cent (Xue, 1977).

The following years witnessed the continuing expansion of the state sector, mainly as a result of 'socialist transformation', a campaign to reorganize urban private industries and trade that had been left untouched immediately after the Revolution into collectives or cooperatives, most of which eventually became, in effect, owned and operated by local governments. The industrialization drive based on primary accumulation in agriculture led to the appearance of massive new state enterprises, which broadened the dominance of the state sector. By the late 1970s, state-owned industries accounted for about 80 per cent of gross national industrial output. Agriculture remained officially in the hands of rural collectives, but the state exercised control over collectives through administration and planning, especially the compulsory procurement mechanism for agricultural products.

Thus, because of the size of the state sector and the existence of central planning, the state not only made all strategic economic decisions, but managed day-to-day economic affairs as well. The distinction between the 'superstructure' and the 'economic base' became blurred since the state served as *de facto* owner, planner and manager of the economy. In this, China was like the Soviet Union to the extent that administration and planning had replaced the market, and the system was founded on the 'fusion of politics and economics' (Goldstein, 1995; see also Bialer, 1980, Chapter 1).

The expansion in the functions of the state during the first three decades of the People's Republic was obviously not determined solely by domestic factors. The Cold War and the absence of a worldwide socialist revolution contributed to a growing statist tendency not only in China, but also in other socialist countries. None the less, despite similarities in ideology and in other areas, such as the one-party political system and central planning, the socioeconomic system in China after the Revolution was quite different from that in the Soviet Union. The separate paths to economic reform and the distinct outcomes highlight this difference.

Leaving aside the question of the advantages and the disadvantages of various paths to reform, one must recognize that the intention to implement reform gradually is one thing, the actual implementation quite another. Gradual reform requires the creation of new political and institutional structures side-by-side with old structures. The ability of the Chinese government to carry out gradual reform has largely been inherited from its experience before the reforms. In contrast to the 'big bang' approach, China's reforms have therefore been more dependent on continuity, most importantly, the continuity of the state in providing leadership and governance during the course of economic transition.

It would be a mistake to conclude that the changes associated with China's economic reorientation have resulted in a weaker state. In some areas, the disengagement of the state administration from economic affairs has indeed led to a replacement of the functions of the state by market forces. In other areas, however, the fusion of politics and economics has continued unabated or even been augmented.

Overall, the issue of the shift in the functions of the state during the market transition in China can be properly understood only if we view the political and institutional structures of the state as a single entity, that is, as a single complex of structures and interactions within and between the central government and local governments. In fact, during the transition, the seemingly weakening of the central authority has been accompanied by the rising power of local governments, from the provinces down to the townships.

As a result of economic transformation, one of the most important tools of the state's management of the economy, the central planning system, has gradually been abandoned. Five-Year Plans are still being used. (The most recent is the Ninth Plan, which covers 1996 to 2000.) However, they have become guidelines for national economic and social development rather than specific, enforced output targets for producers. To various degrees depending on the type of enterprise, producers have gained greater autonomy in determining what and how to produce, as well as where and at what price to sell. This has meant that, in influencing economic growth, direct state control over the behaviour of producers has largely given way to macroeconomic policies.

On the other hand, the reforms have created enormous opportunities for local governments to affect the economy. The obligation to fill central planning quotas is no longer the main focus of the activities of local governments. Easier market entry and greater economic autonomy have become forceful incentives for local governments 'to be entrepreneurial' (Oi, 1995, p. 1137). Based on their extensive bureaucratic endowment, which was substantial before the reforms, local governments have been quick to promote local economic development.

The dynamism of rural industries has been but one outcome of this process, which has combined the authority of local governments and the spontaneous grassroots efforts of villages. Township governments, that is, the bottom layer of the government hierarchy, have been crucial in the rapid growth of rural industries, of which township enterprises account for a large share.

'Local officials act as the equivalent of a board of directors and sometimes more directly as the chief executive officers,' Oi (1995, p. 1132) explains. 'At the helm of this corporate-like organization is the Communist Party secretary.' In rural areas, local authorities are a driving force behind rural industries and enterprises, which constitute the major part of the non-state sector.

To boost the local economy, local governments supply wide-ranging direct and indirect assistance and services to various types of local businesses, including financing, information, training and coordination. It has not been uncommon for local governments and other state institutions to use their official and personal contacts with other localities and with the central government to promote businesses in their jurisdictions. Behind the producers formally competing on the market are often to be found local authorities who are themselves actually the owners of the enterprises or who are acting as patrons of the local producers.

The involvement of local governments in economic initiatives has intensified regional competition, and some local authorities have used their power to protect the local economy against outsiders. In the late 1980s, some local governments erected trade barriers on their borders in order to stop raw materials in short supply from outflowing to other areas. This and other protectionist measures precipitated the so-called 'commodity wars'. An immediate causality was the large state factories in big urban centres that depended on the local supply of raw materials. Similar examples of 'economic localism' are reported periodically even today. The steps taken by local governments in favour either of protectionism or free trade are now depending more on the competitive advantages of the local economy. For this reason, the central government must now coordinate the economic activities of provincial governments, while the latter perform the same function for lower administrative levels.

Encouraged by state policies and supported by local governments, non-state companies and businesses have mushroomed. The relative size of the state sector in the national economy has therefore shrunk. However, once again, this should not be taken as a sign that the state has become less active. And, once again, to understand this, one must view the 'state' as a single entity composed of the central government, local governments, government departments and government organizations. A number of government bodies, including the Liberation Army, has taken advantage of the open market to engage in businesses in nearly all areas of the economy. Profitmaking companies, especially in the service industry, have been established by various government organizations, including ministries, the army, local governments and their branches, public schools and public research institutions. It has thus become usual for nonprofit state organizations to run profitmaking businesses. Precise figures on these 'unit-owned businesses' are hard to obtain, but the aggregate economic weight of the businesses must be substantial. A look at the large conglomerates owned and operated by the army gives a clue.

Under 'local state corporatism', it was not local governments *per se*, but their administrative organs which actually coordinated the conduct of corporations.[3] The development of these 'unit-owned' corporations has worked in the interest of the administrative bodies which own them. These quasi-state businesses, joining forces with the non-state sector, have produced the dynamic growth evident during the reform process. Government organizations are well situated to use their power niche, formal and informal connections, legal status, and so on to gain easier access to lucrative business. However, as in the private sector, the profits generated by these businesses do not go to the state, but are retained by the entities or affiliated organizations which own them. The management of the emerging quasi-state businesses has usually been provided by the employees of the state bodies which own the businesses.

In a way, the state has actually extended its involvement in the economy considerably, since the reforms have tended to draw even non-economic government administrative entities into the business world. The close relationship between government organizations and business suggests that the government and the economy have remained fused. Although the separation of government administration and business enterprises was proclaimed as a reform goal, the penetration of the state into economic life is still profound.

While the central government continues to formulate development strategies and is now frequently resorting to macroeconomic policies to promote growth, the shrinking of the central planning system and the state sector has tended to cut into government revenue. Under the central planning system, the state drew its revenue mainly from the state sector. All business revenues, as well as the expenditures of the state sector, were included in government accounts. State enterprises remitted profits to the state coffers and received in return from the state the expenditure capital necessary for ongoing operations. This permitted the central government to allocate resources for economic projects considered national priorities.

During the transition to a market-oriented economy, the government has had to rely more and more on taxes instead of the remittance of profits as a source of revenue. Several rounds of tax reform have been carried out. However, up to the mid-1990s, government revenue fell substantially. Government budgetary revenue at all levels dropped from 35.5 per cent of GNP in 1978 to about 12 per cent in 1995. The share of the central government in total nationwide tax revenue declined even further, from more than 80 per cent before the reforms to below 40 per cent (Naughton, 1997a; Wang and Hu, 1993).

It has been argued that, in a number of transition economies, the depletion in state revenue is a key indicator of the dwindling authority of the central government (for instance, see Popov, 1997; Wang and Hu, 1993). However, as Naughton points out (1997a, pp. 46–7), the reduction in state revenue in China has mainly affected budgetary outlays for investment and military expenditure, while it has had very little quantitative impact on 'routine' government. None the less, 'revenue power' seems to be accruing to local governments. As local governments have gained greater access to tax revenue, the central government has found it difficult to control or even monitor their 'freewheeling' spending. A newspaper reports that China's finance minister has called attention to the problem of the 'extravagant and wasteful spending' of state money by local governments, which 'freely hand out tax breaks to enterprises, pour money into wasteful construction projects, indiscriminately distribute bonuses and subsidies, and engage in extravagant consumption at the public expense' (Mufson, 1995, p. 4).

Aside from tax evasion by enterprises and individuals and significant spending by local authorities, a more serious cause of the weakening financial base of the central government has been the fact that local governments are withholding a greater portion of tax revenue for their own use. Provinces are now turning over only part of the tax receipts which they owe to the central government. To be sure, this is not a new problem. As Goldstein (1995) has pointed out, the rise in the revenue of local authorities *vis-à-vis* the central government is a process that started long before the onset of the reforms.[4] Still, under the reforms, the local revenue base has broadened enormously, mainly due to the robust growth of local economies following the establishment of massive numbers of locally owned and operated enterprises.

To resolve the problem of 'poor centrality and rich locality', the leadership is trying to strengthen the centre through measures such as more intense tax reform and the creation of a more effective mechanism for revenue collection. These measures may succeed over time. In any case, the central government seems more interested in determining the best way to share economic power between itself and local governments than it is in delegating this power entirely to market forces. The general tendency of the reforms appears to be towards a greater role for the market and a more decentralized or 'localized' economic decision-making process. As local economies have become more dynamic and as governments at various levels have become more involved in economic activities, local authorities have been relatively strengthened. Therefore, if the reforms are seen as a process of marketization, this process has also included the building of the capacity of the state to preside over a more complicated market-oriented economy.

According to world-system analysis, the strength of a state can best be tested by examining its relationship to the 'inter-state' system of the capitalist world economy. From this perspective, the CCP government was perhaps at its strongest during the period of the strategy of self-reliance under Mao. By standing up to the world powers, represented by the US and the USSR, the leadership altered the 100-year-old image of the Chinese government as a weak government always ready to compromise in the face of external pressure, but heavy handed, even merciless, towards its own people. This image became widespread during the late Qing Dynasty and did not change much during the GMD regime. On the other hand, despite the country's economic backwardness, the CCP government made China an actor in world politics. The ability to play off the rivalry between the US and the USSR to enhance its own position in the inter-state system was a sign of China's new-found strength.

However, a country's position within the inter-state system is ultimately determined by its economic strength. During the Mao era, while the political leg of China grew healthier, the economic leg remained weak. The economic reorientation since the late 1970s has been aimed precisely at boosting the country's economic power. After 20 years of record economic growth, China's weight in the world economy seems to have increased. Yet, it is unclear whether the reforms have improved China's overall position within the world system.

The Chinese market has certainly become substantially more attractive for foreign goods and capital. The government can now use the market as a bargaining chip in dealings over political and economic issues with other countries, as well as on a world scale. By the same token, however, because China's economy has become more closely linked to the world market, it is more difficult for the Chinese government simply to say 'no' to the demands of foreign capital, and its ability to withstand external pressure seems to have weakened. The government is less willing or able to resist playing by the so-called 'international rules'. The reform logic seems to be somewhat the opposite of the logic of the pre-reform period. Instead of 'political independence will lead to economic development', the catch-phrase appears now to be 'only through economic growth will there be independence'. Whether this is true remains to be seen. In any case, economic interests have become key factors in the country's conduct in inter-state world politics.

As in the central planning period, during every step of the reform process, the role of the state has been decisive, although the interventions of the state in the economy have taken on a new character. While the socialist tendency has been losing ground to the capitalist tendency, the statist tendency has remained strong. As in the central planning period, the dominance of the state has been justified on the basis of the nationalistic goal to catch up to the West. For the same reason, during the reforms, the government has become more willing to rally all forces deemed useful, whether within the country or outside it. One of the best examples of this is the new alliance of the government and overseas Chinese capitalists. The ties with the Chinese capitalist diaspora have been a rather unique feature of the process of economic reorientation in the country.

12 The Overseas Chinese Capitalist Diaspora

Measured in terms of growth in trade and foreign capital investment, China's outward economic reorientation during the 20 years of reform has been quite successful. The 'success', however, cannot be adequately understood unless it is viewed in the context of Asia as a region. The overseas Chinese capitalist diaspora, particularly Hong Kong and increasingly Taiwan, as well as overseas Chinese businesses located throughout East and Southeast Asia, have been important in the process.[1] Moreover, the Asian economy has evolved into a structure which is favourable for the economic integration of China into the region.

Hong Kong has been the primary trading partner of mainland China during the 20 years of reform, although it has acted more as an entrepôt. Half to nearly two-thirds of China's total exports landed in Hong Kong, but the overwhelming majority were re-exported to third countries.[2] Other countries likewise used Hong Kong as an entrepôt for exports to the mainland. During the reform period, Hong Kong's exports have climbed at a pace which is similar to that for the mainland, with an average annual growth rate of 18 per cent between 1978 and 1993.

There has been far less trade between mainland China and Taiwan, mainly due to the political barriers. During the reform years, Taiwan has had a relaxed export regime towards the mainland, but has maintained heavy restrictions on imports from the mainland. This has resulted in a substantial trade imbalance in favour of Taiwan. None the less, overall, the volume of trade across the Taiwan Straits has been rising quickly. Taiwan still had only negligible exports to China in the early 1980s, but entering the 1990s it surpassed Hong Kong and the US, becoming the top exporter to the mainland after Japan (SSB, 1995, pp. 543–6).

In the late 1980s China began to see a large amount of foreign direct investment. However, most of the investment has not in a sense really been 'foreign' at all. In fact, Hong Kong has been the top investor in mainland China, providing around 60 per cent of the total foreign direct investment during the early years of capital inflow into China. Although its share gradually declined from that peak, investments from Hong Kong were still accounting for over half the total foreign capital invested in the mainland in the mid-1990s.[3] Taiwan has not been as active in the mainland, but direct investments from Taiwan have gone up sharply in the 1990s. In 1993 alone, the investments from Taiwan jumped sixfold. In just a few short years, the share of Taiwan in mainland investment surpassed that of the US. Up to the mid-1990s, nearly 70 per cent of the accumulated contracted foreign investment in China came from Hong Kong and Taiwan, compared with only about 7 per cent from the US and less than 6 per cent from Japan.[4]

Thus, if one takes the overseas Chinese capitalist diaspora into consideration, the opening of China assumes quite a different dimension. Without the input from Hong Kong, Taiwan and Macao, China's performance in trade and foreign investment would have been far less dazzling.

The brisk trade expansion of China during the reforms can be attributed to several factors, including the growing capacity to produce marketable goods. This capacity originated in the industrialization undertaken during the state planning period, but it has been considerably enhanced since then through a nationwide effort at technological upgrading in domestic industries. Investment from the overseas Chinese diaspora in labour-intensive, export-oriented manufacturing in the mainland has been a catalyst in the rapid growth of China's exports. The share of foreign-funded ventures in the country's foreign trade has mounted substantially, from almost zero in the mid-1980s to nearly 47 per cent in mid-1997.[5]

Hong Kong and Taiwan are nodes in a much larger network of overseas Chinese businesses scattered around the world, but concentrated in a number of East and Southeast Asian countries, such as Malaysia, Thailand, the Philippines and Indonesia. In these countries, overseas Chinese are an ethnic minority, but hold a commanding position in local business.[6] In Singapore, one of the Asian NIEs, overseas Chinese are a majority in the population.

The value of the aggregate economic assets of the overseas Chinese is unknown. One hears estimates that in the early 1990s the total 'GNP' of overseas Chinese in East Asia, including Hong Kong and Taiwan, was equal to or greater than that of China, or that the liquid assets held by overseas Chinese were worth some $2 trillion (*Financial Times*, 1995; *International Herald Tribune*, 1996; *The Economist*, 1995–96).

The economic relationships between mainland China and the adjacent 'foreign' areas of the overseas diaspora and overseas Chinese concentration have become close only since the onset of reform, but a long historical process prepared the way. The roots of the overseas Chinese business network can be traced back to the Song Dynasty (960–1276). In the eleventh century, during a period of rapid expansion in the sea trade, Chinese began to migrate to Southeast Asia, and, over the next several centuries, a great number of Chinese settled in the region. Through adaptation to local societies and cooperation with business enterprises in these countries, as well as with local elites and, eventually, European colonizers, a minority of the overseas Chinese became successful merchants and amassed great wealth. Business linkages were formed to control trade routes (Wang Gungwu, 1994; Hui, 1995).

Unlike the overseas Chinese business networks in Southeast Asia, the Chinese capitalist diaspora was the result of China's incorporation in the world economy during the nineteenth century. The military power of the Western colonizers forced the cession of Hong Kong to Great Britain and of Macao to Portugal. From these enclaves, the British and Portuguese penetrated the Chinese coast and established footholds for their commercial interests in adjacent areas. Thus, as a territory within the British Empire, Hong Kong thrived because of its advantageous position at the doorstep of China. The separation of Taiwan from the mainland was the product of Japanese imperialist aggression in the nineteenth century and of US support for the GMD regime, which had retreated to Taiwan after its defeat during the Chinese Revolution.

Ironically, the Communist victory on the mainland represented a fresh stimulus for the economic prosperity of the Chinese capitalist diaspora. On the eve of the Communist takeover, large numbers of businessmen from Shanghai and elsewhere on the mainland relocated, with their capital and other assets, to Taiwan, Hong Kong and other neighbouring areas (Arrighi, 1994b; Wong Siu-lun, 1988). Over the next two decades, the US policy of containment created extremely promising economic opportunities for Japan and other US allies in Asia, including the Chinese capitalist diaspora. That three of the Asian NIEs (Hong Kong, Taiwan and South Korea) are located around China is no accident. The policy of containment may have limited China's access to the world market, but it contributed to favourable conditions for the expansion of trading networks and the accumulation of capital and business expertise among the Chinese capitalist diaspora. This economic power has enabled the diaspora to respond to the reform process and to China's openness in the 1980s and 1990s. In a sense, China's new development strategy has benefited from conditions which have been created because of the attempts of the West to contain China in the first place.

After China undertook the strategy of outward reorientation and economic openness, American, European and Japanese multinational companies adopted a wait-and-see attitude. When the multinationals finally started to operate in China, they were bothered by the business environment, such as certain government rules and regulations on investment, or the difficulties in realizing the profits anticipated in Chinese markets. They therefore tended to keep investments at the minimum level necessary to maintain a foothold in China.

Like Western investors, overseas Chinese have also sometimes complained loudly about the difficulties of doing business on the mainland. However, unlike their Western counterparts, they have demonstrated far more readiness to overcome the difficulties. Playing the trump of cultural affinity, shared ancestral roots, familiar customs and habits, and a common language, many have found ways to evade or bypass formal barriers, especially during the earlier stages of the reform process. Some have resorted to the manipulation of kinship and community ties, which they have made great efforts to strengthen through, for instance, generous donations for schools, sporting events, community waterworks, or road construction. Thus, for instance, to a certain degree, the lack of official ties between the mainland and Taiwan has been overcome because of a common 'Chineseness'.

The active trading and investment in the mainland by overseas Chinese businesses have been encouraged by the climate of reform, but also by the advantageous conditions created by the government in its desire to pursue national unification and in its efforts to obtain outside assistance to upgrade the economy.

Hong Kong was the initial target. Often discriminated against by the British colonial authorities, Chinese businessmen in Hong Kong began receiving VIP treatment in mainland China, where they were granted lucrative business privileges. Some of them were invited to represent Hong Kong in China's highest legislature, the National People's Congress, and to cooperate with the central government in Hong Kong affairs. A close political alliance was thereby established between the Chinese Communist Party and overseas Chinese capitalists in Hong Kong (So and Chiu, 1995, pp. 241–65).

Not least for political reasons, the Chinese government has implemented preferential policies towards Taiwan, which has enjoyed the best conditions for investment and trade in the mainland. Although Hong Kong businesses did not benefit from the same treatment, they were closer, and Hong Kong residents could travel more easily across the border.

The government has also oriented its trade policies to court overseas Chinese capitalists. The reform-era coastal-development strategy has been aimed mainly at overseas Chinese investors. It is therefore not surprising that, in the point project, the first four special economic zones were Shenzhen, which is on the border with Hong Kong, Zhuhai, which is close to Macao, and Shantou and Xiamen, which are located on the Taiwan Straits. (The fifth special economic zone, which was established in 1988, is Hainan, on the South China Sea.)

The alliance between the government and the Chinese diaspora has proved to be far more fruitful than the government policy towards the West. Indeed, the response of the overseas Chinese capitalist diaspora to China's greater openness has apparently impressed the Japanese, American and European multinationals, which are now moving more rapidly to find their own niches in this latest 'miracle' of the East Asian regional economy (Arrighi, 1994b).

To be sure, the enthusiastic response of the overseas Chinese has not been prompted so much by 'patriotism' as by economic interest. If China's economy has benefited from the vigorous involvement of overseas Chinese capitalists, the capitalists have profited at least as much. Hong Kong's role as regional and world financial entrepôt for China has been enhanced. The investment capital from Hong Kong and Taiwan has pried open mainland markets, but it has also been geared towards the use of the mainland as a base for the production of exports. In the last few years, Hong Kong has shifted a great part of production to the mainland. In Guangdong Province, an estimated three million to four million people are working for Hong Kong manufacturing enterprises.

The relocation of production across borders has ultimately been a function of capital seeking cheap labour. Wage rates in Hong Kong were climbing rapidly in the 1980s, thereby reducing the profitability of the labour-intensive industries, such as toy and garment manufacturing, which virtually built the former British colony's economy. These were the first to move production across the frontier. The number of workers employed by Hong Kong companies in Southern China soared to several times that of Hong Kong's entire labour force engaged in manufacturing. In 1992, Hong Kong's re-exportation of goods made in Guangdong Province under 'outside-processing' contracts exceeded the domestic exports of Hong Kong. As a result, the size of Hong Kong's labour force in manufacturing plunged almost by half between 1984 and 1993. With the rapid 'loss' of the manufacturing sector to the mainland, the Hong Kong economy has become even more service based.

Less substantially, but in similar fashion, overseas Chinese businesses in the NIEs and elsewhere have greatly benefited from China's reforms and economic openness. For example, Singapore, which is slim in labour-intensive production, has been involved in some heavy-industry projects and in technology-intensive production in China.

Much of the overseas Chinese investment in the mainland has been profitable. Indeed, the gains by overseas Chinese capitalists are believed to be enormous. The mainland undoubtedly has been an important source of the dramatic new wealth among overseas Chinese in the last couple of decades. For example, despite rapid economic growth after World War II, large transnational enterprises were rare in the Chinese diaspora and among the overseas Chinese until about 20 years ago, when Chinese corporate conglomerates and Chinese billionaires began to emerge in Southeast Asia, Hong Kong and Taiwan. Hui (1995, Chapter 5) shows that, in 1993–94, there were at least 34 ethnic Chinese families or groups each with businesses worth $1 billion to $6.5 billion. They were located in Singapore, Indonesia, Malaysia, the Philippines, and Thailand, but Hong Kong and Taiwan hosted a large share of these businesses. In terms of scale, the Chinese multinationals are not inferior to their Western counterparts. It is probably impossible to measure the 'China factor' in this rapidly growing wealth, but, given the high level of economic integration with the mainland, the expansion of the overseas Chinese capitalists cannot be separated from the dynamic processes under way in China's economy.

China has invested in Hong Kong and perhaps Taiwan, too, although the investments are certainly not as substantial as the capital inflows. The primary destination of external investment from the mainland has been Hong Kong. By the mid-1990s the mainland had poured an estimated $25 billion into Hong Kong (*Far Eastern Economic Review*, 1995b, p. 62). This figure probably also includes the assets owned by Chinese enterprises and government agencies in Hong Kong. These assets have soared in value in recent years because of a real estate boom in the territory. Taiwan prohibits investment from the mainland. However, through overseas subsidiaries, the mainland may also have invested in Taiwan, although the level of investment is certainly less significant.

The growing economic integration between the mainland and the Chinese capitalist diaspora is anchored on a number of nodes, which are centres of investment flows and are also major production sites (for example, see Chen Xiangming, 1994). Hong Kong has been the most important node. Through forward and backward linkages with these nodes, China has become more closely connected to international commodity trade networks.

China's aggressive pursuit of outward-oriented economic development, the positive and active response of overseas Chinese capitalists and the dynamic growth of East and Southeast Asia raise questions about the nature of the emerging regional economy. Three possible models of regional development can be mentioned here. One might be called the model of 'the revival of the Sino-centric order'; another is the 'flying geese' model, and a third is the 'three-stage rocket' model.

According to Hamashita, the economic pattern now emerging in Asia is a revived version of a historical structure, called by him the 'Sino-centric order' (Hamashita 1984, 1988, 1993, 1994; see also Ikeda, 1996). In this view, China dominated commercial relations in East Asia historically by integrating periphery states into a Sino-centric economy through a tributary trade system. The key to the success of this system, according to Hamashita (1988, p. 17), was the huge external demand for Chinese commodities, such as silk, and the consequent differences in commodity prices inside and outside China. A Sino-centric political, military and diplomatic order supported the system on the basis of commodity trade relationships and the movements of Chinese seeking opportunities in other countries.

The old system was eroded by the expansion of the world economy into East Asia. In a very serious challenge to the Sino-centric order, former tributary countries began to use Western political and diplomatic principles and methods to resist Chinese influence (Hamashita, 1988, p. 58). The tributary relationship and the Sino-centric order came to an end in the early twentieth century. Since then, Japan may have finally succeeded in incorporating East and Southeast Asia into its accumulation structure.[7]

The economic expansion of the West into East Asia, however, did not lead to a rise in the West's exports of industrial products, but to the flow of silver into Asia and the flow of goods from Asia to the West. To solve this trade deficit problem, the West used other Asian products to pay for their imports of silk, tea and other commodities, thereby generating more intra-Asia trade, including East Asian trade with South Asia and Southeast Asia (de Vries, 1976, p. 135; Hamashita, 1984, p. 66; Ikeda, 1996). In the nineteenth century and throughout the first three-quarters of the twentieth century, China, like other East and Southeast Asian countries, was a supplier of raw materials, but only a limited buyer of Western manufactured goods. The industrialization drives in China over the years highlighted the country as a potential outlet for Western producer goods, but this finally happened only in the 1970s, when China gained access to the world market. Then, China's trade deficit with the West began to climb rapidly, indicating that the country was not generating enough exports to pay for its needs in producer goods from the West. The situation took a turn, however, and since 1990 China has been maintaining a trade surplus.

Taiwan and Hong Kong have been accumulating foreign reserves already for some time. That, like them, mainland China is now a vigorous exporter of manufactured goods and a holder of substantial foreign reserves is significant for the new regional economy which is taking shape (Ikeda, 1996, p. 72). China's entry among the ranks of nations with a trade surplus seems to be adding a crucial missing link to the revival of the old pattern in the flow of goods and financial claims between East Asia and the West. The economic expansion of Japan, the Asian tigers and some other East and Southeast Asian countries have contributed to this flow throughout the postwar period.

The 'flying geese' model of East Asian development views the economic relationships among East and Southeast Asian economies as forming a pyramid-hierarchy. The pyramid-hierarchy exists because of the labour-seeking investments flowing from the higher income countries towards the lower income countries and the labour-intensive exports flowing in the opposite direction. Ozawa (1993) shows that, over time, these counterflows have generated a stratified regional trading system of growing volume and density, with Japan at the top, the Asian NIEs in the middle and the new tiger cubs at the bottom. China became part of this regional structure after the 1970s, and later Vietnam also joined, both of them at the base of the pyramid. The particular pattern in the flows of capital, labour and goods is regarded as the main dynamic factor in the industrial expansion and economic integration of the entire East Asian region.

Given the structure of exports and the sectors in which foreign capital has been invested, China does seem to fit Ozawa's model, but the placement of China on a level with Vietnam at the bottom of the economic pyramid in East and Southeast Asia is problematic. Because of the size, diversity and energetic evolution of its economy, China is doubtless a potential competitor of any of the 'flying geese'. It has been gaining strength in certain areas of capital and technology intensive production that were once the exclusive domains of Japan and the Asian NIEs. Meanwhile, China has also become a big producer of downstream labour intensive products, in which it is now competing for world market share with the ASEAN countries. For these reasons, although in terms of per capita income China is indeed at the bottom, its overall position in the region's economic 'pyramid' is less than a cut and dried issue. This is also the case because, in the 'flying geese' regional model, only sovereign entities are taken into consideration. This has tended to miss the crucial role of the crossborder business networks centred on the Chinese capitalist diaspora and dominated by overseas Chinese capitalists. The emergence of close economic interactions between mainland China and the Chinese capitalist diaspora makes it difficult to treat each economy separately as a distinct unit. This has become even more obvious since the return of Hong Kong to China in 1997.

As an alternative to the flying geese model, Arrighi (1994b) has proposed the 'three-stage rocket' model of the postwar economic growth of East Asia. During the first stage, the US government was the main agency of expansion. During the second stage, while Japanese businesses became the main agency of expansion, 'the Chinese capitalist diaspora was revitalized and the Chinese government was offered unique opportunities to mobilize this diaspora in the double pursuit of economic advancement for mainland China and of a national unification for Greater China' (Arrighi, 1994b, p. 37). During the incipient third stage, the Chinese government and the Chinese capitalist diaspora seem to have emerged as the leading agencies of regional economic expansion. Although the outcome of the third stage is not yet clear because the process is still unfolding, the role of China and overseas Chinese capitalists in the dynamic development of Asia is expanding.

All three models seem to be based on a conviction that the pattern of growth in the region will continue and, in particular, that Japan or China will maintain economic leadership. However, following the financial crisis which unexpectedly swept through most old and new 'miracle' economies in East and Southeast Asia in late 1997, this expectation has been brought into serious doubt. This has shaken the widespread belief that the region is on a fast track to catch up to the West. Japan's economic slowdown, which has already been evident for several years, has worsened. China's economy, on the other hand, has not been badly affected. However, if the history of the capitalist world economy is any guide, despite the differences in the status of Japan and China in the current Asian economic crisis, it is more likely that Japan will remain in the 'club' of the rich countries than that China will obtain club membership. The Chinese government has shown unprecedented willingness to participate in joint programmes to rescue the Asian economies in crisis. This may well be seen as a sign of China's greater economic role in the region. It also indicates that the economic integration of China with the overseas Chinese diaspora and other economies in the region has proceeded to such a point that China can no longer afford to be indifferent. If the regional pattern of development becomes indeed more closely linked to the performance of China, then the country's sustained and rapid economic growth is crucial for the region.

Under the new strategy of reintegration into the world economy, China has sought to improve its access to external resources. The overseas capitalist diaspora has responded most vigorously. The result has been growth in the networks of trade and capital accumulation in East and Southeast Asia in which overseas Chinese capitalists have traditionally been leading actors. China's exports continue to depend heavily on markets in the rich Western countries, but the close collaboration with the overseas capitalist diaspora and the rapid emergence of an Asian market seem to show a potential for reducing China's exposure to the danger of becoming overdependent on these Western markets.

China's economic 'return' to Asia and the world economy has also involved a conscious policy to promote national unification. The vigorous pursuit of national unification in the 1980s and 1990s has unfolded under the indisputable leadership of the mainland. It is the mainland which has all along nurtured the goals of national independence and national unification, and it is the mainland which has been perceived by others as the home of national pride and dignity. The overseas Chinese business networks in Hong Kong, Macao, Taiwan and elsewhere see themselves and are seen by others as more efficient and prosperous, which indeed they are, but their wealth and efficiency, though crucial, are of secondary importance for national revival. It is the People's Republic and, perhaps paradoxically, the CCP which have managed to safeguard and preserve the idea of national revival through a stormy half-century of cold 'wars', economic ups and downs and political turmoil.

In a historical perspective, the participation of the capitalist diaspora in China's latest effort to catch up to the West has required the bridging of a gap between two models of development and between two parts of China, which has been divided temporarily because of the twists and turns of history. For more than 100 years beginning with the Opium War in 1840, China was the victim of constant Western aggression. Now, one by one, the Western powers have lost their grip: Japan in 1945, the USSR in the late 1950s and the British in 1997 with the return of Hong Kong. Portuguese colonial rule in Macao is to end in 1999. The only remnant of the 'century of humiliation' would then be Taiwan, and the last imperial force that would still, *de facto*, hold Chinese territory would be the US. If Taiwan follows the way of Hong Kong, China would finally complete an anti-imperialist sweep after more than 150 years of struggle with the West. Ironically, even if the sweep is successfully completed and the Chinese diaspora becomes once more an integral part of China, China may by then already have become enmeshed in a new division of labour within the capitalist world economy. Are China and its people winning an anti-imperialist victory, or is yet another defeat by the capitalist world economy looming after all?

13 Catching Up?

Since the onset of reform, the Chinese economy has enjoyed unusually rapid growth. Some observers are even talking of another Asian 'economic miracle' in the making. The high GDP growth rate over a period of nearly 20 years reflects a tremendous level of sustained industrial expansion. Unlike most other transition economies, China has not been plagued by a lack of growth. On the contrary, it has sometimes had difficulty coping with the speed of growth. Several times, the government has had to take measures to allow the economy to cool down.

This success has surprised the public and exceeded the expectations of the government. Even the 'designer of the reforms' himself was surprised. In 1984, at a meeting of the central advisory committee, Deng, with an apparent sense of pride, described his reaction to the economic performance of the country during the previous few years. 'Lately, I have been telling our foreign guests boldly that there is no doubt we will reach our goal of doubling GNP [by 2000],' he said (Deng, 1993, p. 88). 'But, once, we were not so certain. We used to say only that, through extraordinary effort, it would be possible to double our GNP.' Indeed, the original goal of the reforms – to double GNP within 20 years – was realized in only about half that time, and now the economy has nearly tripled in size with respect to 1980.

China's economy has been outperforming almost all the other high performing economies, usually by a wide margin (Table 13.1). Prior to the reforms, China had a relatively good growth record by comparison either to its own pre-1949 experience, or to international standards. However, this record was overshadowed by the even more impressive performance of the Asian tigers. Over the last 20 years, the economic performance of China has not been inferior to that of any country in the world, including the Asian tigers. China's rapid economic growth has been the more spectacular because of the country's huge population. Previously, the largest country to experience comparable growth over so many years was Japan.

Because of data like these, one is tempted to conclude that China's goal of catching up to the West is reachable. However, the issue deserves more scrutiny.

The position of a country within the world economy can be roughly gauged by an examination of the relative share of the country in total world production, industrial output, trade, and so on. In general, such

162

Table 13.1   Average annual growth rate, 1980–95 (in percentages)

	GDP		Industry		Value of exports	
	1980–90	*1990–95*	*1980–90*	*1990–95*	*1980–90*	*1990–95*
China	10.2	12.8	11.1	18.1	12.9	19.1
India	5.8	4.6	7.1	5.1	7.2	11.5
Indonesia	6.1	7.6	6.9	10.1	–0.3	11.7
Philippines	1.0	2.3	–0.9	2.2	3.9	16.2
South Korea	9.4	7.2	13.1	7.3	15.0	12.8
Hong Kong	6.9	5.6	–	–	16.8	15.9
Singapore	6.4	8.7	5.4	9.2	9.9	17.6
Brazil	2.7	2.7	2.0	1.7	5.1	9.0
Mexico	1.0	1.1	1.0	0.5	8.2	13.7
Latin America and Caribbean	1.7	3.2	1.4	2.5	3.0	9.1
Russian Federation	1.9	–9.8	–	–	–	–
High-income countries	3.2	2.0	3.2	0.7	7.8	6.9

Source: World Bank, 1997a, pp. 130–2, 154–6.

data are good indicators of the relative 'weight' of a country among nation-states. Thus, because it commanded nearly half the total world output at the end of World War II, the US was able to establish itself successfully as an hegemonic world power. The rich Western countries have collectively controlled a dominant share of world output, and it is this which distinguishes them among nations.

Yet, China's decades-old goal of catching up to the West has also usually implied that China wishes to attain the 'wealth' status of the most advanced countries. In practice, a country's wealth is measured using the per capita GDP indicator. Thus, we can employ two sets of indicators to assess the extent to which China is moving closer to its goal of catching up: indicators of 'economic weight' and indicators of 'wealth status'.

We can look at China's changing 'economic weight' relative, first, to the world as a whole and, second, to the high-income economies (Table 13.2).

Owing to nearly 20 years of uninterrupted growth at a more rapid rate than that in other countries, China has succeeded in improving its economic standing in the world. In terms of the size of the economy as expressed in GDP relative to the world total and relative to the aggregate for high-income economies, China has managed to raise its share by half a percentage point. It has done particularly well in foreign trade. With the growth rate in trade nearly doubling the world average since

Table 13.2   Changes in China's share of GDP, merchandise exports and
private consumption, 1980–95 (in percentages)

	GDP		Merchandise exports		Private consumption	
	1980	*1995*	*1980*	*1995*	*1980*	*1995*
World	1.9	2.5	0.9	2.9	1.6	1.9
High-income countries	2.6	3.1	1.3	3.7	2.2	2.4

Source: Based on World Bank, 1997a, pp. 134–6, 158–60, 178–80. A definition
of each category is offered in the source.

the early 1980s, China's share in world merchandise exports has tripled.
As a result, the country became the eleventh most important trading
nation in 1992, up from twenty-seventh in 1978, and has succeeded in
maintaining this position since then. Private consumption has also
expanded, although less significantly. In a word, the indicators show a
clear trend: China is gaining economic weight.

In terms of wealth status, that is, per capita GDP, China has not done
so well, as the following data, based on exchange-rate information,
show (Table 13.3).

However, it is widely recognized that per capita income in dollars is
not an ideal indicator of living standards in a country. Data based on
exchange rates, while generally appropriate for the measurement of
international trade and capital movements, are inadequate for the measurement of either the relative size of an economy, or the actual level of
per capita income, because market exchange rates may deviate from
purchasing power parity (PPP) values.[1] For example, to say that per
capita income in the rich countries is 45 times higher than that in China,
or that the average Chinese lives 45 times more 'poorly' than the average person in the rich countries does not have much meaning in terms
of the realities of daily life, since, among many other inadequacies, such
a comparison does not take into account the considerably lower domestic
prices in China. Numerous methods have been employed in an attempt
to overcome this discrepancy. The data in Table 13.4 are based on PPP
comparisons and are derived from alternative estimates of the level of
GDP per capita.

Obviously, the inconsistencies between the two datasets would have
to be explained before a proper assessment of the relative performance
of China could be undertaken with any hope of precision. The first set –

Table 13.3 Index of per capita GNP/GDP relative to the rich countries* (rich countries = 100)

	1980	1995
China	2.7	2.4
India	2.3	1.3
Indonesia	4.1	3.8
Brazil	19.4	14.0
Mexico	19.8	12.8
USSR**	43.1	8.6

Sources: Based on World Bank, 1982, p. 111; World Bank, 1997b, pp. 215, 237.
*The 'rich countries' are classified as 'industrial market economies' in World Bank, 1982. This includes the 19 most developed countries, that is, Canada and the US in America, Austria, Belgium, Denmark, Finland, France, Germany, Ireland, Italy, the Netherlands, Norway, Spain, Sweden, Switzerland, and the UK in Europe, and Japan, Australia and New Zealand in the Asia-Pacific region.
**After 1990, refers to the Russian Federation.

Table 13.4 Index of per capita GDP relative to the US (US = 100)

	1980	1992	1987	1995
China	8.0	14.4	6.3	10.8
India	5.1	6.3	4.4	5.2
Indonesia	10.2	12.8	9.8	14.1
Brazil	28.7	21.5	24.2	20.0
Mexico	28.8	23.7	27.8	23.7
USSR*	35.2	21.6	30.9	16.6

Sources: For 1980 and 1992, based on Maddison, 1995, pp. 196–7, 202–3, 204–5; for 1987 and 1995, based on World Bank, 1997b, pp. 214–15.
*After 1990, refers to the Russian Federation.

the data based on exchange-rate information (see Table 13.3) – suggests that China has not been catching up with the West in terms of 'wealth status', while the alternative estimates (see Table 13.4) tell the opposite story, that China has been narrowing the GDP per-capita gap with the West, represented in this case by the US. If, as many have argued, the alternative GDP estimates (the second dataset) are likely to be more realistic, then one has reason to believe that China's effort to catch up has generated remarkable results during the reform period, although the figures vary considerably, leaving room for doubt about the extent of China's 'advance'.

All the information indicates that China has been doing better than the USSR (and the Russian Federation) and the other big developing countries. According to the first dataset (see Table 13.3), China has been losing much less ground relative to the West than have all these countries. The alternative estimates (see Table 13.4) show that, while Brazil, Mexico and the Russian Federation have been falling further behind the US in terms of income since 1980, China, India and Indonesia have been bridging the gap, although their income levels are still relatively quite low.

The relative success of China should not come as a surprise, since the growth rate of real per capita income has been appreciably higher in China than in most other countries over the last 20 years.[2] The reform era has thus represented another turning point in China's modern history. This is the more remarkable given the worldwide pattern. Since the end of World War II, the gap in real per capita GDP between the industrial countries and the rest of the world (with the exception of East Asia) has widened (IMF, 1994, p. 90). Between 1965 and 1990, the share of world income accounted for by the richest quintile rose by 14 percentage points, to 83 per cent of total world GDP. The average income per head in the richest quintile was 31 times the corresponding income in the poorest quintile in 1965; by 1990, the difference had jumped to a factor of 60 (UNCTAD, 1997).

However, China cannot afford to celebrate this victory. In the mid-1990s, with about 20 per cent of the world's population, China had less than 10 per cent of total world output on a PPP-basis and a negligible 2.5 per cent if the calculation is based on market exchange rates. The population of China was 1.5 times the size of that of the rich countries in Western Europe and North America, but China's GDP was a mere 15 to 20 per cent of the total GDP of these countries on a PPP-basis and a miserable 3 per cent if market exchange rates are used. In foreign trade, where the country's expansion was the most rapid, China's merchandise exports remained a tiny proportion of the world total or of the total of the rich countries. Even the Netherlands, with a population of about 1 per cent of that of China, had a larger share of world merchandise exports.

Although the relative distance narrowed between the per capita income in China and that in the rich countries, the income difference in absolute terms actually became larger (Maddison, 1995; World Bank, 1997b). The per capita GDP of China climbed from 8 per cent to 14 per cent of that of the US between 1980 and 1992, but the difference in absolute terms also went up from $16 808 to $18 460 (in 1990 international dollars). The situation appears much gloomier if figures based on exchange rates are used. In 1980, the per capita income of China lagged behind that of the rich countries by $10 030; the difference had mounted to $26 390 by 1995. This means that, in current dollars, the absolute difference in per capita income between China and the average of the rich countries more than doubled between 1980 and 1995, whereas the inflation in dollar prices reached only about 60 per cent over the same period. Given China's per capita income of $2000–3000 on a PPP-basis, or $620 as compared to $27 010 for the rich countries at the market exchange rate in 1995, the gap that China has yet to bridge is formidable.

In summary, China has been very successful in relinking with the world economy. Its trade has thrived, leading to a substantial rise in its aggregate share in the world market, and the economy has been growing steadily. Yet, to say the country is an economic giant is an obvious exaggeration. Whether China can sustain this high economic growth rate is, of course, a key issue. Under the vigorous new development strategy, China has made tremendous progress by managing 'to harness' economic growth. However, success breeds greater expectations, as well as new contradictions. The most striking evidence is the open confrontation between the government and the mass demonstrators in 1989. The government finally prevailed only after resorting to the use of force, leading to the bloodshed, which in turn seriously discredited the government. If economic success of the reforms is not to become merely another development illusion, like so many of those experienced in so many other developing countries, China must maintain economic expansion and assure that it is not only rapid but democratic and equitable, therefore sustainable.

Economic growth has produced noticeable advances in many areas of life in China. International comparisons have repeatedly shown that countries with similar levels of per capita income may differ widely in terms of human development. Thus, while China is still a relatively low per capita income country, it is ranked on a par with the average for upper-middle income countries in terms of human development. Life expectancy at birth has risen during the reform years, from 67 years in 1980 to 69 years in 1995. The infant mortality rate has dropped from 56 to 34 per 1000 live births. The poverty rate has fallen sharply. While malnutrition continues to exist in poorer localities and among the relatively poor, famine and persistent hunger have been successfully eradicated. As a result of the rapid economic expansion over nearly two decades, the living standards of the population have improved considerably. Today, people are undoubtedly more well fed, clad and housed.

This general progress demonstrates that the fruits of economic growth are being widely shared among the population. This has been due mainly to China's social welfare and income distribution system, which was established during the early stages and still owes much to the Maoist era. Even during the first three decades of the People's Republic, although the income gap with the rich countries was substantial and remained so, China was generally able to move forward in its relative standing in the world in terms of human development. Yet once again, this shows that appropriate government interventions and reasonable social policies can achieve a great deal even at low income levels. Undeniably, socialist ideas have exerted considerable influence on the process of reform, especially during the early stages, so that the majority of the people have not become victims of the market transition. This has provided the social stability which has allowed the reforms to be carried out without serious challenge for nearly 20 years.

None the less, the reforms have led to profound economic and social change. Precisely because of the relative success of the reforms, new tensions have appeared in Chinese society. Market forces are becoming more and more important in the allocation of resources, and patterns of income distribution have been affected.

The rise in national wealth has not been accompanied automatically by fair and equitable income distribution. The concept of the Maoist era – 'poverty in common rather than income inequality' – seems to have given way to a new concept: 'income inequality rather than poverty in common'.[3] In the midst of economic growth, the distribution of income among various social groups and regions, as well as between city and countryside, has become more inequitable.

Constant economic adjustments and the emphasis on market efficiency have generated serious unemployment in urban and rural areas alike. This unemployment is a new phenomenon, which threatens the sense of security of all, rather than just the unemployed. Urban poverty, previously unknown, has begun to emerge, largely as a result of unemployment.

Urban wage-earners have generally been able to benefit from the reforms, as living standards have risen in line with the rapid economic growth. However, for this to continue, the high growth momentum must be maintained in the economy, and a new social security system must be established to cope with unemployment and other labour problems in the free market environment.

The loss of job security in the countryside is perhaps an even more serious issue. 'Collective job allocation' – a mechanism of guaranteed employment in rural areas – ceased to exist following the revival of household production and the elimination of the collective farming system. Under the current land contract system, rural households are granted plots of land for cultivation. The 'contracted' land is an essential source of livelihood, thereby also becoming an important component of the social safety net in the countryside. This is a legacy mainly of pre-reform social structures. Yet, a life dependent on the output from the cultivation of a small plot of land is not very secure, nor does it offer much chance for improvement. More and more rural inhabitants are therefore seeking wage-earning jobs in order to supplement household income. Thus, both rural and urban labourers are becoming more dependent on the job market. A failure of the economic expansion to create more jobs would therefore spell serious social problems for China, with its huge pool of labour and extremely diverse local conditions.

Rapid industrial expansion has been shrinking the amount of available farmland. This is raising the alarming issue of food security. In a country with over one billion people, agricultural production is not merely an economic matter; it is a question of national security. Similarly, the jump in energy consumption that has accompanied economic growth has generated enormous industrial pollution which poses a major threat to the environment. Sustainable development will depend on the successful handling of these and other problems, and this in turn will be a key to the progress of China in its efforts to catch up to the West.

China's reintegration into the world economy has produced substantial external pressure in terms of the country's domestic policies and its strategies in international affairs. As China has become tied more closely to the world division of labour through international trade and capital flows, the domestic economy has grown more susceptible to changes in the world market.

Between 1980 and 1995, measured by market exchange rates, the share of trade in GDP rose from 13 per cent to 40 per cent (World Bank, 1997b, pp. 218–9). This seems to indicate that the Chinese economy today has become indeed export-oriented and deeply integrated with the global economy. This trade/GDP ratio is higher not only than that of some other big developing countries such as India and Brazil, but is also higher than that of Japan and the US. However, if trade is measured against PPP-based GDP, which is a better indicator of the situation, the picture becomes quite different. In 1996, the ratio of trade to PPP-GDP in China was 7.1 per cent, up from 6.6 per cent in 1986. This ratio is lower than the low-income countries' average (excluding China and India) of 15.7 per cent, and far below the middle-income countries' average of 21.8 per cent, the high-income countries' average of 38.9 per cent, and the world average of 29.1 per cent. Among large economies, only India has trade/GDP ratio lower than China's (World Bank, 1998, pp. 310–12). To say that China's economy has become largely dependent on the world market seems to be an overstatement.

However, never before since 1949 the world market had such direct and serious repercussions in trade related sectors, which are influential and visible in the economy. The dependency on the world market has become especially significant in particular industries. In 1997, exports accounted for more than half the total output of the clothing industry. It has been calculated that a one-percentage-point drop in clothing exports would lead to a 0.5-percentage-point decline in total clothing output and a 1.5-percentage-point decline in production below the production capacity of the clothing industry (*Shichangbao* [*Market*], 23 September 1997). Stagnation in exports would result in the closing of a considerable number of factories and the layoff of tens of thousands of workers.

It is thus not surprising that the fear of external dependency has given rise to the periodic resurgence of nationalist sentiments. If long-run economic growth fails to materialize, while the tensions created during the process of reintegration into the world market continue to accumulate, there is a real danger that the repercussions may go well beyond the merely economic.

Overall, the relative economic success of China's new development strategy has been made possible by favourable internal and external socioeconomic conditions. The past 20 years have been the most lengthy period of peace and stability without lasting internal social turbulence witnessed by the country since the early-nineteenth century. This has allowed China to mobilize its human and natural resources in support of the goal of economic growth. The well-established industrial base, the large human capital resources, the existence of a strong state, and the transformation of institutional structures have helped pave the way for the market transition. These initial conditions have principally been the legacy of the Maoist era.

Like many countries, China has attempted to learn from the Asian NIEs. However, there is no universal recipe for sustainable and rapid economic expansion, much less for 'catching up'. No single model of development, no matter how good, can work wonders in all cases. Whether China can translate its initial success into long-term development will now depend on its ability to maintain high economic growth rates and to cope with the inevitable costs of marketization and globalization.

Conclusion

Over the past century and a half China has passed through three distinct phases in its response to the challenge posed by the West. These phases have been marked by three separate 'packages' of development strategies: 'Westernization' (whether a formal 'movement' or otherwise), 'delinking and self-reliance' and 'reintegration'. These strategies have been as much the products of domestic and international circumstances as the subjective choices of the respective governments. They have to a large extent shaped domestic economic and social structures and, at the same time, owing to China's size and its historical importance in East Asia, contributed to an East Asian regional development pattern.

There has been continuity among the three phases. The state has been the major agent in the formulation and implementation of the strategies. The Westernization movement in the late-nineteenth century was an attempt by Qing government officials to initiate a nationwide campaign aiming at national regeneration. The attempt failed, and the approaches in the next two phases, supported, respectively, by surging nationalism and the ideas of socialism, were far more 'statist'. Between 1927 and 1949, the GMD government was unable to provide effective leadership and was itself plagued by domestic rivalries and foreign invasions. A genuine revolution ended with the establishment of a strong state in 1949. The Communist-led government formulated and carried out a development programme within a central planning system that began to revitalize the nation. It then engineered a fundamental shift in development strategy in the late 1970s.

A leading role for the state has been widely recognized as a common feature during industrialization of the late comers. In this respect, China is no exception, although in China it has taken the state a rather long time to position itself at the centre of national development. Judged from a nationalist point of view, the state has made the difference in the modern history of China. In this sense, statism, more than neoclassical economics, explains the country's pursuit of greater status in the world economy.

Despite the changing governments and the diverse outcomes, continuity also exists among the three phases because, explicitly acknowledged or not, the fundamental goals of each of the development thrusts have been similar. As an immediate task, the strategies have been aimed at helping fend off threats to national independence; in the medium run, they have been responses to the challenge represented by the peripheralization of China by the 'core' countries, and, in the long run, the strategies have sought to overcome economic backwardness and to restore China to a place of power and wealth in the world.

However, the process and outcomes of each of the three phases have diverged in other respects because of variances in the commitment of the different governments, in the means available for the realization of concrete plans, in the historical and geopolitical contexts, and in the support of the domestic socioeconomic environment.

The response of the Qing Dynasty to the Western challenge was slow and ineffective. The government shed its parochial arrogance and the drive for change acquired a sense of urgency only after repeated, humiliating defeats by the Western powers. When the government finally began to act, it was already too late to avoid Western encroachment. Moreover, by then, the government was also being confronted by rebellions. The regime turned to the Western countries for military assistance so that it could crush the domestic opposition. This precipitated a nationalistic reaction against the Qing Dynasty, which finally crumbled.

The West had first been drawn towards China in the nineteenth century because of the country's resources and its huge potential as a market. These represented both a prize and a challenge for the West, for even Great Britain, which was then the hegemonic power and which already possessed a vast colonial empire, was unable to control China alone. All the major Western powers soon joined in the attempt: the incorporation of China was to be a collective endeavour. To prevent overheated competition among themselves in the process of partitioning the country, the West, led by the US, a latecomer and the emerging hegemon, eventually formulated an 'Open Door' policy to assure equal access to China's markets.

Meanwhile, benefiting from its geopolitical position in Asia and a rather successful socioeconomic transformation, Japan achieved core status among the world powers. This 'corization' of Japan, as So and Chiu (1995) have called it, represented one of the most difficult stumbling blocks to the independence of China from the West before 1949. Japan had long nurtured the ambition to change the Sino-centric order in East and Southeast Asia. It thus became extremely aggressive in trying to weaken and subordinate China. This culminated in Japan's eight-year occupation of China during World War II.

The collapse of the Qing Dynasty and the emergence of the nationalist government were not real breakthroughs, although the new regime prodded the country further along on the path towards Westernization.

Because the Western powers were preoccupied with events in Europe during and just after World War I and because of the more intense competition among them over the wealth of the world, China acquired some 'breathing room' between the wars and experienced relatively rapid economic growth. Certainly, Westernization during the GMD period – though not an explicit government campaign – involved more than the adoption of Western technology. A domestic modern sector, based on Western ideas, institutions, industrial management methods, corporate culture, and so forth, began to expand with the encouragement of the government and the help of Western personnel and Western-trained Chinese. However, under the GMD regime, this 'Westernization drive' did not reach beyond urban centres, and vast rural areas remained isolated. Given the lack of an industrial base, the Westernization of the economy had to depend on foreign inputs. This meant that the modern sector was dominated by Western capital, while agriculture and traditional handicrafts changed little. This imbalance aggravated the structural problems in the economy, thus indirectly fuelling social stratification.

Economic growth was shortlived and not very widespread. The benefits of the growth were reaped principally by those who controlled the resources, such as foreign investors, government officials and domestic modern-sector entrepreneurs. There was no 'Westernization' in the countryside, and the land problem remained acute. Even at its height in the 1920s and 1930s, the Westernization drive was selective and partial, thereby leaving the rural question unresolved. This was its greatest failure, and the government continued to be little concerned about rural problems and peasant issues. Precisely because of its entirely different attitude towards these problems and issues, the CCP gradually gathered strength and eventually defeated the GMD regime.

If the GMD's 'Westernization' drive further polarized the economy, it proved even less capable of achieving Western-style economic growth. In 1949, after more than 50 years of effort, China was one of the poorest countries in the world; it had the lowest growth rate even among the most poorly performing developing countries in Asia.

The victory of the Revolution in 1949 gave the newly established Communist government an opportunity to plan a different future for the country. Yet, though delinking and self-reliance as a national development strategy departed so sharply from previous experience, they were as much the result of long planning as of unfolding domestic and world events.

Economic backwardness was as serious an obstacle as ever. To deal with it, China needed all the assistance it could garner to overcome the shortages in the capital, technology and other inputs necessary for a healthy drive towards industrialization. This represented a problem for the government: How was it to obtain material assistance without compromising national independence and socialist ideology? The government determined to make a distinction between economics and politics and between technology and ideology. This position was expressed in the Common Programme, which was adopted on the eve of the establishment of the People's Republic and which declared that, on the basis of equality and mutual benefit, the People's Republic would develop commercial relations with other countries, including countries with different socioeconomic systems.

However, this approach could not work. Within the Cold War world order, China could not and did not remain neutral in the fierce rivalry between world capitalism and anti-systemic forces. It could not expect to be and, indeed, was not viewed simply as a trading partner in the world market. The establishment of the People's Republic was considered by the US government as the 'loss' to Communism of a political and military ally. Almost explicit was one condition for China to be accepted into the 'world family': the collapse of the Communist government. Military confrontation between China and the US in the Korean War and across the Taiwan Straits had brought China's brief attempt at limited integration in the world economy on its own terms to an end by the mid-1950s.

The irreconcilable conflict with the West on both nationalist and ideological grounds and a conceptual affinity with the socialist camp led by the USSR caused China to rely on the East as an alternative to limited integration in the world economy. This approach was somewhat successful, for the USSR provided much-needed assistance for the initial drive at industrialization. However, strained by the difficulties of economic integration between an economically weak but strongly nationalist China and the more advanced but dominance-minded USSR, the China–Soviet alliance did not last.

Under the strategy of delinking and self-reliance, though commercial relations with other countries and nongovernmental organizations were maintained, China had limited access to the world market. This was not easy for such a large nation. On the other hand, the strategy helped China achieve a level of economic and political autonomy that it had never before been able to achieve in its modern history. The government established firm control over the allocation of resources. It took advantage of the country's abundant labour force and natural resources and of the size and diversity of the domestic economy and internal markets. It favoured programmes designated as national priorities. The highest priority was assigned to the development of heavy industry, which was considered essential for the creation of a comprehensive industrial base and a viable defence complex. The problem of the primitive capital accumulation needed for heavy industry was solved by extracting surplus from the countryside and suppressing domestic consumption.

Meanwhile, under the leadership of Mao, the government was committed to the creation of a social welfare system with broad coverage. In particular, the poorer segments of the population benefited appreciably from the highly equitable scheme of income distribution. The international 'isolation' of China during delinking was a strong stimulus for national cohesion, which allowed the leadership more room to manoeuvre in the implementation of socioeconomic policies.

After enormous effort and despite great difficulties, China was able to achieve substantial progress, while remaining economically and politically independent. This accomplishment was in sharp contrast to the record of most developing countries. Under delinking, instead of falling into oblivion, China raised its political weight in the world. Although the strategic need of the West to offset the power of the USSR was mainly responsible for the opening of Western markets to China, China had shown that it could stand on its own.

Yet, the failure to narrow the income gap with the West heralded fresh reforms, which have altered China's relationship with the capitalist world economy. The shift in development strategy from 'delinking' to 'relinking' did not require a revolution. The new strategy has been pursued by the same government which pursued the old strategy.

In retrospect, it appears that the government was not propelled to seek a new development path because the economy was doing badly. In fact, China had a relatively good growth record during the period. Rather, the government knew that to do better was possible, a lesson it had learned from observing successful experiences, mainly those of the Asian NIEs, in 'catching up'. The government was convinced that China could also achieve such success if it adopted more flexible economic policies.

As the reform programmes unfolded, the socioeconomic changes which occurred were far more profound than the government had ever anticipated. When 'politics in command' began to be replaced by 'economics in command', that is, when pragmatism and the single-minded pursuit of economic growth began to prevail over other considerations, then China started to move towards a market economy, and socialist ideology was relegated to the background. For the reform-minded government, economic growth and social stability were more important than the conflict between socialism and capitalism. This paved the way for the widespread acceptance of 'Western learning'. The economic policies and institutional practices in the advanced capitalist countries began to be viewed in a neutral way, as 'modern' instead of 'Western' or 'capitalist'.

The strategy shift from delinking to reintegration into the capitalist world economy and to the acceptance of the rules of the game has been radical. However, unlike the changes taking place in the former Soviet bloc, the reforms in China have not meant a sudden and sometimes brutal break with the past, but have been built upon prereform socioeconomic legacies and have been more gradual. Thus, though a market-oriented economy has emerged in China over the past 20 years, the overall socioeconomic context is a hybrid, marked by a mixture of market and state, market and planning, and socialism and capitalism.

In terms of economic integration, the differences between the pre-1949 period and the present are striking. For example, the current process of integration has gone beyond urban centres to involve the countryside, where rural industries are expanding at a phenomenal pace and are becoming quite active in world markets.

On the other hand, regional inequalities still represent an obstacle to the prospects for 'common prosperity'. The old bias in favour of urban coastal areas has now become closely associated with a pattern of profit-driven resource allocations. Likewise, the relatively poor are tending to remain so, as income gaps have widened between countryside and city, between coastal area and inland area, and between high- and low-income groups. The government is being confronted by a constant dilemma: how to balance the promise of a better life for all, the need to maintain popular support for the state and the policy of keeping labour costs low so as to attract foreign capital. Thus, for instance, as the government forms alliances with overseas Chinese capitalists, transnational companies and domestic big business, its ideological identity is being called into question and could become a source of internal political conflict.

The boost in China's share of total world trade and the growth in foreign direct investment in China seem to indicate that the open policy of reintegration has been a success, but the very dynamism of the country's current phase of development, particularly the more active involvement of China in regional and world affairs, has begun to cause anxiety among the core countries that dominate the world economy and that for centuries have fixed the rules of the game. Never mind that China's share of the world's exports stands at less than 3 per cent, while the country has one-fifth of the world's population.

Since the beginning of the 1990s, this anxiety has frequently found an echo in the Western media. Headlines like 'Watch Out For China', 'The New Trade Superpower', 'The Rise Of Mighty China' are becoming common. People are being told that China could become a tremendous problem for the world and the world economy. Some have warned that a united, powerful China is not in the interest of the leading Western capitalist economies. China would disrupt the world trade system, like 'an 800-pound gorilla' (*Business Week*, 1994, p. 25).

The talk is not without the usual Western cultural arrogance, though the worries seem genuine enough. The resurgence of China has been seen by some as merely unwelcome, by others as a challenge or even a threat to the industrial West and by still others as destabilizing to the point that it is comparable to the rise of Germany and Japan that led to two world wars (for example, see, Chace, 1994; Garten 1996; Huntington, 1993; Segal, 1993). Since 'no policy can guarantee good behaviour by the Chinese' (*The Economist*, 1995, p. 13), many believe that the West must do something.

The strategic options for dealing with the 'rise of China' appear to revolve around 'engagement' and 'containment'. An instance of 'engagement' is offered by the recent suggestion that the West should use China's desire to join the World Trade Organization as a collective lever to force the country to establish a 'truly open, free-trading economy'. The WTO 'lever' has been viewed by many as the last 'golden opportunity to influence' China's direction (Dale, 1994, p. 13). Regardless of the particulars in the negotiations between the Chinese government and WTO, the general bias of the US-led alliance of core countries against China's entry has not escaped the notice of some observers.[1] Disguised as concerns about free trade and fair competition, the bottom line is that the Western countries do not want a strong and powerful China, which is, in their eyes, politically unredeemed, culturally alien and socio-historically backward.

The irony is that, although China has chosen a more open, market-oriented economic system, the West is staying aloof, rather than welcoming China with open arms. In fact, despite the reluctance of Western politicians and policy experts to use the word 'containment' due to its Cold War connotations, containment is again being contemplated in the West's dealings with China (*International Herald Tribune*, 1995, p. 1).[2] The threat to the existing world economic order by 'an economically dynamic China' is thought by some to be no less serious than the threat represented by the spread of Communism during the Cold War, which the US with its allies Japan and other Western and non-Communist countries in East Asia, sought to contain.

The economic expansion of China has confronted the West with a dilemma. In the 1950s and 1960s, during the Cold War, containment by outright political and military coercion was justified on the grounds that it was necessary to prevent the spread of Communism. But, in the 1990s, there are no appropriate reasons at hand. China's trade surplus with the US, China's commercial practices, its military spending, or its human rights record are not sufficient grounds. Moreover, containment would also require a different sort of effort. Unlike in the 1950s, the US in the 1990s is a hegemonic power in decline and would be unable to carry out a policy of containment alone. Since American and Western European companies are involved in capital flows and trade with China, whether such a policy might serve or damage their interests is not clear. If containment did not bring down the Communist government or lead to the collapse of the Chinese economy during the 1950s and 1960s, its chances of succeeding now in the 1990s do not seem brighter. Now, many Cold War allies of the US are finding that there is more to gain in doing business with China than there is in fighting with China.

None the less, given a proper occasion, the West is unlikely to stop trying to coerce China to act in certain ways on certain issues. After the government crackdown on demonstrations in China in June 1989, the G-7 economic summit declared sanctions. The sanctions were short-lived and ineffective. In fact, they may have worked to strengthen the regime by evoking nationalist sentiment in the country. The reaction of the Chinese leader Deng Xiaoping is illuminating.

'I am a Chinese, and I know the history of foreign aggression against China,' he told visitors to China in April 1990 (Deng, 1993, pp. 357–8). 'When I heard that the Western G-7 summit had decided to impose sanctions on China, it immediately reminded me of the story of the invasion of China in 1900 by an allied army put together by eight Western nations. Replacing Canada in the G-7 with Czarist Russia and Austria, we have the very same eight countries which organized the invasion of China in 1900.'[3]

In the view of Deng and others in the Chinese leadership, the West is not entitled to lecture China on human rights and social justice. The government could also count on the support of the population. The people may have many differences with their government, but unwillingness to stand up to outside pressure is not one of them, especially in such a huge nation with such a strong sense of history. Nationalism would bond the country together rather quickly if a collective man-oeuvre by the West were undertaken. Containment may be a valid topic for discussion, but it is not a practical or a useful option for action.

For the moment, 'engagement' seems to have been adopted by the core countries in their dealings with China. It is not yet clear how engagement is going to be employed over the long run. However, there is not much reason for optimism. It may even be that engagement will be used to try to achieve the same goals as containment, that is, to keep China weak and subordinate.

Obviously, vast differences exist between China and the West in their perceptions of the rise of China, and the differences are likely to persist as long as China's economy is expanding rapidly. From this point of view, the rise of China is indeed a destabilizing force within the world economic order. Because of the nation's huge population, China's ascendancy would pose a challenge to the world economy and to its domination by a privileged minority of rich countries.

However, China's ascendancy, should it ever occur, is still very far off in time because of the enormous difficulties the nation faces in the effort to narrow the income gap with the Western core countries. Since World War II, with the relative exception of the Asian NIEs, with a total population of 70 million, no developing country has succeeded in catching up to the Western standard of wealth. For China, with a population 17 times as large as that of the Asian NIEs and a much lower 'initial' income level, the process of catching up would take a very long time even if the current growth momentum in the country's economy could be sustained.

Nationalism and socialism were instrumental in supporting the delinking strategy in that nationalism provided the popular base for the government's attempt to maintain the nation's political and economic independence, while socialism justified the government's anti-imperialist orientation in foreign policy. Nationalism and socialism were essential to the state's success in the nationalization of property, in central planning and in the industrialization drive focused on heavy industry. The government could use the banner of 'catching up' to rationalize the sacrifices of the people in terms of popular democracy and short-term material benefits. Though the Communist government failed to deliver on the promise of catching up to the West, it succeeded in achieving the socialist target of more equal income distribution and basic social welfare among the entire population, even at a low level of per capita income. The pressure on the country from outside tended to bind the domestic alliance between workers and peasants more tightly and thereby confirmed the legitimacy of the state.

To become integrated into the world economy, countries must play by the rules in the world market, and domestic production must abide by the logic of worldwide capital accumulation, which tends to boost income inequalities between the rich and the poor. The Chinese government continues to consider itself the legitimate protector of all the people, but Chinese society is becoming more stratified as the country has become more closely integrated within the capitalist world economy. Political tensions may not be kept at bay indefinitely.

The new conditions have generated a compelling pressure on the government to accommodate the interests of big business, both domestic and international. Within the country, a new class alliance is replacing the alliance between workers and peasants. In world-political terms, progressive and anti-systemic forces in other countries are being viewed in the light of their relevance to China's 'modernization'. In place of 'proletarian internationalism', 'the national interest' has become the basis of China's conduct on the world stage. In seeking a better position within the world economy and with, perhaps, a better chance to succeed than many other developing countries, China, knowingly or unknowingly, is helping maintain the existing structure of the world economy. This may in turn contribute to the difficulties of developing countries which are less able to compete.

These tendencies are obviously contradictory, and it is therefore not surprising that the reform-minded government has been relying on nationalist sentiment to garner domestic popular support. The resulting surge in nationalism in China is a source of conflict with the 'core' countries. However, as China moves further towards a market economy and towards closer integration within the world economy, the government can be expected to depend more on economic success and less on nationalism to foster popular support. None the less, the class basis of this support has been changing and may become narrower as income inequality grows. Thus, a failure this time around may have much more serious implications for the Chinese state and society. Similarly, because of China's new linkages with the regional and world economy, failure might not only paralyse China's overall development efforts, but also produce spillover effects in the Asian region and other regions as well.

It is not my intention to end on a pessimistic note, however. Indeed, compared with other developing countries and relative to its own recent past, China today seems to be blessed with an opportunity. The socio-economic foundations laid during the central planning period and changes in the geopolitical situation may now favour the rise of China to a new economic and political status. As the twentieth century draws to a close, the belief that China can catch up to the West is becoming more common both within and outside China, although the time this would take is probably quite long.[4] In fact, the process cannot yet be reduced to a matter of time. The road ahead is certainly not smooth, and the responses of the Chinese society will be decisive in determining the outcomes in the long run.

Notes

Introduction: A Framework for Analysis

1. Some of the typical characteristics of countries on the periphery are a concentration on low-profit, low-technology, low-wage production which is not very diversified, a narrow range of economic tasks, few social strata, weak state machinery, poor standards of living among the majority of the population, a monocultural pattern in the agricultural sector in which cash crops are produced on large estates by dependent labour, and the exportation primarily of low-wage products (cf. Wallerstein, 1979a).

1   The Westernization Movement

1. For nearly 100 years before the Opium War, foreign trade in China was subject to official government approval with regard to location, market entry, trade organization, rules, and, at times, the quality and quantity of the products traded. The trade was essentially a single-port trade centred on Canton, now Guangzhou, in Southern China. (See Fairbank, 1953; Hsu, 1990, Chapters 5 and 7; Zheng, 1984.)
2. Hsu (1990, pp. 191–2) has pointed out that, 'In these treaties three stipulations were particularly injurious to China – the fixed tariff, extra-territoriality, and the most-favoured-nation clause. They were granted partly out of expediency and partly out of ignorance of international law and the concept of national sovereignty. The fixed tariff of 5 per cent *ad valorem*, as suggested by the British, was readily accepted by the Chinese for the simple reason that it was higher than the existing imperial tariff, which averaged only 2 to 4 per cent *ad valorem*, although the irregular fees had been high. Little did the Chinese realize that their assent to a fixed rate precluded a protective tariff in the future. Extra-territoriality was signed away under the expedient notion that the barbarians, who spoke different languages and had strange customs, should be allowed to govern themselves – to show Chinese magnanimity and to ease the task of governing them. The MFN treatment was granted *pro forma* on the ground that the emperor looked upon men from afar with equal benevolence.'
3. For example, Deckers (1994, p. 221) has argued that, 'Deng today, as Mao, Chiang Kai-shek and Sun Yat-sen before, all identified the same problem, lack of industrialization, but their recipes concerning how to cure it were different.'
4. Thus, in a well-known incident, Ci Xi, the empress dowager, diverted funds originally allocated for the Northern Ocean Navy to the construction of an imperial park, the Summer Palace.
5. As the vanquished nation in the Sino–Japanese War, China made the following concessions to Japan: it ceded Taiwan and the nearby Penghu (Pescadores) Islands, recognized Korea's independence, paid 230 million taels

in indemnity (including 30 million taels for not giving up the Liaodong Peninsula to Japan under the pressure of other powers), opened more ports, and gave Japanese nationals the right to engage in trade and manufacturing in China. The Qing court had an annual revenue of 89 million taels at the time (Hsu, 1990, pp. 342, 345–6; So and Chiu, 1995, p. 89).

6. Chiang Kai-shek, the leader of the GMD, considered domestic opposition more dangerous to the regime than foreign expansion. He wrote that, 'The Japanese are a disease of the skin; the Communists are a disease of the heart' (cited in So and Chiu, 1995, p. 126).

7. From 1720 to the early-nineteenth century, the 'compradors' ('maiban' in Chinese) were licensed Chinese agents who assisted foreign merchants in the procurement of daily supplies and the management of servants and money. After 1842, the term was used to refer to the middlemen who conducted business for Western (and later also Japanese) merchants on Chinese markets, especially in urban coastal areas. Compradors might function not merely as servants, but as actual managers. In any case, they worked on behalf of their foreign 'bosses'. Without the compradors, it would have been impossible for foreigners to conclude deals with domestic merchants and producers, not least because of the language barriers (cf. Chen Shijun, 1984, pp. 54–5; Hui, 1995, Chapter 3; Zhang Wenqing, 1985, pp. 313–14, 324–6).

8. *'He yi taguo y yangwu xing, er woguo y yangwu shuai ye?!'* (Liang Qichao, 'Li Hongzhang', *Yinbingshi wenji*, Vol. 44, cited in Chen Biao, 1986, p. 52).

2 Foreign Trade

1. In 1926, there were 141 Chinese-owned banks, 42 foreign banks and 20 joint-venture banks in China (Du, 1991, p. 121).

2. The number of foreign vessels registered in accordance with the Inland Steam Navigation Regulations in 1914 was 1125. Only 211 Chinese vessels were so registered. See Feuerwerker, 1983, p. 203.

3. Robert Hart, a British national, effectively presided over maritime customs as inspector-general for nearly 50 years, from 1863 to 1908, and until 1928 all the inspectors-general were British. Within the customs service, as well as the postal service, all responsible administrative positions were held by Westerners, and before the 1911 Revolution no assistant customs officers at any treaty port were Chinese.

4. Two guiding principles were announced in 1928: treaties and agreements that had expired would be replaced by new ones, while those that had not yet expired would be annulled and renegotiated according to accepted legal procedure. Subsequently, the US, Germany, Norway, Belgium, Italy, Great Britain, France, and Japan entered into new customs agreements with China, recognized China's tariff autonomy and agreed in principle to give up their consular jurisdictions.

5. The government issued a number of rules and regulations concerning foreign-trade matters: for example, *shangren yunhuo chukou ji xiaoshou waihui banfa* (Regulations on exports by merchants and foreign exchange

sales) in 1938 and *shougou chukou wuzi banfa* (Regulations on purchasing goods for export) in 1947.

6. This trend came to an abrupt halt when Japan invaded China in 1937.

7. Moser (1935, p. 45) estimated that China may have absorbed more money from abroad for missionary work than any other country in the world.

8. The Standard Oil Company of New York began to ship kerosene to China in the 1880s. Due to the company's particular efforts to promote distribution networks and employ locally oriented advertising, the company's product reached a consumer base which was wider than that for many other foreign goods. However, it was the innovative idea of selling kerosene, together with the free distribution or sale at a very low price of small tin lamps (the famous *Mei-foo* lamp), that created a real market for the kerosene. A rural survey in 1935 found that 54 per cent of all farming families regularly purchased kerosene. By 1910 Standard Oil was shipping 15 per cent of its total exports of kerosene to China. In 1929, US companies accounted for nearly 70 per cent of the kerosene market in China (cf. Feuerwerker, 1983, p. 196; Moser, 1935, pp. 18–19, 28).

3 The Dual Structure of the Economy

1. The crushing indemnity that China was required by the treaty to pay to Japan had a decisive impact on the subsequent development of Japan up to World War II. In particular, it helped finance Japan's heavy industries, especially the iron and steel industries, and enabled Japan to shift to the gold standard. The end of the war marked the beginning of the shift from China to Japan as the leading state in East Asia (cf. Hsu, 1990, pp. 341–5; So and Chiu, 1995, pp. 89–90).

2. The Shanghai Fachang machine factory, the first factory established with Chinese capital to use modern industrial equipment, such as lathes, was founded a quarter of a century later, in 1869. The Jichang filature, the second such Chinese factory, was established by an overseas merchant, Chen Qiyuan, in Nanhai, Guangdong Province (cf. Wang Fangzhong, 1993, p. 13).

3. According to a Chinese study (Yan *et al.*, 1955, cited in Wang Xiang, 1993, pp. 79–80), in 1936, before the Japanese invasion, foreign enterprises controlled the production of 97 per cent of China's pig iron, 83 per cent of its steel, 66 per cent of its machine-operated coal mining, 55 per cent of its electricity, and 90 per cent of its rail transportation. For the situation in 1933, see Xu and Wu, 1993, p. 50.

4. One argument is that the foreign economic sector was the catalyst for the development of modern industry. According to this view, the foreign involvement in China's economy unintentionally fulfilled the historic mission of breaking the highly stable 'equilibrium trap' in the country (see, among others, Dernberger, 1975; Elvin, 1973; Hou, 1965; Murphey, 1977). An opposing argument points out that, while the foreign economic presence stimulated China's capitalist development, it did not foster economic development, but economic underdevelopment (see, among others, Mao,

1965; Zhang Youyi, 1957, Vol. 3; see also Frank, 1969, 1978, on other developing regions).

5.   Chinese-owned cotton mills, like other Chinese factories, were mostly workshops which were usually much smaller than the foreign-owned facilities. In the early 1930s, about 90 per cent of the factories were Chinese-owned, but they accounted for less than 70 per cent of the value of total output and employment and less than 40 per cent of the industrial capital in the country (Dernberger, 1975, p. 41).

6.   This was reflected in the view of some observers of China at the time that, 'the most severe competition in the Chinese market of the future will not be that encountered by Western nations with each other, but the competition encountered by all of them with articles made in China by Chinese' (Moser, 1935, p. 43).

4   Falling Behind: The Lessons

1.   For instance, Jardine Matheon, an old British company, first engaged in opium smuggling and then expanded into diverse financial, real estate and manufacturing activities.

2.   For a summary of the debate among Chinese and foreign scholars, see Wu, 1988.

3.   As Paul Kennedy (1988, p. 4) has expressed it: 'Of all the civilizations of pre-modern times, none appeared more advanced, none felt more superior, than that of China.' (See also Frank, 1998).

4.   The GDP figures for Japan have not been included in the Asian average (see Maddison, 1989, p. 19).

5.   It has also been argued that, unlike China, Japan was successful because the Japanese people had the capacity to act as a nation with the same degree of patriotic mobilization that nationalism called forth among Western people. In China before 1911, given the minority rule of the Manchu over the majority Han people, the Qing government could not afford to try to mobilize China on the basis of nationalism. The Qing government itself might have been the first target of the aroused nationalistic spirit. In comparison to the maintenance of their own safety, the goal of industrialization was of secondary importance for the ruling class.

6.   However, with respect to the production and trade of silk, the two were rivals on the world market (cf. Moulder, 1977; So, 1981, 1986).

7.   The challenger was the US, which became the new leader of the world system after World War II. As Table 4.3 shows, the US was a 'heavy protectionist' while on the way to succeed the UK.

8.   It contained three main points: (1) Within its sphere of interest or leasehold in China, a power would agree not to interfere with any treaty ports or the vested interests of other powers. (2) Within its sphere of interest or influence, no power would discriminate against nationals of other countries in matters of harbour dues or railway charges. (3) Within each sphere of foreign influence, the Chinese treaty tariff should apply and the Chinese government be allowed to collect customs duties. (Cf. Hsu, 1990, pp. 344–50.)

5 The Formation of a Strategy for Catching Up

1. A fuller text is as follows: 'Apart from their other characteristics, China's 600 million people have two remarkable peculiarities; they are, first of all, poor, and, secondly, blank. That may seem like a bad thing, but it is really a good thing. Poor people want change, want to do things, want revolution. A clean sheet of paper has no blotches, and so the newest and most beautiful words can be written on it, the newest and most beautiful pictures can be painted on it' (cited in Meisner, 1977, p. 213; for an English translation, see *Peking Review*, 10 June 1958).

2. In discussing the cause of the defeat of the GMD regime, Fairbank and Reischauer (1984, p. 481) have pointed out that, 'The Nationalist debacle in 1947–1949 was a failure less of arms than aims. Chiang's forces had superior arms but no capacity for economic revival, no programme for popular mobilization, no new vision of China's future.'

3. The GMD government had long been financially bankrupt. Its reckless issuing of banknotes, coupled with the collapse of the regime, had caused hyperinflation. In only nine months, from May 1949 to February 1950, prices in Shanghai had risen by a factor of 70. The anti-inflation measures of the CCP government quickly and effectively brought order to financial markets (cf. Xu, 1982).

4. In 1996, asked to name the 'most significant event of the last 50 years in Asia', Allen S. Whiting, the former head of the East Asian Section of the Bureau of Intelligence and Research at the US State Department and deputy chief of mission at the US Consulate in Hong Kong, answered, 'the Chinese Revolution' (*Far Eastern Economic Review*, 1 February 1996, p. 34). The message was that, over and above the fact that China is the largest society in Asia, the Revolution had established a central government, which China had lacked from 1911 to 1949. In Whiting's words, 'By comparison, the Sino–Soviet split, and even the Vietnam War, was not as large an event in its historic implications.' This view is perhaps shared explicitly or implicitly by many and may become even more widely accepted as time passes.

5. The concept of 'delinking' in the sense in which it is used here is borrowed from Amin (1990).

6. The property of the Axis Powers had been confiscated by the GMD government after the end of World War II.

7. The total US rejection of the government led by the CCP was symbolized by a widely circulated but unproved story that, during the Bandung Conference in 1956, the US secretary of state refused in public to shake hands with the Chinese prime minister, Zhou Enlai.

8. As a translation of the Chinese term *zili gengsheng*, the English term 'self-reliance' is not accurate and can lead to misinterpretation. The Chinese term means rather 'regeneration or reconstruction through one's own efforts'. For the historical background and a detailed discussion, see Riskin, 1987, pp. 201–22.

9. Self-reliance implied the awareness that technology is not neutral either in terms of the social relationships involved in production, or in terms of lifestyles and consumption patterns. Priority was assigned to indigenous

innovation, while efforts were made to create a mix of modern technologies and adapted and improved traditional technologies that was known as 'walking on two legs'.

6 Industrialization

1. One of the most innovative experiments was the promotion of *Angang xianfa*, the Charter of the Anshan Iron and Steel Company. Approved by the central leadership, the Charter contained the following guiding principles for the management of a socialist enterprise: action according to political doctrine, the Party in a position of leadership, mass mobilization, the participation of cadres in production, the participation of workers in management, the redrafting of irrational or outdated regulations, cooperation among cadres, workers and technicians, and encouragement for technological innovation and revolution.

7 Trade and Trade Performance

1. As Meisner (1977, p. 75) has pointed out, the Korean War was but a pretext for the US to send a fleet to the Taiwan Straits. The fleet remained in the area even after the war had ended in July 1953. The military presence of the US in the Taiwan Straits, in fact, was an important step in the establishment by the US of a military cordon extending around China from Korea to Southeast Asia.
2. Sung (1994) has summarized the various patterns as follows: 1952–59, 'leaning to one side'; 1960–69, crisis, recovery and Cultural Revolution, and 1970–79, revival of economic growth with trade.
3. In the words of a leading China expert, the 'Dullesian cold war against Peking in the 1950s was fundamentally mistaken and unnecessary, based on an utter misconception of Chinese history and the Chinese revolution' (Fairbank, 1972, p. 37).
4. After Nixon's visit, China purchased two satellite earth-stations, 10 Boeing 707s, 40 spare jet engines, 20 tractors for towing aircraft, and large quantities of wheat, corn and cotton from the US.

8 Outcome: A Mixed Package

1. 'The Chinese famine of 1958–61', aptly commented by Drèze and Sen (1989), 'was closely linked with policy failures – first in the debacle of the Great Leap Forward, then in the delay in rectifying the harm done, and along with that in accentuating distributional inequalities through enhanced procurement and uneven sharing' (p. 211). They further pointed out that 'What was lacking when the famine threatened China was a political system of adversarial journalism and opposition' (p. 212).
2. Due to a large drop in production during the famine years, the state target of the Second Five-Year Plan (1958–62) went unmet. The annual growth rate of material output during this period was 0.6 per cent. Industrial out-

put grew at 3.8 per cent annually, and agricultural production fell by 3.8 per cent (see Teng, 1982, pp. 9–10).

3. Meisner (1977, p. 384) concludes that, 'China, long (and not long ago) among the most wretched and impoverished lands, today stands in the world as a powerful, independent and rapidly modernizing nation.'

9 A Different Game

1. Quoted in a 1984 article in *People's Daily*, cited in Deckers, 1994, p. 224.
2. Détente in the 1970s involved the acceptance by the West of the socialist world and of the principle of peaceful coexistence. This meant that the West did not wish to change the borders of China by military force and that it abandoned attempts to gain superiority in the arms race. This became possible largely due to the establishment of the concept of strategic nuclear balance. The USSR, which had been very far behind the US as a nuclear power in the early 1960s, had more or less reached nuclear parity with the US by the beginning of the 1970s.
3. The change in reform objectives can be illustrated by official descriptions of the reform programmes. These run from the 'planned economy utilizing the law of market exchange value' in 1978 to the 'planned economy supplemented by market regulations' during 1979–84, 'the planned commodity economy' in 1985–87, 'state regulation of the market and market regulation of enterprises' in 1988–89, the 'organic integration of the planned economy and market regulation' in 1989–91, and the 'socialist market economy' since 1992. See Fan, 1997.

10 Economic Restructuring

1. *Zhongguo xianzhen qiye nianjian* (*Chinese Township and Village Enterprise Yearbook*) 1993, pp. 272–4, cited in Ishikawa, 1997, p. 58.

11 The State

1. The Chinese state seems to be an anomaly not only because 'it survived "the mass extinction of Leninist regimes",' but also because it 'continues along the path of reform' (Goldstein, 1995, p. 1105). This difference has been noticed by many other students of transitional economies.
2. Also see Xu and Wu, 1993, pp. 603–39, on the massive expansion of the state in various economic sectors.
3. For discussions of the term 'corporatism', see Oi, 1992; Unger and Chan, 1995.
4. Goldstein has noticed that, in addition to the mounting revenue received by local governments through their management of a larger number of central-state-owned enterprises during the process of enterprise relocation, the extrabudgetary income of local governments has also swelled. From 1966 to 1977, the extrabudgetary funds administered by the counties grew from 14.5 per cent of the state budget to 35.6 per cent. 'In one county, this type of income rose 3,000 per cent during the Cultural Revolution to become "a major factor in local planning for the county's economic development"' (Goldstein, 1995, p. 1114).

12 The Overseas Chinese Capitalist Diaspora

1. The 'overseas Chinese capitalist diaspora', as used here, includes Taiwan, Hong Kong and Macao, which are all parts of China, but which, with the exception of Hong Kong, are separated from the mainland and are not under the jurisdiction of China's Communist government. Hong Kong was returned to China in July 1997 after 156 years of British rule, but it is now a 'special administrative region' with essentially the same economic and political system that it had under the British. Meanwhile, the concept of 'overseas Chinese' employed here does not correspond to nationality. It simply indicates ethnic Chinese living outside mainland China.

2. Thus, for instance, according to estimates from Hong Kong (Sung, 1994), of all the mainland's exports to Hong Kong in 1993 (which accounted for 54 per cent of China's total exports that year), only 6 per cent were retained in Hong Kong, while 94 per cent were re-exported to third countries. At the same time, 81 per cent of Hong Kong's total exports to mainland China were re-exported third-country goods, while only 19 per cent represented Hong Kong domestic production.

3. The investments in the mainland by Hong Kong include capital from foreign subsidiary companies incorporated in Hong Kong, as well as from subsidiaries in Hong Kong of mainland enterprises. Precise figures on the share of each source of investment are difficult to come by. (Personal communication to the author by K. Y. Tang, Hong Kong government economist, in Hong Kong in December 1994.)

4. For example, in 1992, the direct investment in China from Hong Kong and Macao was 70 per cent of the total foreign direct investment and from Taiwan, 9.5 per cent, while that from Japan was 6.4 per cent of the total, and from the US, 4.6 per cent (Ministry of Foreign Economic Relations and Trade, various years). Taiwan became the most rapidly growing source of foreign direct investment after the Taiwan authorities sanctioned indirect trade, investment and technical cooperation with the mainland in 1989.

5. Figures released by the customs of the People's Republic, reported in the *People's Daily* (overseas edition), 13 September 1997.

6. The population share of overseas Chinese and the share of private, nonland capital held by overseas Chinese in selected Southeast Asian countries are as follows (Backman, 1995, cited in *Far Eastern Economic Review*, 1995a).

	% of population	*% of private, non-land capital*
Malaysia	29	61
Thailand	10	81
Philippines	2	50
Indonesia	3.5	73

7. According to Ikeda (1994), the key institutions of the postwar Japanese accumulation structure are: 1. the corporate group system, 2. the multi-layered subcontracting system, 3. income-redistributive institutions, 4. emphasis on 'equal' educational opportunities and 'fairness' in school entrance examinations.

13   Catching Up?

1. For a discussion of economic indicators based on PPPs and market exchange rates, see Gulder and Schulze-Ghattas, 1993.
2. Thus, for instance, between 1985 and 1995, the average annual growth of real GNP per capita was 8.3 per cent in China, 3.2 per cent in India, 6 per cent in Indonesia, −0.8 per cent in Brazil, 0.1 per cent in Mexico, and −5.1 per cent in the USSR–Russian Federation, while it was 1.3 per cent in the US and between −0.2 per cent and 2.9 per cent in the 19 rich countries, with the exception of Ireland, where it was 5.2 per cent; in nearly half the rich countries, the rate was between 1 and 2 per cent (World Bank, 1997b, pp. 214–15).
3. Phrases like these sometimes oversimplify the message. Obviously, during the Maoist era, the government did not prefer poverty. Rather, the phrase signified simply that, as a matter of principle, the government objected to policies favouring economic growth at any price, particularly if they meant sacrificing equitable income distribution.

Conclusion

1. 'China's already large exports and even greater future export potential are the reasons that its trade system is being subjected to an unusually high degree of scrutiny in discussions of its participation in the GATT,' Lardy, an American expert on China's trade, has noted (1994, p. 28). 'It is likely that if China were an average-size, low-income developing country with modest exports to market economies, comparable to, say, Polish exports of just under $1 billion at the time of its accession in 1967, it would have been admitted to the GATT some years ago.' A similar point has been raised on the Chinese side: 'Can it really be argued that China's trading regime is less in conformity with the WTO than that of all its existing members?' (Zhu Xiaohua, 1995, p. 44).
2. The same source also reveals that Winston Lord, the then US assistant secretary of state for East Asian and Pacific affairs, said: 'We're not naive. We cannot predict what kind of power China will be in the twenty-first century. God forbid, we may have to turn, with others, to a policy of containment.'
3. In 1900, a joint military force supported by Great Britain, the US, Germany, France, Russia, Japan, Italy and Austria invaded China on the pretext of intervening against the Boxer Rebellion. The Qing government signed a treaty in September 1901. The insult to the country's sovereignty and the damage to its resources were immense. (For detailed accounts and further analysis of this event, see Cohen, 1997; Esherick, 1987; Hsu, 1990, pp. 387–407).

4. According to one estimate, the absolute size of the Chinese economy will not match that of the US economy before 2040, and, in per capita terms, China will not catch up to the US for another century and a half, even if it could sustain a per capita income growth rate at twice that of the US (Lardy, 1994, p. 107).

Bibliography

In China the family name is placed before the given name. This practice has been followed here, except in the case of authors who have become known by their 'Western' names (usually those who have lived in the West or in places where Western influence is relatively stronger, such as Hong Kong).

Abramovitz, Moses (1986). 'Catching Up, Forging Ahead and Falling Behind'. *Journal of Economic History*, XLVI, 386–405.

Abu-Lughod, Janet L. (1989). *Before European Hegemony: The World System, A.D. 1250–1350*. New York: Oxford University Press.

ADB (Asian Development Bank) (1994). *Asian Development Outlook, 1994*. Manila: Asian Development Bank.

ADB (Asian Development Bank) (1997). *Asian Development Outlook, 1997 and 1998*. New York: Oxford University Press.

Adshead, S. A. M. (1988). *China in World History*. London: Macmillan.

Allen, G. C. and A. G. Donnithorne (1954). *Western Enterprise in Far Eastern Economic Development*. London: Allen & Unwin.

Amin, Samir (1983). *The Future of Maoism*. New York: Monthly Review Press.

Amin, Samir (1990). *Delinking*. London: Zed.

Amsden, Alice H. (1989). *Asia's Next Giant: South Korea and Late Industrialization*. New York: Oxford University Press.

Amsden, Alice H. (1990). 'Third World Industrialization: "Global Fordism" or a New Model?' *New Left Review*, 182, 5–31.

Amsden, Alice H. (1994). 'Why Isn't the Whole World Experimenting with the East Asian Model to Develop?: Review of the East Asian Miracle'. *World Development*, 22/4, 627–33.

Appelbaum, R. P. and J. Henderson (eds) (1992). *States and Development in the Asian Pacific Rim*. Newbury Park, CA: Sage.

Ariff, M. (ed.) (1991). *The Pacific Economy: Growth and External Stability*. London: Allen & Unwin.

Arrighi, Giovanni (ed.) (1985). *Semiperipheral Development*. Beverly Hills: Sage.

Arrighi, Giovanni (1990). 'The Developmentalist Illusion: A Reconceptualization of the Semiperiphery'. In W. G. Martin (ed.), *Semiperipheral States in the World-Economy*. Westport, CT: Greenwood Press, 11–42.

Arrighi, Giovanni (1991). 'World Income Inequalities and the Future of Socialism'. *New Left Review*, 189, 39–64.

Arrighi, Giovanni (1994a). *The Long Twentieth Century: Money, Power and the Origins of Our Times*. London: Verso.

Arrighi, Giovanni (1994b). *The Rise of East Asia: World-System and Regional Aspects*. Binghamton, NY: Fernand Braudel Centre, SUNY-Binghamton.

Arrighi, Giovanni and J. Drangel (1986). 'The Stratification of the World-Economy: An Exploration of the Semiperipheral Zone'. *Review*, 10/1, 9–74.

Arrighi, Giovanni, S. Ikeda and A. Irwan (1993). 'The Rise of East Asia: One Miracle or Many?' In Ravi A. Palat (ed.), *Pacific Asia and the Future of the World System*. Westport, CT: Greenwood, 41–65.

Atwell, W. S. (1982). 'International Bullion Flows and the Chinese Economy'. *Past & Present*, 95, 68–90.

Bairoch, Paul (1982). 'International Industrialization Levels from 1750 to 1980'. *Journal of European Economic History*, 11, 2, 269–333.

Banister, T. Roger (1931). *A History of the External Trade of China, 1834–1881*. Shanghai: Inspector General of Chinese Customs.

Barnett, A. Doak (1963). *China on the Eve of Communist Takeover*. New York: Praeger.

Barnett, A. Doak (1981). *China's Economy in Global Perspective*. Washington, DC: The Brookings Institute.

Baum, Julian (1990). 'The Mainland Dilemma'. *Far Eastern Economic Review*, 18 October, 29–36.

Becker, David (1983). *The New Bourgeoisie and the Limits of Dependency*. Princeton, NJ: Princeton University Press.

Bello, Walden, and S. Rosenfeld (1990). *Dragons in Distress: Asia's Miracle Economies in Crisis*. San Francisco: Institute for Food and Development Policy.

Bialer, Seweryn (1980). *Stalin's Successors: Leadership, Stability and Change in the Soviet Union*. Cambridge: Cambridge University Press.

Bianco, Lucien (1971). *Origins of Chinese Revolution, 1915–1949*. Stanford, CA: Stanford University Press.

Blecher, Marc (1986). *China: Politics, Economics and Society*. Boulder, CO: Lynne Rienner.

Boltho, Andrea, Uri Dadush, Dong He and Shigeru Otsubo (1994). 'China's Emergence, Prospects, Opportunities, and Challenges'. *World Bank Policy Research Working Papers*, No. 1339.

Borthwick, Mark (ed.) (1992). *Pacific Century: The Emergence of Modern Pacific Asia*. Boulder, CO: Westview Press.

Brown, Shanno (1979). 'The Ewo Filature: A Study in the Transfer of Technology to China in the Nineteenth Century'. *Technology and Culture*, 20, 550–68.

Brugger, Bill (1981). *China: Radicalism to Revisionism, 1962–1979*. London: Croom Helm.

Brugger, Bill and Stephen Reglar (1994). *Politics, Economy and Society in Contemporary China*. London: Macmillan.

Buchnall, K. (1989). *China and the Open Door Policy*. London: Allen & Unwin.

Business Week (1994). 'World Trade: Will China Agree to Pay its Dues?' 26 December, 25.

Chace, James (1994). 'The World Elsewhere'. *World Policy Journal*, 11/1, 125–6.

Chan, Albert (1982). *The Glory and Fall of the Ming Dynasty*. Norman, OK: University of Oklahoma Press.

Chao, Kang (1975). 'The Growth of a Modern Cotton Textile Industry and the Competition with Handicrafts'. In Dwight H. Perkins (ed.), *China's Modern Economy in Historical Perspective*. Stanford, CA: Stanford University Press, 167–201.

Chase-Dunn, C. (ed.) (1982). *Socialist States in the World-System*. Beverly Hills: Sage.

Chase-Dunn, C. (1983). 'Socialist State Policy in the Capitalist World-Economy'. In Pat McGowan and C. W. Kegley (eds), *Foreign Policy and the Modern World-System*. Beverly Hills: Sage.

Chase-Dunn, C. (1990). *Global Formation: Structure of the World-Economy*. Oxford: Blackwell.

Cheek-Milby, Kathleen and M. Mushkat (1989). *Hong Kong: The Challenge of Transformation*. Hong Kong: Centre of Asian Studies, University of Hong Kong.

Chen Biao (1986). 'Yangwu yundong yu shijie jindai gongyehua chaoliu' ('The Westernization Movement and the Trend of Industrialization in the Modern World'). *Shixue yuekan* (*Historiography Monthly*), 4: 51–7. [In Chinese.]

Chen, Edward K. Y. (1979). *Hyper-growth in Asian Economies: A Comparative Study of Hong Kong, Japan, Korea, Singapore and Taiwan*. New York: Holmes & Meier Publishers.

Chen, Edward K. Y. (1980). 'The Economic Setting'. In D. Lethbridge (ed.), *The Business Environment in Hong Kong*. Hong Kong: Oxford University Press, 1–50.

Chen, Edward K. Y. (1985). 'The Newly Industrialized Countries in Asia: Growth, Experience and Prospects'. In R. Scalapino *et al.* (eds), *Asian Development: Present and Future*. Berkeley, CA: Institute of East Asian Studies, University of California.

Chen, Edward K. Y. (1989). 'The Changing Role of the Asian NICs in the Asian-Pacific Region towards the Year 2002'. In Miyohei Shinohara and Fu-chen Lo (eds), *Global Adjustment and the Future of Asian-Pacific Economy*. Tokyo: Institute of Developing Economies, 207–31.

Chen, Edward K. Y. (1992). 'Changing Pattern of Financial Flows in the Asia-Pacific Region and Policy Responses'. *Asian Development Review*, 10/2, 46–85.

Chen Han-seng (1936). *Landlord and Peasant in China*. New York: International Publishers.

Chen Shijun (1984). 'Lun yapian zhanzheng qian de maiban he jindai maiban zichan jieji de chansheng' ('On the Compradors before the Opium War and the Origin of the Modern Comprador Bourgeoisie'). In Ning Jing (ed.) *Yapian zhanzheng shi lunwen zhuanji xubian*. (*The Sequel of Selected Works on the History of the Opium War*). Beijing: Renmin chubanshe (People's Publishing House). [In Chinese.]

Chen Xiangming (1993). 'China's Growing Integration with the Asia-Pacific Economy: Subregional and Local Dimensions, Determinants and Consequences'. In Arif Dirlik (ed.), *What is in a Rim?: Critical Perspectives on the Pacific Region Idea*. Boulder, CO: Westview Press.

Chen Xiangming (1994). 'The New Spatial Division of Labour and Commodity Chains in the Greater South China Economic Region'. In Gary Gereffi and Miguel Korzeniewicz (eds), *Commodity Chains and Global Capitalism*. Westport, CT: Praeger, 165–86.

Cheng, J. (ed.) (1989). *China: Modernization in the 1980s*. Hong Kong: Chinese University Press.

Chesneaux, Jean (1976). *China from the Opium War to the 1911 Revolution*. New York: Pantheon Books.

Chiu, T. N. (1973). *The Port of Hong Kong: A Survey of its Development*. Hong Kong: Hong Kong University Press.

Cohen, Paul A. (1963). *China and Christianity*. Cambridge, MA: Harvard University Press.

Cohen, Paul A. (1970). 'Ching China: Confrontation with the West, 1850–1900'. In James B. Crowley (ed.), *Modern East Asia*. New York: Harcourt.

Cohen, Paul A. (1997). *History in Three Keys: The Boxers as Event, Experience and Myth*. New York: Columbia University Press.

Copper, John F. (1980). *China's Global Role: An Analysis of Peking's National Power Capabilities in the Context of an Evolving International System*. Stanford, CA: Hoover Institute Press.

Crisswell, Colin N. (1991). *The Taipans: Hong Kong's Merchant Princes*. Hong Kong: Oxford University Press.

Crowley, James B. (ed.) (1970). *Modern East Asia*. New York: Harcourt.

Cuchman, Jennifer W. (1993). 'Fields from the Sea: Chinese Junk Trade with Siam during the Late Eighteenth and Early Nineteenth Centuries'. *Studies on Southeast Asia*. Ithaca, NY: Southeast Asia Programme, Cornell University.

Cumings, Bruce (1979). 'The Political Economy of Chinese Foreign Policy'. *Modern China*, 5/4, 411–61.

Cumings, Bruce (1984). 'The Political Economy of China's Turn Outward'. In Samuel S. Kim (ed.) *China and the World: New Directions in Chinese Relations*. Boulder, CO: Westview Press, 203–36.

Cumings, Bruce (1987). 'The Origins and Development of the Northeast Asian Political Economy: Industrial Sectors, Product Cycles and Political Consequences'. In Frederic C. Deyo (ed.), *The Political Economy of New Asian Industrialism*. Ithaca, NY: Cornell University Press, 44–83.

Cumings, Bruce (1993). 'Pacific-Asia and the Future of the World-System'. In Ravi A. Palat (ed.), *Pacific Asia and the Future of the World-System*. Westport, CT: Greenwood.

Dale, Reginald (1994). 'The West Must Stay Firm with China'. *International Herald Tribune*, 18 November, 13.

Dawson, Raymond S. (1976). *Imperial China*. London: Hutchinson.

de Vries, Jan (1976). *Economy of Europe in an Age of Crisis, 1600–1750*. Cambridge: Cambridge University Press.

Deckers, Wolfgang (1994). 'Mao Zedong and Friedrich List on De-Linking'. *Journal of Contemporary Asia*, 24/2, 217–26.

Deng Xiaoping (1993). *Deng Xiaoping wenxuan (Selected Works of Deng Xiaoping)*, Vol. 3. Beijing: Renmin chubanshe (People's Publishing House). [In Chinese.]

Dernberger, Robert F. (1975). 'The Role of the Foreigner in China's Economic Development, 1840–1949'. In Dwight H. Perkins (ed.), *China's Modern Economy in Historical Perspective*. Stanford, CA: Stanford University Press.

Dernberger, Robert F. (1980). *China's Development Experience in Comparative Perspective*. Cambridge, MA: Harvard University Press.

Dernberger, Robert F. (1986). 'Economic Policy and Performance'. In Joint Economic Committee, Congress of the United States. 1986. *China's Economy Looks Towards the Year 2000*. Washington, DC: US Government Printing Office.

Deyo, Frederic C. (ed.) (1987). *The Political Economy of New Asian Industrialism*. Ithaca, NY: Cornell University Press.

Deyo, Frederic C. (1989). *Beneath the Miracle: Labour Subordination in the New Asian Industrialism*. Berkeley, CA: University of California Press.

Dirlik, Arif (ed.) (1993). *What is in a Rim?: Critical Perspectives on the Pacific Region Idea*. Boulder, CO: Westview Press.

Dittmer, Lowell (1987). *China's Continuous Revolution: The Post-liberation Epoch, 1949–1987*. Berkeley, CA: University of California Press.

Dittmer, Lowell, and Samuel S. Kim (eds) (1993). *China's Quest for National Identity*. Ithaca, NY: Cornell University Press.

Dixon, Chris (1991). 'South East Asia in the World-Economy'. *Geography of the World-Economy Series*. Cambridge: Cambridge University Press.

Dodge, E. S. (1976). *Islands and Empires: The Western Impact on the Pacific and East Asia*. Minneapolis, MN: University of Minnesota Press.

Dong Fureng (1982). 'The Relationship between Accumulation and Consumption'. In Xu Dixin *et al. China's Search for Economic Growth: The Chinese Economy Since 1949*. Beijing: New World Press, 79–101.

Drakakis-Smith, D. (1992). *Pacific Asia*. London: Routledge.

Drèze, Jean and Amartya Sen (1989). *Hunger and Public Action*. Oxford: Clarendon Press.

Drucker, Peter (1989). 'The Futures That Have Already Happened'. *The Economist*, 21–27 October, 19–24.

Du Xuncheng (1991). 'Beiyang shiqi zhongguo xinshi yinhang zai duiwai maoyi zhong de zuoyong' ('The Role of Chinese Modern Banks in Foreign Trade during the Period of the Northern Warlords'). *Lishi Yanjiu* (*Journal of History*), 3: 120–33. [In Chinese.]

Duara, Prasenjit (1988). *Culture, Power and the State: Rural North China, 1900–1942*. Stanford, CA: Stanford University Press.

Eckstein, Alexander (1977). *China's Economic Revolution*. Cambridge: Cambridge University Press.

Economic Research Centre, State Planning Commission (*Guojia jiwei jingji yanjiu zhongxin keti zu*) (1994). 'Wo guo liyong waiguo zhijie touzi wenti de yanjiu baogao' ('*Survey Report of the Utilization of FDI in China*'). *Jingji yanjiu cankao* (*Economic Research References*), Nos 156–7. [In Chinese.]

The Economist (1991). 'Asia: As Close as Teeth and Lips'. 10 August, 21–2.

The Economist (1992). 'Taiwan: China's Snare'. 4 January, 30–1.

The Economist (1995). 'Containing China'. 29 July, 13.

The Economist (1995–96). 'The Overseas Chinese: Inheriting the Bamboo Network'. 23 December 1995–5 January 1996, 85.

The Economist (1997). 'China's State-owned Enterprises: Beijing Rules'. 3 May, 64–5.

Elvin, Mark (1973). *The Pattern of the Chinese Past*. Stanford, CA: Stanford University Press.

Elvin, Mark and G. W. Skinner (eds) (1974). *The Chinese City Between Two Worlds*. Stanford, CA: Stanford University Press.

Eng, Robert Y. (1986). *Economic Imperialism in China: Silk Production and Exports, 1861–1932*. Berkeley, CA: Institute of East Asian Studies, University of California.

Engels, Friedrich (1972). 'Persia and China'. In Karl Marx and Friedrich Engels (eds), *On Colonialism*. New York: International Publishers.

Esherick, Joseph (1987). *Origins of the Boxer Uprising*. Berkeley, CA: University of California Press.

Fairbank, John King (1953). *Trade and Diplomacy on the China Coast: The Opening of the Treaty Ports, 1842–1854*. Cambridge, MA: Harvard University Press.

Fairbank, John King (1967). *China: The People's Middle Kingdom and the USA*. Cambridge, MA: Harvard University Press.

Fairbank, John King (1968). *The Chinese World Order: Traditional China's Foreign Relations*. Cambridge: Cambridge University Press.

Fairbank, John King (1972). 'The New China and American Connection'. *Foreign Affairs*, October, 37.

Fairbank, John King (ed.) (1978). *The Cambridge History of China, X: Late Ch'ing, 1800–1911, Part 1*. Cambridge: Cambridge University Press.

Fairbank, John King (ed.) (1983). *The Cambridge History of China, XII: Republican China, 1912–1949, Part I*. Cambridge: Cambridge University Press.

Fairbank, John King (1986). *The Great Chinese Revolution, 1800–1985*. New York: Harper & Row.

Fairbank, John King and Albert Feuerwerker (eds) (1986). *The Cambridge History of China, XIII: Republican China, 1912–1949, Part 2*. Cambridge: Cambridge University Press.

Fairbank, John King and Kwang-ching Liu (eds) (1980). *The Cambridge History of China, XI: Late Ch'ing, 1800–1911, Part 2*. Cambridge: Cambridge University Press.

Fairbank, John King and Edwin O. Reischauer (1984). *China: Tradition and Transformation*. Sydney: George Allen & Unwin.

Fairbank, John King, Edwin O. Reischauer and Albert M. Craig (1965). *East Asia: The Modern Transformation*. Boston: Houghton Mifflin.

Fan Gang (1997). *Growing into the Market: China's Economic Transition*. Helsinki: UNU/WIDER.

Far Eastern Economic Review (1995a). 'Work Hard, Make Money: Australians Ponder the Success of Overseas Chinese'. 31 August, 61.

Far Eastern Economic Review (1995b). 'Great Leap Southward'. 23 November, 60–2.

Fei, Hsia-tung (1980). *Peasant Life in China: A Field Study of Country Life in the Yangtze Valley*. London: Routledge & Kegan Paul.

Fei, Hsia-tung (1989). *Rural Development in China: Prospect and Retrospect*. Chicago: University of Chicago Press.

Feuchtwang, S., A. Hussain and T. Pairault (eds) (1988). *Transforming China's Economy in the Eighties*, Vol. 1: *The Rural Sector, Welfare and Employment*. Boulder, CO: Westview Press.

Feuerwerker, Albert (1958). *China's Early Industrialization: Sheng Hsuan-huai (1844–1916) and Mandarin Enterprise*. Cambridge, MA: Harvard University Press.

Feuerwerker, Albert (1968a). 'The Chinese Economy, 1912–1949'. *Michigan Papers in Chinese Studies*, No. 1. Ann Arbor, MI: Centre for Chinese Studies, University of Michigan.

Feuerwerker, Albert (ed.) (1968b). *History in Communist China*. Cambridge, MA: MIT Press.

Feuerwerker, Albert (1969). 'The Chinese Economy, ca. 1870–1911'. *Michigan Papers in Chinese Studies*, No. 5. Ann Arbor, MI: Centre for Chinese Studies, University of Michigan.

Feuerwerker, Albert (1970). 'Handicraft and Manufactured Cotton Textiles in China, 1871–1910'. *Journal of Economic History*, 30/2, 371–8.

Feuerwerker, Albert (1976). 'The Foreign Establishment in China in the Early Twentieth Century'. *Michigan Papers in Chinese Studies*, No. 29. Ann Arbor, MI: Centre for Chinese Studies, University of Michigan.

Feuerwerker, Albert (1977). 'Economic Trends in the Republic of China, 1912–1949'. *Michigan Papers in Chinese Studies*, No. 31. Ann Arbor, MI: Centre for Chinese Studies, University of Michigan.

Feuerwerker, Albert (1980). 'Economic Trends in the Late Ch'ing Empire, 1870–1911'. In John King Fairbank and Kwang-ching Liu (eds), *The Cambridge History of China, XI: Late Ch'ing, 1800–1911, Part 2*. Cambridge: Cambridge University Press, 1–69.

Feuerwerker, Albert (1983). 'The Foreign Presence in China'. In John King Fairbank (ed.), *The Cambridge History of China, XII: Republican China, 1912–1949*. Cambridge: Cambridge University Press, 128–207.

Financial Times (1995). 'Chinese Investors Underpin Success in East Asia'. 16 August, 10.

Findlay, Christopher (1992). *Challenges of Economic Reform and Industrial Growth: China's Wool War*. Sydney: Allen & Unwin.

Foot, Rosemary (1995). *The Practice of Power: US Relations with China since 1949*. Oxford: Clarendon Press.

Frank, Andre Gunder (1969). *Capitalism and Underdevelopment in Latin America*. New York: Monthly Review Press.

Frank, Andre Gunder (1978). *Dependent Accumulation and Underdevelopment*. New York: Monthly Review Press.

Frank, Andre Gunder (1994). 'The World Economic System in Asia before European Hegemony'. *The Historian*, 56/4, 259–76.

Frank, Andre Gunder (1998) *ReOrient: Global Economy in the Asian Age*. Berkeley, CA: University of California Press.

Friedland, Jonathan (1994). 'The Regional Challenge'. *Far Eastern Economic Review*, 9 June, 40–2.

Galtung, Johan (1981). 'The Politics of Self-Reliance'. In Heraldo Munoz (ed.), *From Dependency to Development*. Boulder, CO: Westview Press.

Garten, Jeffrey E. (1996). 'How to Accompany the Rise of a Mighty China'. *International Herald Tribune*, 16 January, 8.

Gasster, Michael (1971). *China's Struggle to Modernize*. New York: Cop.

Gereffi, Gary (1989). 'Rethinking Development Theory: Insights from East Asia and Latin America'. *Sociological Forum*, IV/4, 505–33.

Gereffi, Gary and Miguel Korzeniewicz (eds) (1994). *Commodity Chains and Global Capitalism*. Westport, CT: Praeger.

Gereffi, Gary and Donald L. Wyman (eds) (1991). *Manufacturing Miracles: Paths of Industrialization in Latin America and East Asia*. Princeton, NJ: Princeton University Press.

Gergere, Marie-Claire (1989). *The Golden Age of the Chinese Bourgeoisie*. New York: Cambridge University Press.

Gibney, F. (1992). *The Pacific Century: America and Asia in a Changing World*. New York: Charles Scribner's Sons.

Gibson, James R. (1992). *Otter Skins, Boston Ships and China Goods: The Maritime Fur Trade of the Northwest Coast, 1785–1841*. Seattle: University of Washington Press.

Gittings, John (1990). *China Changes Face: The Road from Revolution, 1949–1989*. Oxford: Oxford University Press.

Godley, M. R. (1981). *The Mandarin-Capitalists from Nanyang: Overseas Chinese Enterprise in the Modernization of China, 1893–1911*. Cambridge: Cambridge University Press.

Goldberg, Michael A. (1985). *The Chinese Connection*. Vancouver: University of British Columbia Press.

Goldstein, Steven M. (1995). 'China in Transition: The Political Foundations of Incremental Reform'. *China Quarterly*, 144, 1105–31.

Granovetter, Mark (1985). 'Economic Action and Social Structure: The Problem of Embeddedness'. *American Journal of Sociology*, 91, 481–510.

Gray, J. (1973). 'The Two Roads: Alternative Strategies of Social Change and Economic Growth in China'. In Stuart Schram (ed.), *Authority, Participation and Cultural Change in China*. Cambridge: Cambridge University Press, 191–229.

Greenberg, Michael (1969). *British Trade and the Opening of China, 1800–42*. Cambridge: Cambridge University Press.

Greenhalgh, Susan (1984). 'Networks and their Nodes: Urban Society on Taiwan'. *China Quarterly*, 99, 529–52.

Griffin, Keith and Zhao Renwei (eds) (1993). *The Distribution of Income in China*. London: Macmillan.

Gulder, Anne Marie and Marianne Schulze-Ghattas (1993). 'Purchasing Power Parity Based Weights for the World Economic Outlook'. *IMF Staff Studies for the World Economic Outlook*: 106–23.

Haggard, S. (1990). *Pathways from the Periphery: The Politics of Growth in the Newly Industrializing Countries*. Ithaca, NY: Cornell University Press.

Hahn, Emily (1963). *China Only Yesterday, 1850–1950*. Garden City, NJ: Doubleday.

Halliday, Fred (1988). 'Self-Reliance in the 1980s'. *Monthly Review*, February, 47–55.

Halliday, Jon (1975). *A Political History of Japanese Capitalism*. New York: Pantheon Books.

Hamashita, Takeshi (1984). 'International Financial Relations behind the 1911 Revolution: The Fall in the Value of Silver and Reform of the Monetary System'. In Eto Shinkichi and Harold Z. Scheffrin (eds) (1984). *The 1911 Revolution in China*. Tokyo: University of Tokyo Press.

Hamashita, Takeshi (1988). 'The Tribute Trade System and Modern Asia'. *The Memoirs of the Toyo Bunko*, 46.

Hamashita, Takeshi (1993). 'Tribute and Emigration: Japan and the Chinese Administration of Foreign Affairs'. *Senri Ethnological Studies*, 25, 69–86.

Hamashita, Takeshi (1994). 'Japan and China in the 19th and 20th Centuries'. Paper presented at the workshop 'Japan in Asia'. Ithaca, NY: Cornell University. Mimeo.

Hannan, Kate (ed.) (1995). *China, Modernization and the Goal of Prosperity: Government Administration and Economic Policy in the Late 1980s*. Cambridge: Cambridge University Press.

Hao Yen-ping (1970). *The Comprador in Nineteenth Century China: Bridge between East and West*. Cambridge, MA: Harvard University Press.

Harding, Harry (ed.) (1984). *China's Foreign Relations in the 1980s*. New Haven, CT: Yale University Press.

Harding, Harry (1987). *China's Second Revolution: Reform after Mao*. Washington, DC: The Brookings Institute.

Harding, Harry (1993). 'The Concept of "Greater China": Themes, Variations and Reservations'. *China Quarterly*, 136: 660–86.

Harrison, John A. (1967). *China since 1800*. New York: Harcourt.

Hartland-Thunberg, P. (1990). *China, Hong Kong, Taiwan and the World Trading System*. New York: St. Martin's Press.

He Qinglian (1995). 'Jubian qian de shehui jingji jingguan' ('Social Conditions on the Eve of Great Changes'). In Xu Jilin and Chen Dakai (eds), *Zhongguo xiandaihua shi 1800–1949* (*History of Modernization in China, 1800–1949*). Shanghai: Shanghai Sanlian Shudian (Shanghai Sanlian Publishing House), 31–49. [In Chinese.]

Higgins, Roland (1992). 'The Tributary System'. In Mark Borthwick (ed.), *Pacific Century: The Emergence of Modern Pacific Asia*. Boulder, CO: Westview Press.

Hinton, William (1993). 'Can the Chinese Dragon Match Pearls with the Dragon God of the Sea?' *Monthly Review*, July–August, 87–104.

Hobsbawm, Eric J. (1990). *Nations and Nationalism since 1780: Programme, Myth, Reality*. New York: Cambridge University Press.

Hodder, Rupert (1993). *The Creation of Wealth in China*. London: Belhaven Press.

Hopkins, Terence K. and Immanuel Wallerstein (eds) (1982). *World-System Analysis: Theory and Methodology*. Beverly Hills: Sage.

Hopkins, Terence K. and Immanuel Wallerstein (1986). 'Commodity Chains in the World-Economy prior to 1800'. *Review*, 10, 157–70.

Hopkins, Terence K. and Immanuel Wallerstein (1987). 'Capitalism and the Incorporation of New Zones into the World-Economy'. *Review*, 10, 673–80.

Hou, Chi-ming (1965). *Foreign Investment and Economic Development in China, 1840–1937*. Cambridge, MA: Harvard University Press.

Howe, C. (ed.) (1981). *Shanghai: Revolution and Development of an Asian Metropolis*. Cambridge: Cambridge University Press.

Howell, Jude (1993). *China Opens its Doors: The Politics of Economic Transition*. Boulder, CO: Lynne Rienner.

Hsiao Kung-chuan (1967). *Rural China: Imperial Controls in the Nineteenth Century*. Seattle: University of Washington Press.

Hsu, Immanuel C. Y. (1980). 'Late Ch'ing Foreign Relations, 1866–1905'. In John King Fairbank and Kwang-ching Liu (eds), *The Cambridge History of China, XI: Late Ch'ing, 1800–1911, Part 2*. Cambridge: Cambridge University Press, 70–141.

Hsu, Immanuel C. Y. (1990). *The Rise of Modern China* (4th edition). New York: Oxford University Press.

Huang, Philip C. C. (1990). *The Peasant Family and Rural Development in the Yangtzi Delta, 1350–1988*. Stanford, CA: Stanford University Press.

Huang Yasheng (1995). 'Administrative Monitoring in China'. *China Quarterly*, 143, 828–43.

Huang Yifeng *et al.* (1982). *Jiu zhongguo de maiban zichan jieji* (*The Comprador Bourgeoisie in Old China*). Shanghai: Shanghai renmin chubanshe (Shanghai People's Publishing House). [In Chinese.]

Huang Yiping (1991). 'Guandu shangban he Zhongguo zibenzhuyi' ('Private Enterprises under Government Supervision and Capitalism in China'). *Huadong shifan daxue xuebao (Journal of East China Normal University)*, 2, 44–50. [In Chinese.]

Hui Po-keung (1995). 'Overseas Chinese Business Networks: East Asian Economic Development in Historical Perspective'. Binghamton, NY: SUNY-Binghamton. PhD Dissertation.

Hunt, Michael H. (1983). *The Making of a Special Relationship: The United States and China to 1914*. New York: Columbia University Press.

Huntington, Samuel (1993). 'The Clash of Civilizations?' *Foreign Affairs*, 72/3, 22–49.

Hyde, Francis E. (1973). *Far Eastern Trade, 1860–1914*. London: Adam & Charles Black.

Ikeda, Satoshi (1994). 'Japanese Accumulation Structure and the Postwar World-System'. *Social Justice*, 21/2, 24–49.

Ikeda, Satoshi (1996). 'The History of the Capitalist World-System vs. the History of East-Southeast Asia'. *Review*, XIX, 1, 49–77.

IMF (International Monetary Fund) (1994). *World Economic Outlook*, October. Washington, DC: IMF.

International Herald Tribune (1995). 'A Resurgent China Sets off Alarms over "Containment"'. 7 July, 1.

International Herald Tribune (1996). 'Chinese Money Returns Home'. 4 January, 15.

Iriye, Akira (1986). 'Japanese Aggression and China's International Position, 1931–1941'. In John King Fairbank and Albert Feuerwerker (eds), *The Cambridge History of China, XIII: Republican China, 1912–1949, Part 2*. Cambridge: Cambridge University Press, 492–546.

Ishikawa, Shigeru (1997). 'China's "Open Door" and Internal Development in Perspective of the Twenty-First Century'. In Fumio Itoh (ed.), *China in the Twenty-First Century: Politics, Economy and Society*. Tokyo: UNU Press, 48–71.

Itoh, Fumio (ed.) (1997). *China in the Twenty-First Century: Politics, Economy and Society*. Tokyo: UNU Press.

Jacobson, Harold K. and Michel Oksenberg (1990). *China's Participation in the IMF, the World Bank and GATT: Towards a Global Economic Order*. Ann Arbor, MI: University of Michigan Press.

Jao, Y. C. and C. K. Leung (1986). *China's Special Economic Zones: Policies, Problems and Prospects*. Hong Kong: Oxford University Press.

Jie Fang Daily (1997). 'Xin pi duzi qiye shuliang da zeng, shouci chaoguo zhongwai hezi qiye' ('Increase in Authorizations for Foreign-funded Enterprises: Joint Ventures Surpassed'). 8 September.

Kao, John (1993). 'The Worldwide Web of Chinese Business'. *Harvard Business Review*, March–April, 24–34.

Kapur, Karish (1987). *The Awakening Giant: China's Ascension in World Politics*. Alphen, the Netherlands: Sijthoff & Noordhoff.

Kennedy, Paul (1988). *The Rise and Fall of the Great Powers: Economic Change and Military Conflict from 1500 to 2000*. London: Unwin Hyman.

Kim, Samuel S. (ed.) (1984). *China and the World: New Directions in Chinese Relations*. Boulder, CO: Westview Press.

Kleinberg, R. (1990). *China's Opening to the Outside World*. Boulder, CO: Westview Press.

Kraar, Louis (1992). 'A New China without Borders'. *Fortune*, 5 October, 124–8.

Kraus, Richard C. (1979). 'Withdrawal from the World-System: Self-Reliance and Class Structure in China'. In Walter L. Goldfrank (ed.), *The World-System of Capitalism*. Beverly Hills: Sage, 237–59.

Kueh, Y. Y. (1989). 'The Maoist Legacy and China's New Industrializing Strategy'. *China Quarterly*, 119: 420–47.

Kwon, Jene (1994). 'The East Asian Challenge to Neoclassical Orthodoxy'. *World Development*, 22/4: 635–44.

Lardy, Nicholas R. (1987). *China's Entry into the World Economy*. Lanham, MD: University Press of America.

Lardy, Nicholas R. (1992). *Foreign Trade and Economic Reform in China, 1978–1990*. New York: Cambridge University Press.

Lardy, Nicholas R. (1994). *China in the World Economy*. Washington, DC: Institute for International Economics.

Lasek, Elizabeth (1983). 'Imperialism in China: A Methodological Critique'. *Bulletin of Concerned Asian Scholars*, 15/1, 50–64.

Lee, Dinah (1991). 'Asia: The Next Era of Growth'. *Business Week*, 11 November: 56–9.

Leeming, Frank (1993). *The Changing Geography of China*. Oxford: Blackwell.

Li Kuo-ting (1995). *The Evolution of Policy behind Taiwan's Development Success* (2nd edn). Singapore: World Scientific Publishing Co.

Liang Wensen (1982). 'Balanced Development of Industry and Agriculture'. In Xu Dixin *et al.*, *China's Search for Economic Growth: The Chinese Economy since 1949*. Beijing: New World Press, 52–78.

Liao Kuang-sheng (1990). *Antiforeignism and Modernization in China*. Hong Kong: Chinese University Press.

Lieberthal, Kenneth (1995). *Governing China: From Revolution through Reform*. New York: W. W. Norton.

Limlingan, Victor S. (1986). *The Overseas Chinese in ASEAN: Business Strategies and Management Practices*. Manila: Vita Development Corporation.

Lin Yifu (1995). 'The Needham Puzzle: Why the Industrial Revolution did not Originate in China'. *Economic Development and Cultural Change*, 43/2, 269–92.

Lin Yifu, Cai Fang and Li Zhou (1994). *Zhongguo de qiji: fazhan zhanlue yu jingji gaige* (*The China Miracle: Development Strategy and Economic Reform*). Shanghai: Shanghai Sanlian Shudian. (Shanghai Sanlian Publishing House). [In Chinese.]

Linder, S. B. (1986). *The Pacific Century: Economic and Political Consequences of Asian-Pacific Dynamism*. Stanford, CA: Stanford University Press.

Liu Fuyuan (1990). *Gong nong ye shouru chayi* (*Income Differences between Industry and Agriculture*). Chongqing: Chongqing chubanshe (Chongqing Publishing House). [In Chinese.]

Liu Guoguang (ed.) (1988). *Zhongguo jingji tizhi gaige de moshi yanjiu* (*Models of China's Reforms of Economic Institutions*). Beijing: Zhongguo sheke she (China Social Science Press). [In Chinese.]

Luo Rongqu (1991). 'Zhongguo zaoqi xiandaihua de yanwu – yi xiang bijiao xiandaihua yanjiu' ('The Delay of China's Early Modernization: A Study of

Comparative Modernization'). *Jindaishi Yanjiu* (*Journal of Modern History*), 1, 28–49. [In Chinese.]

Ma Hong (1983). *New Strategy for China's Economy*. Beijing: New World Press.

Ma Hong and Sun Shangqing (eds) (1981). *Zhongguo jingji jiegou wenti yanjiu* (*Problems of Economic Structure in China*). Beijing: Renmin chubanshe (People's Publishing House). [In Chinese.]

Ma Jun and Zou Gan (1991). 'Lun woguo neilu bianjing shengqu de duiwai kaifang' ('Issues Surrounding the Opening of the Inland Frontier Provinces'). *Jingji yanjiu* (*Economic Research*), 3: 61–9. [In Chinese.]

Mabbett, Ian W. (1985). *Modern China: The Mirage of Modernity*. London: Croom Helm.

Maddison, Angus (1982). *Phases of Capitalist Development*. Oxford: Oxford University Press.

Maddison, Angus (1989). *The World Economy in the 20th Century*. Paris: Organization for Economic Cooperation and Development.

Maddison, Angus (1991). *Dynamic Forces in Capitalist Development*. Oxford: Oxford University Press.

Maddison, Angus (1995). 'Monitoring the World Economy, 1820–1992'. *OECD Development Centre Studies*. Paris: Organization for Economic Cooperation and Development.

Mann, Susan (1987). *Local Merchants and the Chinese Bureaucracy, 1750–1950*. Stanford, CA: Stanford University Press.

Mao Zedong (1965). 'The Chinese Revolution and the Chinese Communist Party'. In Mao Zedong, *Selected Works of Mao Tse-Tung* (Vol. II). Oxford: Pergamon Press, 305–34.

Mao Zedong (1967). 'On the People's Democratic Dictatorship'. In Mao Zedong, *Selected Works of Mao Tse-Tung* (Vol. IV). Peking: Foreign Language Press, 411–24.

Mao Zedong (1977). *A Critique of Soviet Economics*. New York: Monthly Review Press.

Maruya, Toyojiro (1992). 'The Development of the Guangdong Economy and its Ties with Beijing'. *China Newsletter* (Japan Export Trading Corporation), 96, 2–14.

Maxwell, Neville and B. McFarlane (eds) (1986). *China's Changed Road to Development*. Oxford: Pergamon.

McNeill, William H. (1982). *The Pursuit of Power: Technology, Armed Force and Society since A.D. 1000*. Chicago: University of Chicago Press.

Meisner, Maurice (1970). 'Yanan Communism and the Rise of the Chinese People's Republic'. In James B. Crowley (ed.), *Modern East Asia*. New York: Harcourt.

Meisner, Maurice (1977). *Mao's China: A History of the People's Republic*. New York: The Free Press.

Meisner, Maurice (1986). *Mao's China and After: A History of the People's Republic*. New York: The Free Press. [A new edition of Meisner, 1977]

Michael, Franz (1964). 'State and Society in Nineteenth Century China'. In Albert Feuerwerker (ed.), *Modern China*. Englewood Cliffs, NJ: Prentice-Hall.

Michael, Franz (1986). *China Through the Ages: History of a Civilization*. Boulder, CO: Westview Press.

Ministry of Foreign Economic Relations and Trade. (Various years). *Almanac of China's Foreign Relations and Trade*. Beijing: Zongguo jingji chubanshe (China Economics Publishing House).

Moise, Edwin E. (1987). *Modern China: A History*. London: Longman.

Montinola, Gabriella, Qian Yingyi and Barry R. Weingast (1995). 'Federalism, Chinese Style: The Political Basis for Economic Success in China'. *World Politics*, 48, 50–81.

Moore, Barrington Jr (1966). *Social Origins of Dictatorship and Democracy*. Boston: Beacon Press.

Moser, Charles K. (1935). 'Where China Buys and Sells'. *Trade Information Bulletin*, 827. Washington, DC: US Government Printing Office.

Moulder, Frances V. (1977). *Japan, China and the Modern World-Economy: Towards a Reinterpretation of East Asian Development, ca. 1600 to ca. 1918*. Cambridge: Cambridge University Press.

Mufson, Steven. (1995). 'China's Tax Woes Revealed in Budget'. *International Herald Tribune*, 4 March, 4.

Murphey, Rhoads (1977). *The Outsiders: The Western Experience in India and China*. Ann Arbor, MI: University of Michigan Press.

Myers, Ramon H. (1965). 'Cotton Textile Handicrafts and the Development of the Cotton Textile Industry in Modern China'. *Economic History Review*, 18/3, 614–32.

Nathan, Andrew (1990). *China's Crisis*. New York: Columbia University Press.

Naughton, Barry (1988). 'The Third Front: Defence Industrialization in the Chinese Interior'. *China Quarterly*, 115, 351–86.

Naughton, Barry (1996). *Growing out of the Plan: Chinese Economic Reform, 1978–1993*. Cambridge: Cambridge University Press.

Naughton, Barry (1997a). 'Economic Reform in China: Macroeconomic and Overall Performance'. In Doowon Lee (ed.), *The System Transformation of the Transition Economies: Europe, Asia and North Korea*. Seoul: Yonsei University Press, 27–64.

Naughton, Barry (ed.) (1997b). *The China Circle: Economics and Technology in the PRC, Taiwan and Hong Kong*. Washington, DC: Brookings Institution Press.

Nee, Victor and David Stark (eds) (1989). *Remaking the Economic Institutions of Socialism: China and Eastern Europe*. Stanford, CA: Stanford University Press.

Needham, Joseph (1981). *Science in Traditional China: A Comparative Perspective*. Hong Kong: Harvard University Press.

Newsweek (1994). 'Purr of the Tiger Cubs'. 28 November, 28.

Oi, Jean C. (1992). 'Fiscal Reform and the Economic Foundations of Local State Corporatism'. *World Politics*, 45/1, 99–126.

Oi, Jean C. (1995). 'The Role of the Local State in China's Transitional Economy'. *China Quarterly*, 144: 1132–49.

Oksenberg, Michel (1982). 'Economic Policy-making in China: Summer 1981'. *China Quarterly*, 90: 165–94.

Oksenberg, Michel and Bruce J. Dickson (1991). 'The Origins, Processes and Outcomes of Great Political Reform'. In Dankwart A. Rustow and Kenneth Pau Erickson (eds), *Comparative Political Dynamics: Global Research Perspectives*. New York: Harper and Row, 235–61.

Oksenberg, Michel and Steven M. Goldstein (1974). 'The Chinese Political Spectrum'. *Problems of Communism*, XXIII, 2, March–April.

Olson, Mancur (1982). *The Rise and Decline of Nations: Economic Growth, Stagflation and Social Rigidities*. New Haven, CT: Yale University Press.

Overholt, William H. (1993). *China: The Next Economic Superpower*. London: Weidenfeld and Nicolson.

Ozawa, Terutomo (1979). *Multinationalism, Japanese Style: The Political Economy of Outward Dependency*. Princeton, NJ: Princeton University Press.

Ozawa, Terutomo (1993). 'Foreign Direct Investment and Structural Transformation: Japan as a Recycler of Market and Industry'. *Business & the Contemporary World*, 5/2, 129–50.

Ozawa, Terutomo (1994). 'Exploring the Asian Economic Miracle: Politics, Economics, Society, Culture, and History, A Review Article'. *Journal of Asian Studies*, 53/1: 124–31.

Palat, Ravi A. (ed.) (1993). *Pacific Asia and the Future of the World System*. Westport, CT: Greenwood.

Parsh, William L. (ed.) (1985). *Chinese Rural Development: The Great Transformation*. Armonk, NY: M. E. Sharpe.

Parsonage, James (1992). 'Southeast Asia's "Growth Triangle": A Subregional Response to Global Transformation'. *International Journal of Urban and Regional Research*, 16, 307–17.

People's Daily (1997). 'Woguo liyong waizi tupo liang qian yi meiyuan' ('China's Utilized Foreign Direct Investment Exceeds $200 Billion'). 28 November (overseas edition), 1.

Perkins, Dwight H. (1966). *Market Control and Planning in Communist China*. Cambridge, MA: Harvard University Press.

Perkins, Dwight H. (1969). *Agricultural Development in China, 1368–1968*. Chicago: Aldine.

Perkins, Dwight H. (ed.) (1975). *China's Modern Economy in Historical Perspective*. Stanford, CA: Stanford University Press.

Perkins, Dwight. H. (1991). 'China's Industrial and Foreign Trade Reform'. In A. Koves and P. Marer (eds), *Foreign Economic Liberalization*. Boulder, CO: Westview Press, 269–82.

Perkins, Dwight H. (1997). 'History, Politics and the Sources of Economic Growth: China and the East Asian Way of Growth'. In Fumio Itoh (ed.), *China in the Twenty-First Century: Politics, Economy and Society*. Tokyo: UNU Press, 25–41.

Perry, Elizabeth J. and Christine Wong (eds) (1985). *The Political Economy of Reform in Post-Mao China*. Cambridge, MA: Council of East Asian Studies, Harvard University.

Pfeffer, Richard M. (1972). 'Serving the People and Continuing the Revolution'. *China Quarterly*, 52, 620–53.

Piore, Michael J. and Charles F. Sabel (1984). *The Second Industrial Divide: Possibilities for Prosperity*. New York: Basic Books.

Pollard, D. E. (1985). 'The Controversy Over Modernism'. *China Quarterly*, 104, 641–56.

Pomfret, R. (1991). *Investing in China: Ten Years of the Open Door Policy*. Ames, IA: Iowa State University Press.

Popov, Vladimir (1997). *Investment in Transition Economies: Factors of Change and Implications for Performance*. Helsinki: UNU/WIDER. Mimeo.

Rawlinson, John L. (1967). *China's Struggle for Naval Development, 1839–1895*. Cambridge, MA: Harvard University Press.

Rawski, Thomas G. (1978). 'China's Republican Economy: An Introduction'. *Discussion Papers*, No. 1. Toronto: University of Toronto.

Rawski, Thomas G. (1989). *Economic Growth in Prewar China*. Berkeley, CA: University of California Press.

Redding, S. G. (1991). *The Spirit of Chinese Capitalism*. Berlin and New York: Walter de Greuter.

Riedel, James (1991). 'Intra-Asian Trade and Foreign Direct Investment'. *Asian Development Review*, 9/1, 111–46.

Riskin, Carl (1987). *China's Political Economy: The Quest for Development since 1949*. London: Oxford University Press.

Rosenbaum, Arthur L. (ed.) (1992). *State and Society in China: The Consequences of Reform*. Boulder, CO: Westview Press.

Rossabi, Morris (ed.) (1983). *China among Equals: The Middle Kingdom and its Neighbors, 10th–14th Centuries*. Berkeley, CA: University of California Press.

Rozman, Gilbert (ed.) (1981). *The Modernization of China*. New York: The Free Press.

Rozman, Gilbert (1992). 'The Confucian Faces of Capitalism'. In Mark Borthwick (ed.), *Pacific Century: The Emergence of Modern Pacific Asia*. Boulder, CO: Westview Press.

Ryoshin, Minami (1994). *The Economic Development of China: A Comparison with the Japanese Experience*. London: Macmillan.

Saich, Tony (ed.) (1990). *The Chinese People's Movement: Perspectives on Spring 1989*. Armonk, NY: M. E. Sharpe.

Sarker, P. C. and A. P. Gaur (1994). 'Socio-economic and Human Development in South and East Asian Countries'. *Asia-Pacific Development Journal*, 1/2, 73–90.

Schram, Stuart (ed.) (1973). *Authority, Participation and Cultural Change in China*. Cambridge: Cambridge University Press.

Schurmann, Franz (1966). *Ideology and Organization in Communist China*. Berkeley, CA: University of California Press.

Scobell, Andrew (1988). 'Hong Kong's Influence on China'. *Asian Survey*, 28/6, 599–612.

See Chong-su (1919). *The Foreign Trade of China*. New York: Columbia University Press.

Segal, Gerald (1993). 'The Coming Confrontation between China and Japan?' *World Policy Journal*, 10/2, 27–32.

Selden, Mark (1971). *The Yanan Way in Revolutionary China*. Cambridge, MA: Harvard University Press.

Selden, Mark (ed.) (1979). *The People's Republic of China: A Documentary History of Revolutionary Change*. New York: Monthly Review Press.

Selden, Mark (1993). *The Political Economy of Chinese Development*. Armonk, NY: M. E. Sharpe.

Seligson, Mitchell A. and John T. Passé-Smit (eds) (1993). *Development and Underdevelopment: The Political Economy of Inequality*. Boulder, CO: Lynne Rienner.

Shambaugh, David (1993). 'Introduction: The Emergence of "Greater China"'. *China Quarterly*, 136, 653–9.

Shambaugh, David (ed.) (1995). *Greater China: The Next Superpower?* Oxford: Oxford University Press.

Sheridan, James E. (1975). *China in Disintegration: The Republican Era in Chinese History, 1912–1949*. New York: The Free Press.

Shinohara, Miyohei and Fu-chen Lo (eds) (1989). *Global Adjustment and the Future of Asian-Pacific Economy*. Tokyo: Institute of Developing Economies.

Shirk, Susan L. (1993). *The Political Logic of Economic Reform in China*. Berkeley, CA: University of California Press.

Skinner, G. W. (1964). 'Marketing and Social Structure in Rural China'. *Journal of Asian Studies*, 24, 3–43.

Skinner, G. W. (1985). 'The Structure of Chinese History'. *Journal of Asian Studies*, XLIV, 271–92.

Skocpol, Theda (1979). *States and Social Revolutions*. Cambridge: Cambridge University Press.

Smart, Josephine and A. Smart (1991). 'Personal Relations and Divergent Economies: A Case Study of Hong Kong Investment in South China'. *International Journal of Urban and Regional Research*, 15, 216–33.

So, Alvin Y. (1981). 'Development inside the Capitalist World-System: A Study of the Chinese and Japanese Silk Industry'. *Journal of Asian Culture*, 5, 33–56.

So, Alvin Y. (1984). 'The Process of Incorporation into the Capitalist World-System: The Case of China in the Nineteenth Century'. *Review*, VIII/1, 91–116.

So, Alvin Y. (1986). *The South China Silk District: Local Historical Transformation and World-System Theory*. Albany, NY: SUNY Press.

So, Alvin Y. (1988). 'Shenzhen Special Economic Zone: China's Struggle for Independent Development'. *Canadian Journal of Development Studies*, 9, 313–24.

So, Alvin Y. and Stephen W. K. Chiu (1995). *East Asia and the World-Economy*. Newbury Park, CA: Sage.

Solinger, Dorothy J. (ed.) (1984). *Three Visions of Chinese Socialism*. Boulder, CO: Westview Press.

Solinger, Dorothy J. (1993). *China's Transition from Socialism: Statist Legacies and Market Reforms, 1980–1990*. Armonk, NY: M. E. Sharpe.

Srinivasan, T. N. (ed.) (1994). *Agriculture and Trade in China and India: Policies and Performance since 1950*. San Francisco: ICS Press.

SSB (Office of Fixed Assets Investment, State Statistical Bureau) (1987). *Zhongguo guding zichan touzi tongji ziliao 1950–1985 (Statistical Data on China's Investments in Fixed Assets, 1950–1985)*. Beijing: Zhongguo tongji chubanshe (China Statistical Publishing House). [In Chinese.]

SSB (State Statistical Bureau) (1990). *Zhongguo tongji nianjian 1990. (China Statistical Yearbook, 1990)*. Beijing: Zhongguo tongji chubanshe (China Statistical Publishing House). [In Chinese.]

SSB (State Statistical Bureau) (1992). *Zhongguo tongji nianjian 1992. (China Statistical Yearbook, 1992)*. Beijing: Zhongguo tongji chubanshe (China Statistical Publishing House). [In Chinese.]

SSB (State Statistical Bureau) (1995). *Zhongguo tongji nianjian 1995. (China Statistical Yearbook, 1995)*. Beijing: Zhongguo tongji chubanshe (China Statistical Publishing House). [In Chinese.]

SSB (State Statistical Bureau) (1997). *Zhongguo tongji zhaiyao 1997 (A Statistical Survey of China, 1997)*. Beijing: Zhongguo tongji chubanshe (China Statistical Publishing House). [In Chinese.]

Steven, R. (1990). *Japan's New Imperialism*. London: Macmillan.

Sung Yun-wing (1991). *The China–Hong Kong Connection: The Key to China's Open-Door Policy*. Cambridge: Cambridge University Press.

Sung Yun-wing (1994). 'An Appraisal of China's Foreign Trade Policy, 1950–1992'. In T. N. Srinivasan (ed.), *Agriculture and Trade in China and India: Policies and Performance since 1950*. San Francisco: ICS Press, 109–53.

Taira, Kimiaki (1988). 'Hong Kong: Ever Entrepôt'. *China Newsletter*. Japan Export Trading Corporation, 77, 1.

Tang Wenqi and Lin Gang (1987). 'Shilun 1927–1937 nian Nanjing chengshi jingji fazhan yu nongcun fudi zhi guanxi' ('On the Relationship between Urban Economic Development in Nanjing and the Rural Hinterland during 1927–1937'). *Minguo dangan (Archives of the Republic of China)*. [In Chinese.]

Tawney, R. H. (1932). *Land and Labour in China*. London: Allen & Unwin.

Teng Weizao (1982). 'Socialist Modernization and the Pattern of Foreign Trade'. In Xu Dixin et al., *China's Search for Economic Growth: The Chinese Economy since 1949*. Beijing: New World Press, 167–92.

Teng Weizao et al. (eds) (1988). *Transnational Corporations and China's Open Door Policy*. Lexington, MA: Lexington Books.

Thomas, Stephen C. (1984). *Foreign Intervention and China's Industrial Development, 1870–1911*. Boulder, CO: Westview Press.

Tickner, J. Ann (1987). *Self-Reliance versus Power Politics*. New York: Columbia University Press.

Tsai, Jung-fang (1993). *Hong Kong in Chinese History: Community and Social Unrest in the British Colony, 1842–1913*. New York: Columbia University Press.

Tsao, James T. H. (1987). *China's Development Strategies and Foreign Trade*. Lexington, MA: Lexington Books.

Tuan, Francis C. (1990). 'Performance of China's Agricultural Trade in the 1980s'. *CPE Agriculture Reports*, March–April, 2–5.

UNCTAD (United Nations Conference on Trade and Development) (1997). *Trade and Development Report, 1997*. Geneva: UNCTAD.

UNDP (United Nations Development Programme) (1994). *Human Development Report, 1994*. New York: Oxford University Press.

Unger, Jonathan and Anita Chan (1995). 'Corporatism and the East Asian Model'. *Australian Journal of Chinese Affairs*, 33, 29–54.

United Nations (1993). *World Economic Survey, 1993*. New York: United Nations.

Van Ness, Peter and George Barney (1989). *Market Reform in Socialist Societies*. Boulder, CO: Lynne Rienner.

Viraphol, Sarasin (1977). *Tribute and Profit: Sino–Siamese Trade, 1652–1853*. Cambridge, MA: Council on East Asian Studies, Harvard University.

Vogel, Ezra (1989). *One Step Ahead in China: Guandong under Reform*. Cambridge, MA: Harvard University Press.

Wade, Robert (1990). *Governing the Market: Economic Theory and the Role of Government in East Asian Industrialization*. Princeton, NJ: Princeton University Press.

Wade, Robert (1992). 'East Asia's Economic Success: Conflicting Perspectives, Partial Insights, Shaky Evidence'. *World Politics*, XLIV, 2.

Wakeman, R. Jr (1966). *Strangers at the Gate: Social Disorder in South China, 1839–1861*. Berkeley, CA: University of California Press.

Wallerstein, Immanuel (1974). *The Modern World-System I: Capitalist Agriculture and the Origins of the European World-Economy in the Sixteenth Century*. New York: Academic Press.

Wallerstein, Immanuel (1979a). *The Capitalist World-Economy*. New York: Cambridge University Press.

Wallerstein, Immanuel (1979b). 'Dependence in an Interdependent World: The Limited Possibilities of Transformation within the Capitalist World-Economy'. In Immanuel Wallerstein, *The Capitalist World-Economy*. New York: Cambridge University Press, 66–94.

Wallerstein, Immanuel (1980). *The Modern World-System II: Mercantilism and the Consolidation of the European World-Economy, 1600–1750*. New York: Academic Press.

Wallerstein, Immanuel (1982). 'Socialist States: Mercantilist Strategies and Revolutionary Objectives'. In E. Friedman. (ed.), *Ascent and Decline in the World-System*. Beverly Hills: Sage, 289–300.

Wallerstein, Immanuel (1989). *The Modern World-System III: The Second Era of Great Expansion of the Capitalist World-Economy*. Cambridge: Cambridge University Press.

Wallerstein, Immanuel (1990). 'Antisystemic Movements: History and Dilemmas'. In Samir Amin *et al.* (eds), *Transforming the Revolution: Social Movements and the World-System*. New York: Monthly Review Press.

Wallerstein, Immanuel (1991a). *Geopolitics and Geoculture*. Cambridge: Polity Press.

Wallerstein, Immanuel. (1991b). 'The Cold War and Third World: The Good Old Days?'. *Economic and Political Weekly*, XXVI, 7.

Wallerstein, Immanuel (1992). 'The Concept of National Development, 1917–1989'. In G. Marks and L. Diamond (eds), *Reexamining Democracy: Essays in Honour of Seymour Martin Lipset*. Newbury Park, CA: Sage.

Wallerstein, Immanuel (1993). 'Foes as Friends'. *Foreign Policy*, 90, 145–57.

Wang Fangzhong (1982). *Zhongguo jindai jingji shigao* (*History of China's Modern Economy*). Beijing: Beijing chubanshe (Beijing Publishing House). [In Chinese.]

Wang Fangzhong (1993). *Zhongguo minzu zibenzhuyi de xingshuai* (*The Rise and Fall of National Capitalism in China*). Beijing: Gaodeng jiaoyu chubanshe (Higher Education Press). [In Chinese.]

Wang Gungwu (1993). 'Greater China and Chinese Overseas'. *China Quarterly*, 136, 926–48.

Wang Gungwu (1994). *Zhongguo yu haiwai huaren* (*China and the Chinese Overseas*). Hong Kong. Shangwu yinshuguan (Shangwu Printing House). [Chinese translation of a 1991 English-language publication.]

Wang Jingyu (1982). 'The Birth of the Chinese Bourgeoisie'. *Social Sciences in China*, 3, 1.

Wang Jingyu (1991). 'Qian yi jindai zhong wai jingji guanxi de pingjia wenti' ('On the Assessments of Modern Sino–Foreign Economic Relations'). *Jindai shi yanjiu (Journal of Modern History)*, 1, 1–27. [In Chinese.]

Wang Shaoguang and Hu Angang (1993). *Zhongguo guojia nengli baogao (A Report of State Capability of China)*. Shenyang: Liaoning renmin chubanshe (Liaoning People's Publishing House). [In Chinese.]

Wang Xiang (1993). 'Zhongguo jindai jingjishi yanjiu zhong de ruogan lilun wenti' ('Some Theoretical Issues in the Study of Modern Chinese Economic History'). *Lishi yanjiu (Journal of History)*, 4, 77–92. [In Chinese.]

Wank, David (1995). 'Private Business, Bureaucracy and Political Alliance in a Chinese City'. *Australian Journal of Chinese Affairs*, 33, 55–74.

Watson, Andrew (1985). 'Agricultural Reform and China's Foreign Trade'. *Australian Journal of Chinese Affairs*, 14, 39–63.

Watson, Andrew (ed.) (1992). *Economic Reform and Social Change in China*. London: Routledge.

White, Gordon (1983). 'The Postrevolutionary Chinese State'. In V. Nee and D. Mozingo (eds), *Contemporary China*. Ithaca, NY: Cornell University Press.

White, Gordon (ed.) (1988). *Developmental States in East Asia*. New York: St. Martin's Press.

Wilson, Jeanne (1990). 'Labour Policy in China: Reform and Retrogression'. *Problems of Communism*, 39, 44–65.

Wong, Christine P. W. (1988). 'Interpreting Rural Industrial Growth in the Post-Mao Period'. *Modern China*, 14/1, 3–29.

Wong, Kwan Yiu *et al.* (1988). *Perspectives on China's Modernization: Studies on China Policy and Special Economic Zones*. Hong Kong: Chinese University Press.

Wong, R. Bin (1992). 'Chinese Economic History and Development: A Note on the Myers–Huang Exchange'. *Journal of Asian Studies*, 51, 600–11.

Wong Siu-lun (1988). *Emigrant Entrepreneurs: Shanghai Industrialists in Hong Kong*. Hong Kong: Oxford University Press.

World Bank (1982). *World Development Report, 1982*. New York: Oxford University Press.

World Bank (1992). 'China: Strategies for Reducing Poverty in the 1990s'. *World Bank Country Studies*. Washington, DC: World Bank.

World Bank (1993). *The East Asian Miracle: Economic Growth and Public Policy*. New York: Oxford University Press.

World Bank (1994a). *World Development Report, 1994*. New York: Oxford University Press.

World Bank (1994b). *China: Foreign Trade Reform*. Washington, DC: World Bank.

World Bank (1996). 'The Chinese Economy: Fighting Inflation, Deepening Reforms'. *World Bank Country Studies*. Washington, DC: World Bank.

World Bank (1997a). *World Development Indicators, 1997*. Washington, DC: World Bank.

World Bank (1997b). *World Development Report, 1997*. New York: Oxford University Press.

World Bank (1998). World Development Indicators, 1998. Washington, DC: World Bank.

Wright, Tim (1986). 'Imperialism and the Chinese Economy: A Methodological Critique of the Debate'. *Bulletin of Concerned Asian Scholars*, XVIII/1, 36–45.

Wright, Tim (ed.) (1992). *The Chinese Economy in the Early Twentieth Century*. New York: St. Martin's Press.

Wu Chengming (1988). 'Zhongguo jindai jingjishi ruogan wenti de sikao' ('Thoughts on Issues in China's Modern Economic History'). *Zhongguo jingji shi yanjiu* (*Journal of Chinese Economic History*), 2, 153–60. [In Chinese.]

Wu Chengming (1991). 'Jindai zhongguo gongyehua de daolu' ('The Road to Industrialization in Modern China'). *Wenshizhe* (*Literature–History–Philosophy*), 6, 65–70. [In Chinese.]

Wu Chengming (1992). 'A Brief Account of the Development of Capitalism in China'. In Tim Wright (ed.), *The Chinese Economy in the Early Twentieth Century*. New York: St. Martin's Press, 29–43.

Xiao Gongquan (1975). *A Modern China and a New World: K'ang Yu-wei, Reformer and Utopian, 1858–1927*. Seattle: University of Washington Press.

Xu Dixin (1982). 'Transformation of China's Economy'. In Xu Dixin *et al.*, *China's Search for Economic Growth: The Chinese Economy since 1949*. Beijing: New World Press, 1–27.

Xu Dixin *et al.* (1982). *China's Search for Economic Growth: The Chinese Economy since 1949*. Beijing: New World Press.

Xu Dixin and Wu Chengming (eds) (1985). *Zhongguo zibenzhuyi fazhangshi* (*The History of Capitalist Development in China*), Vol. 1: *Zhongguo zibenzhuyi de mengya* (*The Sprouts of Chinese Capitalism*). Beijing: Zhongguo renmin daxue chubanshe (Chinese People's University Press). [In Chinese.]

Xu Dixin and Wu Chengming (eds) (1990). *Zhongguo zibenzhuyi fazhangshi* (*The History of Capitalist Development in China*), Vol. 2: *Jiu minzhuzhuyi geming shiqi de zhongguo zibenzhuyi* (*Capitalism during the Period of the Old Democratic Revolution in China*). Beijing: Renmin chubanshe (People's Publishing House). [In Chinese.]

Xu Dixin and Wu Chengming (eds) (1993). *Zhongguo zibenzhuyi fazhangshi* (*The History of Capitalist Development in China*), Vol. 3: *Xin minzhuzhuyi geming shiqi de zhongguo zibenzhuyi* (*Capitalism in China during the Period of the New Democratic Revolution*). Beijing: Renmin chubanshe (People's Publishing House). [In Chinese.]

Xue Muqiao (1977). 'The Two-Road Struggle in Economic Field during the Transition Period'. *Beijing Review*, 50, 12–15.

Yan Zhongping (1955). *Zhongguo mianfangzhi shigao* (*Draft History of China's Cotton Textile Industry*). Beijing: Kexue chubanshe (Science Press). [In Chinese.]

Yan Zhongping (1986a). 'Shi lun zhongguo maiban zichanjieji de fasheng' ('On the Formation of China's Comprador Bourgeoisie'). *Zhongguo jingji shi yanjiu* (*Journal of Chinese Economic History*), 1, 81–98 (Part 1). [In Chinese.]

Yan Zhongping (1986b). 'Shi lun zhongguo maiban zichanjieji de fasheng' ('On the Formation of China's Comprador Bourgeoisie'). *Zhongguo jingji shi yanjiu* (*Journal of Chinese Economic History*), 3, 71–96 (Part 2). [In Chinese.]

Yan Zhongping *et al.* (1955). *Zhongguo jindai jingjishi tongji ziliao xuanji* (*Selected Statistical Data on the Modern Economic History of China*). Beijing: Kexue chubanshe (Science Press). [In Chinese.]

Yang, Dali (1991). 'China Adjusts to the World Economy: The Political Economy of China's Coastal Development Strategy'. *Pacific Affairs*, 64, 42–64.

Yao Xiangao (1963). *Zhongguo jindai duiwai maoyishi ziliao (Historical Materials on China's Modern Foreign Trade)*. Beijing: Zhonghua shuju (China Book Company). [In Chinese.]

Yeats, Alexander J. (1991). *China's Foreign Trade and Comparative Advantage: Prospects, Problems and Policy Implications*. Washington, DC: World Bank.

Young, Ernest (1970). 'Nationalism, Reform and Republican Revolution'. In James B. Crowley (ed.), *Modern East Asia*. New York: Harcourt, 151–79.

Young, G. (ed.) (1985). *China: Dilemmas of Modernization*. London: Croom Helm.

Yu Heping (1993). *Shanghui yu zhongguo zaoqi xiandaihua (Chambers of Commerce and the Early Modernization of China)*. Shanghai: Shanghai renmin chubanshe (Shanghai People's Publishing House). [In Chinese.]

Yu Yong-ding (1989). 'China's Economic Policy towards Asian-Pacific Economies'. In Miyohei Shinohara and Lo Fu-chen (eds), *Global Adjustment and the Future of Asian-Pacific Economy*. Tokyo: PMC Publications, 176–204.

Zarrow, Peter (1991). 'Review Essay: Social Change and Radical Currents in Republican China, 1912–49'. *Bulletin of Concerned Asian Scholars*, 23, 49–60.

Zhang Keming (1935). 'Hankou linian jinchukou zhi fenxi 1867–1932' ('Analysis of Import and Export in Hankou Port, 1867–1932'). *Hankou shangye yuekan (Business Monthly of Kankou)*, 22. [In Chinese.]

Zhang Li (1988). 'Jianqiang Min–Tai jingji hezuo cujin xiangzhen gongyie fazhan' ('Strengthening Fujina–Taiwan Economic Cooperation and Facilitating the Development of Township Industries'). *Tequ yu kaifang chengshi jingji (Special Zone and Open City Economy)*, 3, 58–62. [In Chinese.]

Zhang Wenqing (1985). 'Ming qing guangzhou zhongxi maoyi yu zhongguo jindai maiban de qiyuan' ('Sino–Western Trade in Ming-Qing Guangzhou and the Origin of Modern Chinese Compradors'). In Guangdong Lishixuehui (Association of Historians of Guangdong Province). *Ming qing guangdong shehui jingji xingtai yanjiu (Studies of Socioeconomic Formation in Guangdong during the Ming and Qing Dynasties)*. Guangzhou. Guangdong renmin chubanshe (Guangdong People's Publishing House). [In Chinese.]

Zhang Youyi (1957). *Zhongguo jindai nongyeshi ziliao (Materials on the Agricultural History of Modern China)*, Vols. 2–3. Beijing: Sanlian Shudian (Sanlian Publishing House). [In Chinese.]

Zheng Youkui (1984). *Zhongguo de duiwai maoyi he gongye fazhan (Foreign Trade and the Industrial Development of China)*. Shanghai: Shanghai sheke chubanshe (Shanghai Social Sciences Publishing House). [In Chinese.]

Zhu Cishou (1987). 'Jiu Zhongguo gongye suo shou waili yapo, qinduo he pohuai' ('Industry in the Old China under Foreign Pressure, Encroachment and Sabotage'). *Caijing yanjiu (Journal of Finance and Economics)*, 7, 52–6. [In Chinese.]

Zhu Xiaohua (1995). 'Double Standards for China'. *Far Eastern Economic Review*, 7 December.

Zong Yumei (1992). '1927–1937 nian Nanjing guomin zhengfu de jingji jianshe shuping' ('A Review of Economic Construction under the GMD Government in 1927–1937'). *Minguo dangan (Archives of the Republic of China)*, 1, 94–100. [In Chinese.]

Zweig, David (1991a). 'Internationalizing China's Countryside: The Political Economy of Exports from Rural Industry'. *China Quarterly*, 128, 716–41. December.

Zweig, David (1991b). 'Rural Industry: Constraining China's Leading Growth Sector'. In Joint Economic Committee, Congress of the United States. *China's Economic Dilemmas in the 1990s: The Problems of Reforms, Modernization and Interdependence.* Washington, DC: US Government Printing Office.

Index

Note: 'n.' after a page reference indicates the number of a note on that page.

acquisitions 43
Agricultural Bank 89
agricultural sector 6
    economic restructuring 131
    food security 169
    foreign trade 34, 39
    industrialization 86, 88, 90, 91
    Nanjing regime 24
    processing activities 49
    state role 145
aid, foreign 83, 98
airlines 24
Angang xianfa (Anshan Iron and Steel
    Company Charter) 188n.1
Argentina 45, 58
arms 19, 20, 21
Asia 6, 7–8, 12–13
Association of Southeast Asian
    Nations (ASEAN) 78, 98,
    100, 102
autarchy 11, 76

balance of trade
    agricultural developments 34
    Chinese capitalist diaspora 158
    economic restructuring 134–5
    reform programme (1978) 128
    silver, fall in price of 38
    Soviet loans and trade 98
    Westernization movement 19
banking sector 24, 30–1, 89
Bank of China 89
Boxer Rebellion 31, 61
Brazil 45, 58, 127, 135, 166
bricks 49
budget deficit 25
bureaucrat capital 26, 46, 74
business firms 32–3

Canada 5
capital accumulation 83, 87, 88
capital formation 46

'catching up' 7, 8–9, 72–85, 162–71,
    180–2
centralization 89–90
central planning 141
    abandonment 121, 123, 139, 146
    appraisal 114
    economic restructuring 132
    government revenue 148
    industrialization 87, 88–90,
        92–3, 94
    problems 122–4
    reform 126, 127
    strengthening 121
    trade and trade
        performance 104–5, 107
Ceylon 35
Chen Qiyuan 185n.2
Chiang Kai-shek 184n.6
Civil War 23, 61
Ci Xi 183n.4
class alliance 181
coal industry 43, 45
coastal areas 137–8, 139
Cold War 145, 175
collective job allocation 169
collective property ownership 111
colonization 5, 16, 22–3
    internal 139
commodity wars 147
Common Programme 77, 175
commune system 88, 130
Communist Party, Chinese
    (CCP) 142, 172, 174
    'catching up' strategy 72–4
    and Guomindang, conflict
        between 23, 61
    industrialization 93
    national revitalization, call for 67
    overseas Chinese capitalists 154,
        155, 161
    state role 144–5
    strength 150

215

competition, regional 147
comprador capital 26, 74
compradors 29, 33
Confucianism 143–4
consumer goods 44, 104
consumption, growth of 164
containment strategy 78, 178–80
corporatism, local state 148
cotton industry 20, 34, 36
   dual structure of economy 49–50, 53, 54
   foreign involvement 43
credit 24
Cultural Revolution 90, 93–4, 99, 109
currency 24
customs service 31–2

defence, national 86, 95
delinking 10–11, 71, 76–7, 79–84, 95, 175–6
   appraisal 112, 114, 116
   Cultural Revolution 94
   economic growth 123
   move away from 121–2
   trade and trade performance 96–7, 101, 106
Deng Xiaoping 9, 108, 121
   on economic growth 162
   economic restructuring 130
   reform programme 124, 125, 128
   on sanctions 179
'development by invitation' 116, 127
direct foreign investment *see* foreign direct investment
diversity of economy 6
dual structure of economy 42–54

Eastern Europe 79, 98
economic restructuring 130–40
education 111
efficiency
   economic 95
   industrial 90, 92
electricity industry 45
emigrants 151, 152–61
employment 168–9
   full 83, 88, 111
   industrialization 91, 92

structure 91, 132
   see also labour force
energy consumption 169
engagement strategy 178, 180
entrepreneurialism 54
environmental issues 169
exchange rate 89
experimental approach to reform 2
exports 29–30, 34–40, 103–7
   dependency on 170
   economic restructuring 134, 135–6, 137, 138, 139
   growth 163, 164
   industrialization 93
extra-territoriality 17, 24, 28, 51

Fachang machine factory 185n.2
famine 109, 111, 167
Five-Year Plans
   1st (1953–57) 90–1, 98
   2nd (1958–62) 188n.2
   9th (1996–2000) 146
flour milling 49
'flying geese' model of East Asian development 159–60
food 59, 169
foreign aid 83, 98
foreign direct investment 1
   dual structure of economy 42–7, 52–4
   economic restructuring 133–4, 136, 137
   overseas Chinese capitalists 152–3
foreign-earnings retention system 133, 135
foreign exchange 24, 30, 93
foreign loans
   customs revenue 31, 32
   delinking and self-reliance strategy 84
   dual structure of economy 42, 43
foreign owned enterprises 42–3
   cotton mills 49–50, 186n.5
   economic restructuring 131, 134, 136
   Korean War 78
   Westernization movement 21

foreign reserves   135, 158–9
foreign trade   1, 28–41, 97, 99–107
   delinking and self-reliance
      strategy   84
   economic restructuring   133,
      134–6, 138
   growth   163–4
   industrialization   89, 93, 94
   Opium Wars   17, 18
   proportion of world total   166
   reform programme (1978)   128
France
   annexation of Vietnam   62
   Chinese territory leased to   22
   invasion (1884)   21
   Opium Wars   17, 60
   peasant rebellions   19
   Sino–French War   60, 62
   trade with China   37
free-rider effect, communes   130
Fujian Province   137
full employment   83, 88, 111

General Agreement on Tariffs and
   Trade (GATT)   5
Germany   22, 37
glass industry   49
gold standard   38
gradualism   2, 126, 145
Great Britain   173
   dual structure of Chinese
      economy   43, 44
   free trade   65
   Hong Kong   12, 22, 154
   incorporation of China into world
      economy   15
   Opium Wars   16–17, 55, 60
   peasant rebellions   19
   trade with China   34, 37, 38
   World War II   24
Great Leap Forward   85, 90, 99,
   109, 113–14
gross domestic product (GDP)   58
   growth rates   109–10, 113, 163–7
   index   163
   trade/GDP ratio   169–70
gross national product (GNP)   1,
   109, 162, 165
growth without development   47

Guangdong Province   33, 137, 138,
   156
Guomindang (GMD)   23, 172, 174
   bankruptcy   187n.3
   and Chinese Communist Party,
      conflict between   23, 61
   foreign trade   32, 33
   state role   143, 144
   transformation of society not
      effected by   63
   Western models   25–6, 60

Hainan   156
handicraft sector   47–54, 86
Hart, Robert   184n.3
Hay, John   65
health care   111
heavy industry
   economic restructuring   131–2
   industrialization   86, 87, 88, 90–2,
      94, 176
hong (business firms)   32–3
Hong Kong
   cession to Great Britain   12, 17,
      154
   Chinese capitalist diaspora   152–7
   foreign reserves   158
   investment in China   137, 152
   relationship with China   12
   tiger economy   12, 108
   trade with China   37, 78, 99, 100,
      102
Hong Kong Bank   30
household responsibility
   system   130–1
human rights   179
Hunan Province   138
hundred-day reform   22
hunger   109, 111, 167
hyperinflation   25, 187n.3

imperialism   60–3
imports   29–30, 34–40, 104
   economic restructuring
      134, 135
   handicrafts, competition with   50
   industrialization   93
   military sector   20
import-substitution   97, 99, 106, 127

income distribution   111, 132, 168,
       176
income gap
   between countries   112, 115, 116,
       166, 176
   within China   138, 139, 177
income levels   57–9, 87–8, 164–7
incrementalism   2, 126, 145
India
   colonialization   5, 16
   foreign direct investment   45
   imports   135
   income levels   58, 166
   periphery status in world
       economy   5
   size of economy   56
   tea   35
   trade/GDP ratio   170
Indian subcontinent   16, 35
Indonesia   45, 58, 153, 166
industrial goods   89–90
industrialization   6, 86–95
   appraisal   109–12, 114, 121–2
   failure   59–60, 63–4
   foreign aid, lack of   83
   Nanjing regime   25
   state   141
   trade and trade performance
       101, 106
   Westernization movement   18–19,
       20–1, 22
industrial sector
   dual structure of economy   47–54
   foreign direct investment   44
   industrialization   92
   Nanjing regime   24–5
   see also heavy industry; light
       industry
inertia, social   59, 60
infant mortality rate   111, 167
inflation   25, 187n.3
insurance companies   30
integration into world economy
       2–3, 6–7, 9
   dual structure of economy
       53, 54
   Westernization movement   15,
       16–17
internal colonialization   139

internationalization of the
       countryside   138
International Monetary Fund
       (IMF)   5
investment
   foreign *see* foreign direct
       investment
   industrialization   87, 91
   Nanjing regime   24
   vs profit distribution   20
involution   47
iron industry   45
Italy   127

Japan
   accumulation structure   158
   Chinese territory leased
       to   22
   core status in world economy   5,
       12, 173
   dual structure of Chinese
       economy   42, 43–4
   East Asian geopolitics,
       restructuring of   62
   economic growth   162
   economic slowdown   160
   imperialism   23, 154
   international politics,
       weight in 6
   invasion of China   61
   investment in China   153
   Northeastern provinces annexed
       by   38, 61
   peripheralization, avoidance
       of   22, 61
   Russo–Japanese War   23
   Sino–Japanese War   21, 42, 60
   trade with China   37, 78, 98–100,
       102
   Westernization   61–2
Jardine Matheon   186n.1
Jiangnan Arsenal   20
Jichang filature   185n.2
joint ventures   134, 136

kerosene   40, 48, 49
Korea   62, 183n.5
   see also North Korea;
       South Korea

Korean War 77–8, 81, 96, 175, 188n.1
    nationalism, Chinese 97
Kuomintang *see* Guomindang

labour force
    economic restructuring 136–7
    industrialization 92
    rural areas 131
    see also employment
laissez-faire economy 142, 143
land contract system 169
land reform 74
Latin America 65
    see also specific countries
Liang Qichao 27
Liao Chengzhi–Takasaki
    Tatsunosuke Memorandum 99
Liaodong Peninsula 184n.5
Liberation Army 147
life expectancy 67, 111, 167
light industry
    economic restructuring 131–2
    industrialization 87, 90, 91
List, Friedrich 80
Liuqiu Island 62
living standards *see* standards of living
local governments 146–8, 149
local state corporatism 148
Lord, Winston 191n.2

Macao 153, 154, 155
Malaysia 78, 100, 153
malnutrition 167
Manchus 17
manufactured goods, exports 136, 137, 138
manufacturing sector *see* industrial sector
Mao Zedong 9, 176
    death 124
    and Deng, comparison between 124
    goal of government 84
    population size, views of 83
    on poverty 72
    self-reliance 79–80
    Sino-Soviet treaty of alliance 79
    on Soviet Union 79
    victory declaration 67
    on Westernization 27
Maritime Customs Service of China 31
Marxist theory 52, 82, 142
Mei-foo lamps 185n.8
merchants 29
mergers 43
Mexico 45, 58, 127, 166
migration
    overseas Chinese capitalists 151, 152–61
    within China 92
military
    Communist regime 74
    delinking and self-reliance strategy 83–4
    Nanjing regime 26
    Opium Wars, lessons from 19–21, 22
Ministry of Foreign Trade 89, 105
Ministry of Railways 24
missionaries 38
modernization 9, 53, 124
    theory 52
modern sector
    dual structure of economy 47, 49, 50, 51–4
    foreign investment 45, 46
money houses 30
Mongols 17
most-favoured nation (MFN) status 17, 28, 42
multinational corporations 154–5, 157
Muslim rebellion 21, 60

Nanjing 47
Nanjing (Nanking) regime 23–6
    see also Guomindang
Nanking, Treaty of 17
nationalism 179–81
    Communist era 82
    Korean War 97
    Nanjing regime 23
    Qing Dynasty 186n.5
nationalization 74, 77, 89
    see also state sector
National People's Congress 155

national unification 161
neoclassical economics 81
Netherlands 65, 166
new democratic stage 76–7
Nian rebellion 21
Nixon, Richard 100
'Nixon shock' 100, 101
North Korea 77
nuclear capability 11, 189n.2

Open Door policy 65–6, 173
openness, economic 11, 121,
  125–6, 133
  Opium Wars 16–17
  overseas Chinese capitalists 154
opium 34, 36, 48
Opium Wars 15, 16–18, 28, 55, 60
Ottoman empire 16
output
  dual structure of economy 51
  foreign involvement 43, 45
  global manufacturing 56
  Nanjing regime 24
overseas Chinese capitalists 151,
  152–61

papermaking 49
peasant rebellions 19, 21, 60
Penghu Islands 183n.5
People's Bank of China 89
People's Construction Bank 89
Pescadores Islands 183n.5
pollution 169
population levels 57, 83
ports 46
  treaty *see* treaty ports
Portugal 154
postal service 24
pottery 49
poverty 67, 95, 167, 168
  Deng's views 124
  foreign trade 41
  Mao's views 72
power generation 45
prices 88
private sector 21, 77, 87
producer goods 40, 44, 104
profits 20, 89
protectionism 33–4, 54, 64–5, 125

Prussia 80
public sector *see* nationalization;
  state sector
public utilities 45
Pudong New Area 133
purchasing power parity (PPP) 164,
  169–70

Qing Dynasty 16–21, 172, 173
  Boxer movement 60–1
  change, resistance to 63
  foreign loans 31, 42
  foreign trade 32
  legacy 23
  protectionism, lack of 54

railroads 24, 43
rapeseed 49
raw materials, allocation of 89–90
Red Army 74
reform programme (1978) 1–2,
  121–9
regional competition 147
regional development 138–9
regions, self-reliance 83–4
reintegration 119–20, 176–7
residence registration scheme 92
Revolutions
  1911 23, 61
  1949 72, 74–5, 142, 174
  Cultural 90, 93–4, 99, 109
rubber industry 78
rural areas
  dual structure of economy
    47, 48
  dynamism 146
  economic restructuring 130–1
  expansion 127
  industrialization 88, 92
  internationalization 138
  labour force 92
  Nanjing regime 26
  national cohesiveness, lack of 73
  unemployment 169
Russia
  Chinese territory leased to 22
  dual structure of Chinese
    economy 44
  economic performance 166

occupation of Ili   62
'seizing the chance'   127
Russian empire   16
Russo–Japanese War   23

sanctions   179
savings   24, 83
scientific development   111
security, national   86, 121
'seizing the chance'   127–8
self-reliance   10–11, 71, 76, 79–84,
    95, 175–6
  appraisal   112, 114, 116
  Cultural Revolution   94
  economic growth   123
  move away from   121–2
  reform programme (1978)
      125, 127
  trade and trade performance
      96–7, 100–1, 106
self-strengthening   18, 19, 26
self-sufficiency   48, 53, 82
semi-colonialization   16, 23,
    24, 52
service sector   147, 156
Shanghai
  dual structure of economy   46
  Fachang machine factory   185n.2
  foreign direct investment   43
  Pudong New Area   133
Shantou   155–6
Shenzhen   137, 155
Shimonoseki, Treaty of   42
shipping industry   31, 45
silk   34, 35
silver   38
Singapore   12, 100, 108, 153, 156
Sino-centric model of East Asian
    development   158–9
Sino–French War   60, 62
Sino–Japanese War   21, 60
size of Chinese economy   56
smoking   51–2
socialism   108, 116, 180
  'catching up' strategy   75–6, 79
  influence on reform process   168
socialist market economy   126
socialist transformation   87, 144
Song Dynasty   153

South Korea
  Chinese capitalist diaspora   154
  economic growth   110
  Korean War   77
  tiger economy   12, 108
  US alliance with   78
sovereignty   24, 32
Soviet Union *see* Union of Soviet
    Socialist Republics
soybeans   49
special economic zones   133, 137,
    155–6
Stalin, Joseph   79
Standard Oil Company   185n.8
standards of living   1, 87, 92, 108
  entitlements   111
  improvements   167–8
  measurement   164
  reform programme (1978)   125
starvation   109, 111, 167
state   141–51, 172
  economic restructuring   130
  foreign trade   84, 105
  industrialization   6, 20–1, 22, 86,
      93
State Planning Commission   89–90
state property ownership   111
state revenue   148–9
state sector
  economic restructuring   131, 132
  expansion   144–5
  industrialization   87
  see also nationalization
steel industry   45
subsistence goods and services   88
Sun Yat-sen   27, 73

taban (general manager)   33
Taiping rebellion   19, 20, 60
Taiwan
  Chinese capitalist diaspora   152–7
  economic growth   110
  foreign reserves   158
  future   161
  investment in China   137, 152–3
  'miracle'   143
  occupation by Japan   62
  relationship with China   12
  separation from mainland   12, 154

Taiwan – (*continued*)
    Sino–Japanese War   183n.5
    tiger economy   12, 108
    US alliance with   78
    US Seventh Fleet   78, 175
tariffs
    autonomy, recovery of   24, 34
    dual structure of economy   51
    Westernization   17, 31, 32
    world economy   64
taxation   25, 28, 148–9
tax evasion   149
tax-farming   20
tea   29, 34, 35
technology   19, 111
telecommunications   24
terms of trade   104–5, 127, 139
textile industry   34, 45, 50
    see also cotton industry
Thailand   153
'third line' policy   95
'three-stage rocket' model of East
    Asian development   160
tiger economies
    growth   110, 162
    strategy   114, 115–16
    see also Hong Kong; Singapore;
        South Korea; Taiwan
tiles   49
tobacco   52
township and village enterprises
    (TVEs)   138
township governments   146
trade balance *see* balance of trade
trade organizations   105
transportation   24
treaty ports   9, 23, 28–30, 32, 33
    dual structure of economy
        46, 47
tributary trade system   7

unemployment   168–9
Union of Soviet Socialist
    Republics
    collectivization   109
    economic performance   166
    industrialization   86
    loans to China   84
    nuclear capability   189n.2

Sino–Soviet political split   98,
    99, 175
Sino–Soviet treaty of
    alliance   79
state role   145
trade with China   79, 98
UN Security Council   5
United Kingdom *see* Great Britain
United Nations (UN)   100
    Security Council   5
United States of America
    Chinese capitalist diaspora
        154
    Cold War   175
    containment strategy   78, 179
    core status in world economy   5
    détente with China   100–1,
        112–13
    dual structure of Chinese
        economy   44
    investment in China   153
    Korean War   77, 78, 96, 175,
        188n.1
    nuclear capability   189n.2
    Open Door policy   65–6, 173
    Opium Wars   17
    protectionism   186n.7
    Seventh Fleet   78, 96, 175
    trade with China   37, 40, 101
    Vietnam War   99
    World War II   24
unit-owned businesses   147–8
urban areas
    dual structure of economy
        46, 47
    industrialization   87–8, 89
    unemployment   168
urbanization   92

vegetable oil extraction   49
Vietnam   62, 159
Vietnam War   99

wages   87–8, 156
'walking on two legs'   188n.9
war indemnities   31, 32, 184n.5
wealth, pursuit of   18
welfare system   88, 132, 168
West Africa   16

Westernization   9, 15, 55–6, 61–2,
     67, 174
   movement   18–22, 26, 27,
      59–60, 172; foreign
      trade   33
   Nanjing regime   25, 26
Whiting, Allen S.
     187n.4
World Bank   5
world-system analysis
     81, 150

World Trade Organization
     (WTO)   178
World War II   24
Wuhan   46

Xiamen   137, 155–6

Yuan Dynasty   17

Zhou Enlai   124, 187n.7
Zhuhai   155